DISCARDED

APR 2 3 2025

D1713471

Ancient Earthen Enclosures
of the Eastern Woodlands

The Ripley P. Bullen Series
Florida Museum of Natural History

Ancient
Earthen
Enclosures

of the Eastern Woodlands

Edited by
Robert C. Mainfort, Jr.
and
Lynne P. Sullivan

University Press of Florida

Gainesville Tallahassee Tampa Boca Raton
Pensacola Orlando Miami Jacksonville

03 02 01 00 99 98 6 5 4 3 2 1
Library of Congress Cataloging-in-Publication Data
Ancient earthen enclosures of the Eastern Woodlands / edited by Robert C. Mainfort, Jr.,
and Lynne P. Sullivan
p. cm.--(Ripley P. Bullen series)
Includes bibliographical references (p.) and index.
ISBN 0-8130-1592-8 (c: alk. paper)
1. Indians of North America--East (U.S.)--Antiquities.
2. Earthworks (Archaeology)--East (U.S.). 3. Woodland Indians--
Antiquities. 4. East (U.S.)--Antiquities. I. Mainfort, Robert
C., 1948-. II. Sullivan, Lynne P. III. Series.
E78.E2A585   1998   98-5507
974--dc21

The University Press of Florida is the scholarly publishing agency for the State University System
of Florida, comprising Florida A&M University, Florida Atlantic University, Florida International
University, Florida State University, University of Central Florida, University of Florida, University
of North Florida, University of South Florida, and University of West Florida.

University Press of Florida
15 Northwest 15th Street
Gainesville, FL 32611
http://nersp.nerdc.ufl.edu/~upf

Contents

Figures

Tables

Foreword

Earthen enclosures were once a prominent feature of the precolumbian land-scape of the eastern United States. Built by the ancestors of present-day American Indians, the enclosures—some huge and encompassing many acres, others small and situated on hilltops or in other locations—have remained enig-matic. Who built them? How? When? For what use? What did they symbolize? These are tough questions, and the answers have eluded nineteenth-century antiquarians and twentieth-century archaeologists.

In this book editors Robert Mainfort and Lynne Sullivan have assembled a group of scholars who use new techniques and theories to reexamine the archaeology of earthen enclosures. The results, which draw on a host of new data, are provocative and, in some instances, controversial.

Ancient Earthen Enclosures of the Eastern Woodlands, perhaps the first book to focus entirely on precolumbian Native American enclosures, will influence how all future archaeologists study and interpret these unique struc-tures from our country's past.

Jerald T. Milanich,
series editor

Preface

In eastern North America, earthen enclosures occur throughout a span of nearly three millennia and in a number of topographically and physiographically diverse regions. Once, before many were destroyed through Euroamerican agricultural practices and the processes of urbanization, these features formed prominent components of the cultural landscape of Native America. Researchers formerly relied on two standard interpretations for enclosures, designating them as ceremonial sites or forts. Only within the past few decades have we begun to understand the wide range of variation in the physical characteristics of enclosures and the equally varied purposes for which they were built.

Considering this now-recognized variation among enclosure sites and the lengthy period during which these structures were created in eastern North America, a single explanation for all embankment designs and the cultural materials found within them is not to be expected. Indeed, there is no reason to believe that there is a single best research orientation or excavation strategy for the study of these diverse earthworks. This volume amply documents these points. Its authors also demonstrate that while earthen enclosures remain poorly understood and under-investigated, a variety of experimental approaches for their examination are beginning to bear fruit.

While we are not so pretentious as to believe that publication of this volume will usher in a new era of enclosure research, it is appropriate to note that we have assembled here the first collection of essays exclusively devoted to prehistoric enclosures in eastern North America. The volume had its genesis in two conference symposia that were independently organized by the editors. Earlier versions of the chapters by Thunen, Lepper, Byers, Jones and Kuttruff, Riordan, and Connolly were presented at a symposium entitled "Middle Woodland Enclosures: The Archaeology of Structured Space" and chaired by Robert Thunen and Robert Mainfort at the 1994 joint meeting of the Southeastern Archaeological Conference and the Midwest Archaeological Conference in Lexington, Kentucky. The symposium abstract aptly describes the essays assembled in this volume: both theoretical and recent archaeological results are presented to further our understanding of individual enclosures and the larger phenomenon of creating ritual space. At the 1995 Society for American Archaeology annual meeting in Minneapolis, Sarah W. Neusius and Lynne P. Sullivan presented a more broadly focused symposium entitled "Earthworks, Forts, and Villages: Unraveling the Sacred from the

Secular." Among the participants, Gibson, Milner and O'Shea, Riordan, Belovich, and S. Neusius et al. contributed to this volume. That session highlighted questions about the purposes of enclosures and methodologies for discerning enclosure use from archaeological data.

The resulting collection of essays addresses the full range of issues involved in enclosure research—from the "dirt archaeology" to the theoretical—and discusses examples of the variety of enclosure sites in the Eastern Woodlands, across time and space. The authors also offer analytical approaches that range from culture-historical to post-processual. This volume is thus a statement on the current state of the art of enclosure research; it is far from the last word or "the answer" to the enclosure problem. Instead, the volume clearly shows the difficulties, the frustrations, and the ambiguous results that characterize investigations of these enigmatic sites, as well as the rewards in the form of steadily increasing knowledge reaped through patient and thoughtful study. At present there is little glory in enclosure research, but as archaeological questions about these features become increasingly more sophisticated, these essays demonstrate that we may expect research on enclosures to enrich significantly our understanding of many aspects of the behaviors of prehistoric peoples.

Several people deserve our sincere thanks for their efforts toward making this volume possible. We especially thank Buzz Thunen and Sarah Neusius for their work in organizing the original conference symposia. Their advice and ideas significantly shaped not only the list of contributors but the variety of questions about enclosures that the volume addresses. Several reviewers also provided valuable assistance and guidance: Vernon James Knight, Martha Rolingson, and Jerald Milanich. We thank them for their support of the project and for pointing out places where improvements could be made as well as parts they liked; constructive, balanced criticism is a real gift for any manuscript. We also thank John Hart for securing two reviews. The encouragement and support of Meredith Morris-Babb, Jerald Milanich, and the staff of the University Press of Florida were unfailing, and we appreciate their enthusiasm and patience. Thanks, too, to the contributors for being both timely and tolerant of our queries and requests.

Without the artistic talents of Patricia Miller, this volume would have suffered; we thank her for making the graphics for the various chapters more attractive and coherent. Lindi Holmes (Sponsored Research Program, Arkansas Archeological Survey) prepared the manuscript for the University Press of Florida, compiled the conflated bibliography, and greatly assisted in preparing the volume index. Finally, we appreciate the patience of Mary, Brian, and John who continually endure the rigors of being the spouses and offspring, respectively, of archaeologists. We hope the rewards are sufficient.

Chapter 1

✖ Explaining Earthen Enclosures
Robert C. Mainfort, Jr., and Lynne P. Sullivan

Nineteenth-century antiquarians (Atwater 1820; Larkin 1880), surveyors (Cheney 1859; Squier and Davis 1848), and more scientifically inclined investigators (Fowke 1902; Holmes 1892; Thomas 1889) documented hundreds of ancient earthen walls and enclosures across the eastern United States. Early speculation about these and other earthen constructions attributed them to ancient races of moundbuilders (Silverberg 1970), but as more rational thinking prevailed, investigators firmly established that these monuments were constructed by American Indians.

During the ensuing years, archaeological research and knowledge concerning ancient enclosures has progressed slowly. Although the mounds often associated with enclosures have received considerable attention from archaeologists (particularly those associated with the Hopewellian societies of the Ohio Valley), few archaeological investigations have focused on the enclosures themselves (e.g., Baby 1954; Clay 1988; Essenpreis and Moseley 1984; Shane 1974; Thunen 1990a; Willoughby and Hooton 1922; G. Wright 1990). Several factors are probably responsible for this lack of study. First and perhaps most importantly, many mounds associated with enclosures contain human burials and grave inclusions of considerable artistic merit. In contrast, artifacts of any kind are generally much less common within earthen embankments and enclosure interiors (excepting mounds). A second contributing factor may simply be one of scale; most archaeologists are unaccustomed to dealing with features that cover many acres. Finally, the paucity of investigations itself has perhaps dissuaded researchers from addressing the archaeology of earthen enclosures. There has been little, if any, guidance to be found in previous work at comparable sites.

Particularly in southern Ohio, where a considerable number of large and elaborate enclosure sites occur, research traditionally focused on the mounds (many containing burials) within enclosures, rather than the enclosures themselves. This emphasis has had several important effects on interpretations of enclosures and the societies that built them. First, overall site structure was ignored, essentially removing the mounds from their contexts. Second, enclosures and associated mounds were perceived as static features; there was no sense of the architectural evolution of enclosure sites.

The chapters in this volume document a markedly different research approach to enclosures, one in which the enclosures themselves are the focus of archaeological inquiry. We now know that earthen (and occasionally stone) enclosures were constructed in various regions in eastern North America during a period spanning roughly 3000 years, between approximately 1500 B.C. and A.D.1500. Current interpretations suggest that there was also considerable diversity in the subsistence bases of the societies that constructed these structures. During Poverty Point times (circa 1500 B.C.) in the Lower Mississippi Valley, there is no evidence of agriculture, although the rich environment probably provided stable subsistence resources based on intensive seasonal collecting. The Hopewellian farmers of the Ohio River Valley tended crops of native cultigens (B. Smith 1992), but the scale of agriculture and the relative dietary contribution of crops is not clear. Between A.D. 800 and 1300, maize became an important staple of many societies throughout eastern North America, and earthen enclosures were constructed by some of these groups (e.g., Cottier and Southard 1977).

The essays in this volume discuss sites that span this range of temporal and geographic settings represented by earthen enclosures in the eastern United States (fig. 1.1). Although the authors clearly show the difficulties in interpreting these sites, they demonstrate that the purposes for which these structures were built are equally diverse. We can no longer assume that such sites served solely defensive or ceremonial purposes, nor can we assume that the purposes for which an enclosure originally was constructed remained constant throughout its use-life. What is eminently clear is that we cannot generalize as to the temporal context or the use of enclosure sites; each site requires investigation to approach these questions. European archaeologists (e.g., Drewett 1977) recognized this dilemma long ago in dealing with the varied forms of enclosure sites found on that continent, and their experiences may prove instructive to North Americanists, a point to which we shall return.

The volume begins with the earliest known enclosure in North America— Poverty Point. Most reported enclosures are located in the upper Midwest, but Poverty Point is located in northeastern Louisiana. The appearance of the Poverty Point site has long seemed enigmatic, and although recent research demonstrates that mound construction along the Gulf coast and environs predates Poverty Point by several millennia (Gibson and Shenkel 1988; Russo 1994), the site remains unique in terms of architectural form and scale (see Gibson, this volume and elsewhere). Not only does the site exhibit enclosure architecture unlike that seen at any later site, but it also includes two of the largest earthen mounds in all of North America. Still puzzling is the lack of any remotely comparable enclosure sites until over 1000 years after Poverty Point ceased to be used.

Most recorded enclosures were constructed and used in eastern North

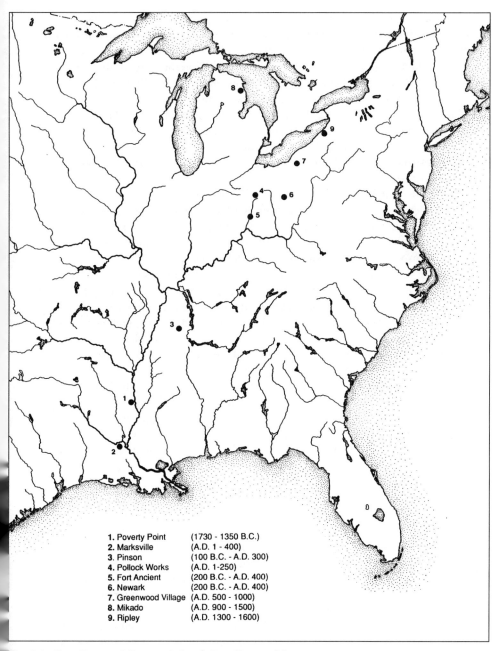

1. Poverty Point	(1730 - 1350 B.C.)
2. Marksville	(A.D. 1 - 400)
3. Pinson	(100 B.C. - A.D. 300)
4. Pollock Works	(A.D. 1-250)
5. Fort Ancient	(200 B.C. - A.D. 400)
6. Newark	(200 B.C. - A.D. 400)
7. Greenwood Village	(A.D. 500 - 1000)
8. Mikado	(A.D. 900 - 1500)
9. Ripley	(A.D. 1300 - 1600)

Fig. 1.1. Locations and time periods of sites discussed in text.

America during the Middle Woodland period (circa 200 B.C.–A.D. 400), and the majority of these are located in southern Ohio. Indeed, the mounds and elaborate enclosures of this region served as the focal point for the "mound-builder debate" of the nineteenth century (e.g., Silverberg 1970). It is therefore fitting that four of the eleven essays assembled here (those by Riordan, Connolly, Lepper, and Byers) discuss these structures. The chapters on the Ohio Valley sites also help fill a conspicuous gap in the 1979 Hopewell Conference volume (Brose and Greber 1979). The scant discussion of enclosures in that volume is rather incongruous, as earthen enclosures and the finely crafted artifacts from mortuary contexts are the two hallmarks of Hopewell in the Ohio Valley.

Middle Woodland enclosures are not, however, strictly limited to the Ohio Valley; examples are known from the Lower Mississippi Valley and the Midsouth (Faulkner 1968; Mainfort 1988, 1993; Thunen 1988a). Chapters by Jones and Kuttruff and by Thunen address the large and complex Marksville and Pinson mound sites, respectively, in these regions.

After A.D. 500, enclosure construction appears to have been substantially curtailed, although not stopped, throughout the Eastern Woodlands. The nature and function of later period enclosures remain poorly understood at present, but several authors (Belovich, Milner and O'Shea, and Neusius et al.) offer important new insights. Some later enclosures evidently do represent defensive structures that surround village sites, while others served (in the broadest sense) a ceremonial purpose.

In grappling with the intricacies presented by the archaeology of enclosure sites, the various authors present a number of fruitful lines of inquiry. The use and function of earthen enclosures is one topic that figures prominently in these chapters. This issue has been a particular focus of musings by antiquarians (e.g., Squier and Davis 1848) as well as by modern archaeologists. The nature of activities conducted at the sites and how these activities may be discerned archaeologically are of specific concern. A second major topic is that of symbolism, which the authors approach in several contrasting but complementary ways. Questions address the connection of the earthworks to systems of cultural beliefs as well as iconography. This leads to the third topic, namely, the architecture of enclosures. Issues addressed include site planning, the physical construction of enclosures, the evolution of individual enclosures over time, and the appearance that enclosures presented to their builders. It should be self-evident that these issues are interconnected.

While all of the papers in this volume examine the social and economic contexts of enclosures at some level, the authors have left us latitude to take a broad perspective on these aspects of enclosure construction and use. We take the opportunity to provide this somewhat lofty view as an epilogue to our consideration of the three main topics addressed by the authors. In so doing, we make comparisons with Neolithic Europe by contemplating commonalities in the subsistence bases and degrees of sociopolitical complexity of the monument builders in both areas, as well as by considering the integration of these features into regional settlement patterns and the role of enclosures in social relationships.

The Uses of Enclosures

The function or functions of the earthen enclosures of eastern North America have intrigued scholars since the days of antiquarianism, and it is therefore not surprising that the subject is alluded to in virtually every chapter. It is with no disrespect to the other authors that we will suggest that the classes of data recovered from archaeological investigations are probably unsuited to address questions of function. Rather, archaeological remains may contribute to our understanding of enclosure *use*, but not *function*, a similar point having been made some years ago by Clay (1988).

One classic interpretation of earthwork use in the Eastern Woodlands is as "ceremonial centers." The "sacred" nature of geometric enclosures (particularly those associated with Ohio Hopewell) is a theme that began with antiquarians. Squier and Davis (1848) devoted considerable attention to the topic of enclosure use, and their speculations illustrate early musings on the sacredness of the enclosures. Not only are their statements outstanding examples of mid-nineteenth-century speculation, elements of their ideas are echoed by modern interpretations.

> As has already been intimated, they were probably, like the great circles of England, and the squares of India, Peru, and Mexico, the sacred enclosures, within which were erected the shrines of the gods of the ancient worship and the altars of ancient religion. They may have embraced consecrated groves, and also, as they did in Mexico, the residences of the ancient priesthood. Like the sacred structures of the country last named, some of them may have been secondarily designed for protection in times of danger. . . . we know that it has been a practice, common to almost every people in every time, to enclose their temples and altars with walls of various materials, so as to guard the sacred area around them from the desecration of animals or the intrusion of the profane. Spots consecrated by tradition, or rendered remarkable as the scene of some extraordinary event, or by whatever means connected with the superstitions, or invested with the reverence of men, have always been designated in this or some similar manner. (Squier and Davis 1848:102)

> If we are not mistaken in assigning a religious origin to that large portion of ancient monuments, which are clearly not defensive, nor designed to perpetuate the memory of the dead, then the superstitions of the ancient people must have exercised a controlling influence upon their character. If, again, as from reason and analogy we are warranted in supposing, many of these sacred structures are symbolical in their forms and combinations, they indicate the prevalence among their builders of religious beliefs and conception, corresponding with those which prevailed among the early nations of the other continent. (ibid., 304)

In a critique of Squier and Davis, Cyrus Thomas (1894:69) offered some comments worthy of consideration by modern researchers: "But their further classification into enclosures for defense, sacred and miscellaneous enclosures, mounds of sacrifice, temple mound, etc. is unfortunate, as it is based on supposed uses instead of real character, and has served to graft into our archaeological literature certain conclusions in regard to the uses and purposes of these various works that in some cases, at least, are not justified by the evidence."

The notion of sacred enclosures later became linked in the era of modern archaeological research to the idea that enclosures were ceremonial centers, which in some sense they no doubt were. The comments of Morgan and Griffin in *Archeology of Eastern United States* (Griffin 1952) neatly illustrate this point:

> These geometrical enclosures were used as centers by the Hopewell peoples for social, religious and burial purposes. Their sacred character is testified to by the achieving of privacy by walls and connecting passageways, their symbolic form, and their use for the burial of important personages in the group. . . . Although the hill-top enclosures have been termed "forts," it is evident that they were used as ceremonial centers as well as for defense. (Morgan 1952:89)

> The areal extent of some of these major Hopewell sites, such as Turner, the large number of earthworks and mounds in what is now the heart of Cincinnati, of Portsmouth, of Circleville, Newark, and other large Ohio sites, indicates that these people had a definite plan in mind as to the type of earthworks which were to be constructed and that this major plan was recognized and carried out over a considerable period. The majority of them are certainly not defensive structures, but are part of a ceremonial and sacred precinct. (Griffin 1952:359)

Prufer (1964a, b) called attention to another aspect of some Eastern Woodlands enclosures: their lack of abundant associated artifacts and features. Subsequent to the publication of his articles, it is rare to find references to earthen enclosures as "ceremonial centers" without the preceding adjective "vacant":

> I suggest that it [the lack of extensive habitation debris at enclosure sites] reflects a settlement pattern similar to the classic Mesoamerican situation of the vacant ceremonial centers–semi-permanent shifting agricultural village type. In other words, what we are facing here seem to be elaborate ceremonial centers based upon a mortuary cult and surrounded by very small dependent villages of little permanence. (Prufer 1964a:71)

> While reflecting on all these factors, I was struck by a possible parallel between the Ohio Hopewell sites and the classic ceremonial sites of certain areas in Middle America, where the religious center remained vacant except on ritual occasions and the population lived in scattered hamlets surrounding the center. (Prufer 1964b:94)

Indeed, Griffin is virtually the only researcher to call attention to what appears to be domestic habitation debris within some of the large Ohio enclosures (see Brose and Greber 1979:64). Unfortunately, much of the material to which Griffin refers was recovered prior to the advent of modern archaeological field techniques and reporting. Identification of this material as "domestic" rather than special purpose or "ceremonial" occupation debris remains uncertain.

Recent discussions of enclosures continue to invoke the notion of ceremonial center in reference to enclosure sites, and this is often accompanied by suggestions that enclosures represent localities at which various social groups convened to "interact" in some fashion. For example, DeBoer and Blitz (1991:62) comment that "In this context, the ceremonial center is the key institution at which the Chachi periodically aggregate. During these aggregations, large or small, participants reassert their identity as Chachi, exchange information concerning both local and global matters, and expose and attempt to alleviate internal disputes. . . . The ceremonial center, then, can be seen as a rather clever device for integrating the dispersed population."

As several of the quotations above indicate, the second longstanding interpretation of enclosure use is as fortifications. Fowke (1902:153) cites a number of nineteenth-century writers in this regard:

> The large [enclosures] may have been walls, surrounding their towns and cultivated fields, and even used to protect their fields from predatory animals. The smaller ones may have been designed to

guard their temples and sepulchral mounds from profane intrusion–
Foster, 176.

A few of these enclosures may possibly owe their origin to a religious sentiment, but of a large majority of them it may be safely said, in view of recent investigations, that they were simply fortified villages. Self-protection was the primary object of the people who lived behind these walls–Carr, *Mounds*, 555.

Fowke (1902:268) himself expressed the now largely discredited notion that hilltop enclosures "are unmistakably defensive in their nature; and their size indicates warfare of no small proportions." More recently, Stothers and Graves (1983:119) reiterate this view for late prehistoric enclosures and embankments in the upper Midwest:

The phenomenon of earthwork enclosures (distributed throughout the area of northwest Ohio, southeast Michigan, and southwest Ontario) appears to be directly related to the suggested military interaction between the Western Basin and Sandusky traditions. . . . More specifically, we suggest these earthwork enclosures represent defensive fortification measures taken by opposing Western Basin and Sandusky tradition peoples. . . . the earthwork enclosures in question represent a series of prehistoric "Maginot" lines of military defense that fluctuate though time and terminate with the eventual evacuation of the Western Basin Tradition peoples by ca. 1400 A.D.

While ceremonial centers and fortifications are the uses most typically cited for enclosures in the eastern United States, the interpretive framework proposed by Drewett (1977) for the causewayed enclosures of the early Neolithic in England is useful to consider. As we note, both the early (or "Primary") English Neolithic and Hopewellian societies of the Eastern Woodlands of North America (particularly, Ohio Hopewell) are characterized by the construction of various forms of enclosures and also seem to share elements of subsistence and settlement.

Drewett (1977:222) proposes seven uses for English Neolithic enclosures, of which all but "cattle enclosures" are potentially applicable to examples from eastern North America, and indeed reference to most can be found in the chapters here. The uses include burial sites, cult or ritual centers, communal meeting places, trade centers, settlements, and defensive structures. It is clear that mortuary activities were conducted within some enclosures in eastern North America (see Neusius et al., this volume), certain Ohio Hopewell structures being outstanding examples (e.g., Greber 1976, 1979). Yet many, perhaps most, enclosures lack specific evidence of mortuary rituals (e.g., Clay 1987, 1988). Drewett's centers for cult or ritual purposes remain a popular interpretation among contemporary archaeologists of eastern North America, but as Drewett suggested (1977), such postulations all too often mask the inability of researchers to explain data from enclosures.

There seems little reason to doubt that many enclosures were communal meeting places, if only because the scale of their construction would seem to require fairly sizable workforces. In this volume, Milner and O'Shea conclude that a Late Woodland enclosure in northern Michigan was used as a meeting and trading place by geographically separated social and political groups. They report the occurrence of stylistically nonlocal ceramics to advance this argument. Enclosures as trade centers is a theme not often found in eastern North America; besides Milner and O'Shea's interpretation, a notable exception is Jackson's 1991 discussion of the Poverty Point site.

In the Eastern Woodlands, enclosures are not generally viewed as long-term loci of domestic activity, particularly in the case of geometric enclosures. On the other hand, the Poverty Point site (Gibson, this volume) exhibits considerable accumulation of domestic artifacts and refuse. Abundant remains of domestic habitation, including midden deposits, are present on and within the earthen ridges. Poverty Point is the only site represented in this volume at which there seems to be an abundance of both domestic and "ritual" artifacts associated with an enclosure, thus providing no indication of a straightforward sacred/secular dichotomy. The degree to which the secular and sacred are virtually inseparable at Poverty Point further underscores the unique nature of this site. In contrast, within Hopewellian enclosures artifacts are not generally numerous, and most can be attributed to specialized, nondomestic contexts (e.g., Baby and Langlois 1979; Prufer 1964a, b).

Corresponding with Prufer's observations, some excavated enclosure sites provide virtually no evidence about use; these include Marksville (Jones and Kuttruff, this volume), Old Stone Fort (Faulkner 1968), Pinson Mounds (Thunen, this volume), and Pollock Works (Riordan, this volume), all of which have produced minimal artifact assemblages from within the enclosures. This situation is especially striking in the case of the Pinson enclosure (Thunen 1990a and this volume; Mainfort 1986, 1988), where nearly half of the enclosure interior was disked and surface-collected prior to planting a suitable ground cover. Artifacts are very sparse throughout the entire mound complex, including the geometric enclosure (Mainfort 1986; Thunen 1990a). Some later enclosure sites also seem to be characterized by low artifact density and few, if any, subsurface archaeological features. This implies, but by no means proves, short-term, specialized use.

Based on the artifact assemblage at Peter Village, Kentucky, Clay (1988) infers that processing and perhaps distribution of barite/galena was conducted, but specialized activities have not been identified at other enclosures.

On the other hand, later enclosures more often continue to be interpreted as "defensive." While it seems quite certain that the hilltop enclosures of Ohio Hopewell were not constructed *primarily* for defensive purposes, fortified villages may be characteristic of certain geographic regions in post-Hopewell times (see Belovich, and Neusius et al., this volume).

Whatever the uses of the enclosures (a point we will revisit), it clearly is not necessary to construct earthen embankments, some of elaborate form, to delimit a ritual activity area or ceremonial center, a gathering place for trade, a locus for societal integration, or a boundary marker. While these uses may characterize enclosures, the architectural features themselves should not be viewed solely in such functionalist terms; they represent something more. This point has been forcefully argued by Byers, who states in reference to Ohio Hopewell enclosures, "this dissertation will establish that they [enclosures]) were more than and possibly not even best conceived as enclosures at all. As I will argue later, it might be quite appropriate to dismiss this term entirely and refer to them as iconic features that represent and participate in the nature of the cosmos while necessarily but quite possibly unintentionally they took on the form of being 'containers'" (1987:66). This perspective brings us to discussion of the second topic addressed in this volume, enclosure symbolism.

Symbolism of Enclosures

Recent developments in archaeological theory recognize material culture as an active medium of symbolic communication (e.g., Hodder 1982, 1987; Seeman 1995). The earthen enclosures of eastern North America, like roughly comparable architectural features throughout the world, represent material culture on a grand scale, and the symbolic character of some of these earthworks (particularly the geometric Hopewellian enclosures) was mentioned by some of the earliest antiquarian writers. For example, Squier and Davis (1848:304) comment that "many of these sacred structures are symbolical in their forms and combinations [and] indicate the prevalence among their builders of religious beliefs and conceptions."

In this volume, Gibson approaches symbolism in a manner somewhat reminiscent of Robert Hall by drawing parallels between the Poverty Point earthworks, the associated artifact assemblage, and the rich corpus of Native American mythology in the Mississippi Delta region. While inferences drawn in such a manner are probably untestable in the strict sense, placing prehistoric iconography (including mounds and embankments) into a broader cultural context is worthy of pursuit.

A much different perspective on the symbolism of enclosures has been advanced by A. Martin Byers (1987 and this volume), who has applied structural analysis to Hopewellian enclosures as a means to understanding the under-lying deep structures manifested in and by the enclosures. Byers (1987:26) views these enclosures as "symbolic material features. As symbols they would have evoked in the participants of the social system the world as it really existed to them in virtue of their cultural structures. Their cultural structures were both the medium and context that constituted both the enclosure and the construction and use as intelligible." Applying Douglas's (1966, 1970, 1975) notion of warrants, Byers argues that the earthworks are iconic warrants built and used to immanentize the sacred authority of the cosmos.

Following Byers, it is important to recognize the profound worldview consequences of physically enclosing and systematically scarring nature. Any major act of construction/enclosure constitutes a reworking or modifi-cation of the natural world and therefore its cultural order. The building materials of enclosures and mounds are derived from the visible world, and the action of human construction is not only a reworking of the natural order but also a juxtaposition of the cosmology that structured it. Societies objec-tify themselves through their acts in nature. Earthworks, therefore, can act as physical expressions of social structure, and their lasting nature means they can represent and preserve that which is past, thus potentially generating and expressing a temporal segmentation.

Although for Byers (1987) the Hopewell enclosures themselves are al-most incidental by-products of the activities and rites that went into their creation, it is important to note that enclosure and other monumental con-struction often commemorates and enshrines specific sets of actions and the created landscape remains as a social framework and medium. Moreover, these structures can be physical reminders and manifestations of success-fully completed rituals. The endurance of monuments can serve to distance the code of society from its current members by demonstrating time depth or plurality. Therefore monuments can influence social development in the sense that tradition structures social behavior and can be manipulated (e.g., Giddens 1979).

The Architecture of Enclosures

Two fundamental attributes are shared by all enclosures, whether in eastern North America or elsewhere in the world, regardless of function. First, enclo-sures do, in fact, enclose space—hardly a profound revelation. Second, the locations at which enclosures were built were specifically chosen by mem-bers of the social groups responsible for these structures. In the case of enclo-sures linked to corporate or ritual, rather than purely defensive, purposes, the locations themselves probably were viewed in part as "natural monuments" (Bradley 1991). That is, even as certain logistic parameters obtain for the placement of defensive enclosures, it seems likely that a set of ideological parameters had to be satisfied in choosing a location for constructing a prehistoric ceremonial enclosure. But even here, the distinction between "defensive" and "ceremonial" may become somewhat blurred. Use of monumental architecture in marking social boundaries has been noted by Chapman (1981, 1995) and others (e.g., Charles and Buikstra 1983), so one might conceive of the logic-in-use as requiring placement that is both ideologically appropriate and politically expedient.

In this regard, if on some level enclosures are attempts to impose a structure on inter- and intragroup relationships, we might expect the sites to be positioned in relation to their function within a broader community and with regard to the nature of the activities taking place at the enclosures. For example, a central location could be disadvantageous if Hopewell enclosures were the focus of world renewal rites (Wright 1990) or other rituals of major importance and if these rites were conceived of as potentially very dangerous. The fate of the world, or at the very least society, literally hung in the balance. Therefore it would be appropriate to locate ritual centers (enclosures) outside the main settlement zone on the boundary of community territory.

In the case of the northern Michigan enclosures (Milner and O'Shea, this volume), the marginal location of these structures might reflect not just ecotonal settings but also an attempt to remove locations within which political and/or social (rather than ritual) activities could be potentially dangerous. Hence, placement of these gathering points well away from major settlements would be advantageous.

Another important point made by several authors, notably Connolly and Riordan, is that enclosures are not to be understood as static creations entailing only a single construction episode (see Thunen 1988b:100–101). Their patient investigations at Fort Ancient and Pollock Works, respectively, have revealed complex histories of construction stages, some of which dramatically altered the appearance, or "presentation," of the enclosures.

In a similar vein, it is interesting to note that major structural changes are recorded for the earliest of the excavated Ohio Valley enclosures, Peter Village (Clay 1988), which may have been started around 300 B.C. with the erection of a wooden stockade. This was subsequently burned and an earthen embankment and ditch were added. Similar architectural evolution apparently occurred at the Mt. Horeb earthwork (Webb 1941), a relatively small "Adena sacred circle."

On a larger scale, it should come as no surprise that the complex architecture manifested at Fort Ancient was produced over a period spanning two or three hundred years (Connolly, this volume). Especially impressive in this instance are the long-term commitment to the Fort Ancient locality and the execution of planned design over a number of generations. In this regard it is

perhaps important not to impart a Eurocentric sense of awe to our appreciation of long-term planning and execution of projects by prehistoric Native
Americans; after all, many of the great cathedrals of Europe were also created
over a span of generations.

Indeed, it may be that much of our misunderstanding of enclosures
stems from treating these structures as closed, stable monuments, rather than
considering the social context of their execution. Perhaps it is more appropriate to view prehistoric enclosures as "projects" rather than to focus on the
criteria of formal design and architecture. That is, to some extent these structures were resolved only through their construction, and certain spatial
attributes may have become manifest only during the sequence of their construction. Importantly, since some of these structures existed and were the
focus of various activities over considerable periods of time, and therefore
were modified and redefined, enclosures and other monuments should not be
treated as static, unchanging artifacts. Their final form cannot necessarily be
assumed in their initial construction because form was accumulative and
resolved only through a sequence of events, including additive construction.

The Social and Economic Contexts of Enclosures

We turn now to the broader contexts of enclosure construction: the social
and economic conditions that accompany such endeavors. Western Europe is
another area of the world where earthen enclosures are found as features of
prehistoric sites. Even though prehistoric Native Americans of the Eastern
Woodlands did not construct megalithic structures such as the henges and passage graves of prehistoric Europe, the enclosures of the Eastern Woodlands certainly must be considered examples of monumental architecture on par with
the earthworks of Neolithic Europe. An appreciation of monumental scale can
be obtained by comparing the linear embankments erected in the two regions.
For example, the Dorset Curcus, the largest Neolithic monument in England,
consists of an embankment and ditch that traverses a distance of approximately 10 km and attained a maximum height of about 2 m (Barrett et al.
1991). Yet this magnificent structure easily is surpassed in both scale and
architectural complexity by several North American sites, including Poverty
Point and Newark (Gibson and Lepper, this volume).

European archaeologists (e.g., Sherratt 1990) typically associate the rise of
"monumental architecture" (especially large funerary monuments) with major
changes in social organization inferred to have occurred concomitantly with
the rise of cereal grain production during the Neolithic. This inferred social
reorganization presumably gave rise to ranked societies that provided a context for the mobilization of large workforces for monument construction.
Such a model is compatible with ethnographic and archaeological data from

many areas of the world which generally support the proposition that monumental architecture is produced primarily by sedentary agricultural societies that roughly conform to Service's (1975) chiefdom or state levels of social and political organization (Trigger 1990). The Eastern Woodlands case and newer data from Europe, however, raise significant issues concerning these presumed economic and social underpinnings of monumental construction.

New data and interpretations call into question the rapid adoption of full-scale agriculture, especially in northern and western Europe. Moreover, the last ten years have provided data that greatly modify or expand upon earlier interpretations of Middle Woodland subsistence in eastern North America. Specifically, the onset of the Middle Woodland period (circa 200 B.C.) is marked by a dramatic upsurge in the utilization of native cultigens (Johannessen 1984; B. Smith 1992). Thus, subsistence differences between Middle Woodland and early Neolithic peoples may not be very pronounced (e.g., Chapman 1995; C. Evans 1988; J. Evans et al. 1988).

Parenthetically, Bender (1985; see also Clay 1987) correctly calls attention to the architectural parallels between Middle Woodland and the European Neolithic (specifically, in Brittany), but errs in interpreting the former societies as nonagricultural because they were not maize horticulturists. In fairness to Bender, it should be noted that a large body of evidence about the domestication and use of native cultigens in eastern North America has accumulated in the years since her paper was written.

Thus in both western Europe and eastern North America, the emergence or intensification (in the Eastern Woodlands) of agriculture does appear to coincide with the rise of monumental architecture (see also Seeman 1992). This correlation is not surprising since the development of agriculture represents a major shift in the relationship between humans and land (or between culture and nature); an agrarian subsistence base transforms nature in contrast to previous modes of its immediate exploitation (Goodelier 1977). This of course says nothing of potential social and political correlates.

The social contexts of monumental constructions are much less clear. Although sites such as Poverty Point and Newark clearly required labor on a scale comparable to or greater than that required for some Neolithic structures, there is no ready explanation for either area as to how the necessary labor force was assembled and maintained. There is little evidence in the Eastern Woodlands of marked social ranking through which key individuals commanded sufficient authority and power (sensu Brown 1981) to demand and/or coerce construction of the Hopewell or later enclosures (e.g., Greber 1976, 1979; Sullivan and Coffin 1996). Collaborative efforts by several small-scale sociopolitical groups can be invoked to account for the presumed requisite numbers of participants (e.g., Mainfort 1986), and while such a scenario may be essentially correct, the mechanism by which numerous individuals were brought together and organized for large construction projects during either the Middle Woodland period or later prehistory in the Great Lakes region (to say nothing of Poverty Point) remains unknown.

The settlement patterns associated with both the early Neolithic and at least the Middle Woodland enclosures (and possibly later ones as well; see Milner and O'Shea, and Neusius et al., this volume) suggest that these constructions may be associated with relationships among groups living in dispersed residences. Early (but not later) Neolithic settlement in northern and western Europe is now seen as consisting of small, dispersed habitations, not large, centralized towns or villages (Sherratt 1990). This pattern is comparable, at least in a general sense, to the pattern of small, dispersed farmsteads that characterizes Hopewellian societies in Ohio (B. Smith 1992). Sherratt's statement that "the element of permanence seems to have been provided not by the settlements themselves, but by monumental tombs and enclosures" (1990:149) seems appropriate to both early Neolithic and Hopewell.

Some English scholars (J. Evans et al. 1988) view enclosures as monuments that served on one level to bind the dispersed early Neolithic farmsteads of agricultural communities together and to formalize relationships between different groups. It seems reasonable that at least some North American enclosures served a similar function. Interpretation of specific activities taking place at enclosures represents another, separate level, and such activities could have varied regionally.

It is interesting to note that Goldstein (1995) has proposed a model for construction of late prehistoric effigy mounds (A.D. 650–1200) in the upper Great Lakes and eastern edge of the Great Plains regions that echoes many of the themes of current models of enclosure construction, although construction of these earthworks is not clearly linked with agricultural intensification. While not of the monumental proportions of the geometric Hopewell enclosures, these low (<2 m) mounds range from 20 to 50 m in length, occur in groups of up to eighty mounds, and often contain burials. She interprets the mound sites as periodic aggregation points for dispersed groups, but points out that it is counterproductive to view them simply as mortuary sites, territory markers, astronomical markers, or symbolic totems. It is likely they may represent all of these things in certain contexts, and they must be viewed against an overall social and physical landscape. In the case of the effigy mounds, Goldstein (1995:118) believes they served as "maps"–"symbolic representations of both form and space to the people who built and used the mounds"–and that they may have functioned as indicators or pointers to resources controlled by a particular group.

We submit that interpretations of earthen enclosures as ceremonial and/or social aggregation sites also probably contain elements of truth but fall short of addressing the question of why the enclosures were built. The same can be said for linkages between monumental architecture and social boundaries. The multifaceted discussions of enclosure use, symbolism, and architecture in this volume all are aspects of understanding the enclosures. This multidimensionality leads us to point to Greber's (1992) concept of the enclosures as "corporate centers." This concept seems both appropriate and useful, as the term subsumes a full range of potential activities and shifts attention away from what may be illusory dichotomies. We suggest that it is the very integration of the various uses, meanings, and constructions of the enclosures that will lead us to explanations.

Chapter 2

✵ Broken Circles, Owl Monsters, and Black Earth Midden

Separating Sacred and Secular at Poverty Point
Jon L. Gibson

The Poverty Point site in the Lower Mississippi Valley is a good place to try to make sense out of a long-standing problem in Eastern North American archaeology: Are prehistoric earthworks sacred or secular constructions or both? How do we tell? Is the distinction recognizable empirically, or are sacred and secular dimensions too inseparable for us to untangle?

Poverty Point is a terminal Archaic earthwork complex built sometime between 1730 and 1350 (cal.) B.C. Construction may have spanned all or part of these four centuries. When completed, there were six concentric C-shaped ridges, enclosing a 14 ha plaza, and five or more mounds, including two towering bird effigies rising over 21 and 15 m high (fig. 2.1). Construction fill totaled about three-quarter million steres of dirt, a lot of dirt by any standards but especially impressive for hunter-gatherers.

Four decades ago, Poverty Point was the oldest large earthwork known in the American South, and that made it hard to explain under the normative, progressive evolutionary framework that guided our thinking at the time (J. Ford 1955). Discoveries in Louisiana and Florida have since revealed mound-building antecedents. Several mounds and mound groups have yielded radiocarbon dates that predate Poverty Point by more than twenty-five centuries, and, what is more, many of these Archaic mounds are not the small, unimposing affairs we might expect of mounds of such antiquity but are as big as any constructed during Poverty Point times, except for the two giant bird mounds at Poverty Point, which are among the largest mounds ever built in the United States.

Joe Saunders, Thurman Allen, and associates are presently working one of these early sites, Watson Brake on the Ouachita River in northeastern Louisiana, some 75 km west of Poverty Point (Saunders 1995; Saunders et al. 1994). Watson Brake dates sometime between 3300 and 3900 (cal.) B.C. (Saunders 1995), but what is just as intriguing as its age is the fact that this late Middle Archaic site has eleven mounds set in an artificial earthen ring about 280 m in diameter (Saunders et al. 1994:143–145). The largest mound, an aproned conical, stands 7 m high. No, Watson Brake is not as large as Poverty Point. It would fit comfortably inside Poverty Point's plaza, but the

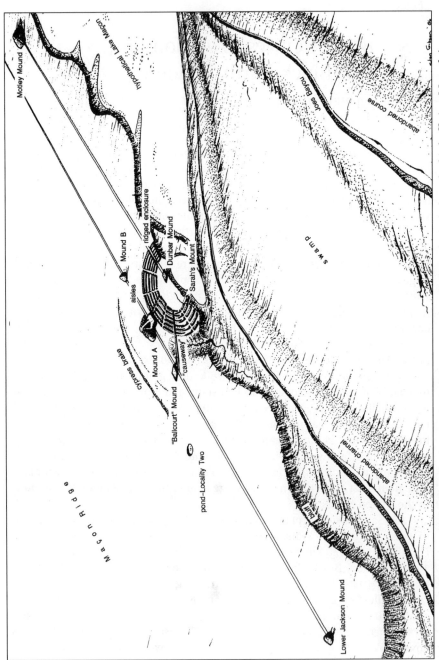

Fig. 2.1. Poverty Point earthworks, showing central ridged enclosure and mounds, including the bird effigies, Mound A and Motley Mound.

point is this: large-scale mound building was going on in the Poverty Point vicinity more than 2500 years before the Poverty Point earthworks were constructed. One of these early mounds may even have been incorporated into Poverty Point's main north-south axis.

We now realize that Poverty Point is not the earliest earthwork complex in the South, nor is it the only truly ambitious Archaic construction (J. Gibson 1994; Russo 1994; Saunders et al. 1994). Whatever was going on at Poverty Point had precedents in the Lower Mississippi Valley and Gulf South, and just knowing that enables us to view Poverty Point as an outgrowth of preexisting cultural conditions rather than having to grapple with it as a precocious developmental oddity.

This is not the first attempt to separate sacred from secular at Poverty Point. In fact, this very issue has held center stage in Poverty Point archaeology for more than four decades. After digging at Poverty Point in the early 1950s, James Ford and Clarence Webb (1956:128) claimed the earthworks were house foundations for a large group of permanent residents, but concluded that religion was responsible for the enormity of earth moving. Gordon Willey (1957:198–199) took issue with Ford and Webb, likening the geometric rings to Adena and Hopewell "sacred" circles. William Haag (1961:322) sided with Ford and Webb, citing the extent and depth of midden and multitudes of artifacts as indications that Poverty Point was no mere ceremonial center visited only on holy days but a large, thriving village as well. Later, Clarence Webb (1968:319) and James Ford (1969) reaffirmed their earlier view but put more emphasis on its ceremonial nature than they had before. Then Philip Phillips (1970:872) and Jeffrey Brain (1971) went along with Willey, maintaining that Poverty Point was a vacant "ceremonial center for a large community scattered over a wide area in small hamlet-type settlements." I took exception (J. Gibson 1973) and, joining with Ford, Webb, and Haag, went on to boast that Poverty Point was North America's first chiefdom, a theocratic chiefdom (J. Gibson 1974). Webb (1982) concurred. Now Edwin Jackson (1991) disagrees with everybody and proposes that Poverty Point is neither ceremonial nor residential but is instead a periodic meeting ground where peoples from near and far met to swap rocks and other stuff.

A while back, Webb and I tried to identify sacred areas on the Poverty Point site by analyzing the distributions of more than a hundred thousand provenience-controlled, surface-collected artifacts (J. Gibson 1970, 1972, 1973; C. Webb 1970, 1982). We concluded the west sector of the rings was a sacred precinct because it had a disproportionate number of finished, hard stone lapidary objects, which we assumed belonged to civic and religious personages. Unfinished lapidary items were concentrated in the south sector of the rings. This seemed like clear evidence of activity segregation, perhaps separate production and demonstration areas. What better location, we surmised, for a sacred precinct than the area around the large bird mound, which we presumed to be a shrine or religious edifice.

In 1991, I spent a field season digging in the western rings, trying to confirm the sacred-precinct notion (J. Gibson 1993). I had no luck. I was looking for what James Knight (1986) calls sacra, a lot of sacra. What I found was typical-looking domestic residue, such as loess ball fragments and flint flakes and chips. But did the abundance of such residue mean the west sector was strictly a domestic area, and not a sacred zone or a staging area for ceremonial activities on the bird mound? Over 90 percent of the recovered artifacts were fragments of loess balls, which were used in cooking. Even religious celebrants had to eat. Maybe ceremonies had all been accompanied by feasts. I was still puzzled. Why had so many stone beads and other polished stone objects been found on the surface of the rings and so few in our excavations?

In hindsight, I realize I wouldn't have recognized a sacred area if I had been standing on one, and, to be perfectly frank, I'm still not sure I would. My expectations of sacred ground were too general to distinguish sacred from secular.

Methods

Back then, Webb and I assumed the presence of or nearness to mounds and the heavy occurrence of ornaments to be indicators of sacred areas. We assumed the presence of thick black midden, fire pits, and other structural features to be indicative of residential areas. But this simplistic and uncritical slate of correlates produced mixed signals, which is why conflicting views of Poverty Point—as a vacant ceremonial center and as a municipal center—have managed to coexist so long. The issue was set up to have an either-or resolution. Both perspectives were based on the same too-general criteria, and the prevailing view at any given moment was usually the last one published.

Who published last gave no answer to the real nature of Poverty Point. That lay in a fresh approach, in a more suitable dialectic and new correlates for separating sacred from secular. I dusted off Durkheim, Lowie, Radin, Levi-Strauss, Gill, and other cultural anthropologists, inquiring after contextual and rational bases of native religion, hoping to come up with a better evaluative framework. I reviewed ethnographic literature on rituals, ceremonies, and lore of Lower Mississippi and other southern tribes (Bushnell 1909; Stouff and Twitty 1971; Swanton 1911, 1928a, 1931, 1946; Wright 1828) looking for common elements, no matter how general. My search focused on the Natchez, Chitimacha, Tunica, Koroa, Caddo, Choctaw, Chickasaw, Cherokee, and Creek. The working assumption was that commonalities among these tribes stemmed from their common linguistic ancestry as Gulf-speaking peoples (Haas 1956, 1958). Similar rites and ideas about the great mysteries might approximate those of Poverty Point people 3500 years ago—approximate, not duplicate. I did not expect identity, but I did hope to recognize enough common ground between archaeological materials and native views to be able at least to distinguish sacred from secular in a broad sense.

Knight (1986) documented an essential continuity between historic tribes and Mississippian groups in terms of the religiosity of platform mounds. I wondered if some threads of continuity didn't go back even further, back 3000 more years to Poverty Point, perhaps even back 6000 years to the beginning of mound-building itself. I, in fact, count on it.

Sacred beliefs and stories are among the most conservative elements of traditional cultures, and though culture is always changing, peoples' sacred explanatory stories are tenaciously preserved because they are inseparable from their social consciousness and perceptions of identity. Even if there is no historical continuity, the methods employed here provide a refined set of ethnographically based correlates for our archaeological data.

How Secular Can Sacred Be?

So how secular can sacred be and still be considered sacred? That is a real problem at Poverty Point, where we lack mortuary remains and artifacts smack of common, everyday utility.

That people congregated at Poverty Point in considerable numbers is obvious by the tons and tons of trash they left. At the site, dark midden underlies the elevated rings and it formed on top of the finished rings and along their lower edges. Dark midden incorporates abundant domestic remains—charcoal, chipped and ground stone tools and residue from tool making, fire-cracked gravel, angular pieces of sandstone and other rocks and minerals, loess cooking balls, and many other artifacts. Sometimes densities in the dark middens reach an artifact per cubic centimeter. The black staining comes from charcoal and other organic residues, leftovers from cooking. Fire pits, earth ovens, postmolds, and remnants of other stationary facilities occur both underneath and on temporary building-module surfaces within the rings.

There have been too few large, contiguous excavations to reveal house patterns, and the paucity of evidence for extensive post-in-ground housing is the key to the vacant ceremonial center argument. Only at Poverty Point, it seems, do you find archaeologists ready and willing to ignore the long-held assumption that thick, black, artifact-laden midden means substantial and prolonged occupation. Even though the assumption implies nothing about the kind of occupation, it speaks emphatically about its intensity, and, in my mind, that intensity is plainly out of kilter with a small resident group of religious caretakers, a periodic influx of religious pilgrims, or a regularly held camp meeting.

The full assemblage—at least the materials from the last midden to form, the one on top of the rings—conveys an overwhelming impression of domesticity. It is made up mainly of broken equipment and fabrication by-products, signs of people hard at work, doing everyday jobs, leading routine lives. But is this really the case? Is this all there is to it?

Artifacts found in the artificial fill of the rings are different from those in the dark surface midden. Although the same tool classes are generally present, there are very few unbroken, finished tools in the fill, and those usually have been resharpened or transformed into other tools. Most tools from the fill are informal; they are predominantly flakes and blades that have been expediently modified or used. Comparatively greater numbers of unbroken and unreworked bifacial tools, as well as formal tools on flakes and other materials, are found in the dark surface midden. It seems the builders were curating tools and conserving rock supplies when they were working on the rings, suggesting that construction work kept them pretty busy. The building project evidently curtailed toolmaking and economic exchange and may even have temporarily shut down exchange entirely. Economic inflation, precipitated by construction's drain on resources and labor, was even felt at small contemporary sites nearby, like Orvis Scott (J. Gibson 1996), where stone shortages were also being experienced and tool conservation being practiced.

Although this doesn't necessarily mean that religion was the prime cause of this situation at Poverty Point, I think by the time we add up all the evidence, we can make a strong case that it was deeply involved.

Sacred Places and Sacred Symbols

Religion cannot really be separated from daily life in traditional societies (Renfrew 1994:47); it is just too interwoven. Sacred objects are not sacred intrinsically (Gill 1982); they are sacred because people say they are. They are symbols and can be fully understood only within their makers' perceptions of reality and cosmos. We are never going to grasp the fullness or emic meaning of Poverty Point's sacred worldview, but I think we can perceive some of its basic functional and structural elements and maybe even understand a bit of its general nature.

Earthworks as Ritual Space

Most peoples have special places where they conduct ritual and ceremony, although worship and spirituality per se have no such bounds. If there is one thing that distinguishes Poverty Point from contemporary sites, it is the gigantic earthworks. A few other Poverty Point period sites have earth-works—single midden rings or mounds (J. Gibson 1994:170–172), but none have six concentric rings or as many mounds built on such a sweeping scale. And size is not a consequence of a protracted building span either. At Poverty Point, construction only took a couple of centuries or less (J. Gibson 1992). The earthworks were meant to be big from the start, and a lot of people worked on them to make sure they reached the desired magnitude (J. Gibson 1987:table 2).

The scale is too large to appreciate the geometric layout from ground level or even from the top of the tallest tree. It had to be "seen" with the mind and not the eye, and that, to me, makes it out of the ordinary—supernatural, if you will—an interpretation also supported by its C-shape. The broken-circle (actually arcuate) plan is a recurrent theme of sacred areas, ritual activities, and dance movements of peoples linked linguistically to ancient Gulf or proto-Gulf language speakers (DuPratz [1774] 1975; Gill 1982:30, 33). Poverty Point's rings open to the east, along a thirty-foot-high bluff, providing a perfect vista for observing the rising sun over the treetops or across a lake, which is hypothesized to have lain alongside the site (fig. 2.2). The sun was the pri-mary celestial being of Gulf language-linked tribes (Swanton 1911:175, 1928b:206–213; Hudson 1976:126, 1984:13, 1987:141), and its widespread importance undoubtedly reflects the antiquity of that belief. The opening in the rings gave a clear view of the awakening sun each day during its sol-stice-to-solstice journey along the horizon; such sighting paths were used in historic times by holy men to awaken the sun and summon its blessings (LePetit in Swanton 1911:174).

Not only did broken-circle architecture provide a direct link to the sun, it also provided an exit for tensions and imbalances built up inside an area, whereas completely enclosed spaces trapped evil inside (Gill 1982:30). But openings in enclosures allowed outside ghosts, witches, and other evil super-naturals to enter, unless prevented by water barriers, ashes, or other means (Hall 1976:360–363). The opening in Poverty Point's rings was protected by a water barrier, either a bayou or possibly a lake. Thus, Poverty Point's design fits with indigenous beliefs about ways of getting rid of evil within and keep-ing external evil out.

Another widely held historical view was that geometric figures kept evil spirits at bay (Hall 1976:362). If this concept is embodied in Poverty Point's earthworks, then we can envision the uniformly concentric, elliptical sym-metry of the rings as a protective shield around those sections of the inner area that were unprotected by the water barrier. Even the swales between the concentric rings, which held water during rainy times only, might have been magical impediments to the spread of disharmony within the enclosure.

Possibly another evil-mediating feature of the site's geometry is the

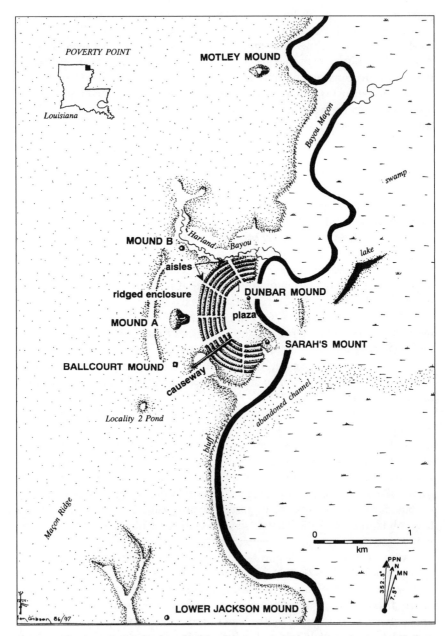

POVERTY POINT

Louisiana

MOTLEY MOUND

Bayou Maçon

swamp

MOUND B

Harland Bayou

aisles

lake

ridged enclosure

DUNBAR MOUND

MOUND A

plaza

SARAH'S MOUNT

BALLCOURT MOUND

causeway

abandoned channel

Locality 2 Pond

bluff

Maçon Ridge

0   1
km

PPN
N
MN
352.5°
7.5°

LOWER JACKSON MOUND

Fig. 2.2. The east-facing, broken-circle arrangement of the geometric rings and the north-south alignment of mounds at Poverty Point.

recurring number six (or seven). There are six concentric elevated rings. They are divided into six sectors by bisecting aisles. They enclose a central open space, or plaza. Because the earthworks are axially aligned with cardinal directions, they may embody the numerical elements of the Gulf-Muskogean cosmos (Hudson 1984:11–12): this world, the upper world, and the lower world (three cardinal points, corresponding to the center, up, and down); and four value-laden directions emanating from the center (east, south, west, and north), a total of seven sacred positions—six directions and a center.

In this connection, it may also be significant that mounds were placed outside the ringed enclosure on the west and north (fig. 2.2), the directions of death and of witchcraft and social disharmony, respectively (Hudson 1984:12). The Motley Mound, due north of the northern compartment of rings, and Mound A, positioned immediately west of the outer opening of the western aisle, are massive bird-shaped structures (Ford and Webb 1956:128), size and bird form perhaps being essential for combating the powerful, anti-social, supernatural forces originating from those directions.

Two smaller mounds may have helped: Mound B, a conical, lay outside the northwest sector of rings; and Ballcourt Mound, a square platform, lay outside the southwest sector. Unlike Mound A, these two do not block aisle entrances. Mound B is positioned radially 250 m northwest of the approximate arcuate center of the northwest sector. Ballcourt Mound is about 185 m radially southwest of the upper end of the southwest sector.

Ballcourt Mound, Mound A, and Mound B all fall along the same north-south axis, which bears an azimuth of 352.5°. The Motley Mound is off line, but its long axis (or "wing") is perpendicular to the main north-south axis. Thus, the placement and axial geometry of some Poverty Point mounds are congruent with the protective-shield concept: the rings protecting the inner sanctum (the center, or plaza) and the axial square formed by the mounds— possibly a microcosmic representation of the earth island (Hudson 1987:140)—protecting the rings and their occupants.

Poverty Point has other mounds, including two inside and several more outside the enclosure toward the south. Most of these are later, but even if some are Poverty Point constructions, they would not have fit the axial symmetry of the other mounds. But this fact does not compromise the protective shield. The benevolent spirit forces, which resided in the south, didn't need guarding against.

Aside from Gulf-linked concepts about geometry, the mere presence of mounds and a plaza embodies sacred concepts. Symbolically, mounds were regarded as microcosmic earth mothers (Knight 1989; Swanton 1931:37). They were integral to virtually all intensification rites, especially those of purification and renewal (Knight 1986:680, 1989). Even the dirt of which they were made was sometimes regarded as sacred, especially when it had been swept up from plazas where ceremonies so charged the ground with supernatural power that it was deemed unsafe or improper for regular people to tread on. Knight (1989) links this powerful, swept-up dirt, or *tadjo*, to Mississippian sacred symbolism of a thousand or so years ago. I look at the mounds and plaza at Poverty Point, the same physical manifestations of tadjo as in Mississippian and historic contexts, and ask why not there too? The symbolic linkage between ceremonially charged dirt and earthworks had to start sometime, somewhere. Maybe it was a basic principle of mound-building from the beginning, and, if so, its roots may predate Poverty Point by three thousand years.

Symbolic Artifacts and Tribal Stories

Poverty Point is different from contemporary sites in another way. It has a large number of artifacts with probable symbolic meaning, including engraved, carved, and molded objects of polished stone and baked loess (C. Webb 1982). Animal, human, and hybrid animal and animal-human figures occur, as do geometric designs and other glyphs. Our data are not good enough to tell if Poverty Point has more of these objects per capita than surrounding components, but there is no question that it has absolutely more. Their presence, along with the earthworks, is really what distinguishes Poverty Point from coeval sites.

There are a number of ways to look at these objects, but here I focus on similarities between Poverty Point representational artifact imagery and ethnohistorical information on native southeastern cosmology and other sacred beliefs (J. Gibson 1990).

Beads, pendants, and carved designs on soapstone vessels, plummets, bannerstones, and gorgets represent a variety of birds. Owls are most prominent. There are large owls, small ones, and middle-size ones, possibly portraying the great horned, screech, and barred species respectively (fig. 2.3a–c). The so-called fox-man designs on plummets and gorgets probably represent owls too (C. Webb 1975), not foxes: special owls—owl monsters with deer antlers (fig. 2.3d), owl-masked and costumed performers or shamans (fig. 2.3e–f), and owl-human hybrids (fig. 2.3g). In addition, there is a crow (fig. 2.4a), a nestling with open beak (fig. 2.4b), and crested (fig. 2.4c), long-billed (fig. 2.4d), big-headed (fig. 2.4e), and song bird forms (fig. 2.4f).

Birds are prominent in the sacred beliefs of native southeastern peoples. Thunder and lightning were considered great birds (Swanton 1931:212); crows were thought to bring bad luck (Swanton 1931:204); doves and pigeons symbolized kindness; woodpeckers were considered guardians (Swanton 1931, 1946:776); wrens were informants (Stouff and Twitty 1971:62–63); and wild canaries (?) foretold the weather (Swanton 1946:781). Owls, screech owls especially, were associated with death and witchcraft (Swanton 1931:198–199,

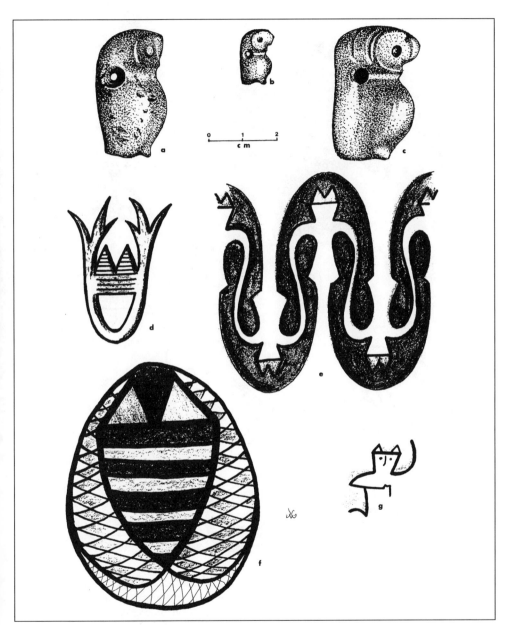

Fig. 2.3. The sacred birds: *a–c,* owl pendants (to scale); *d,* owl monster with deer antlers, carved on plummet; *e–f,* owl-masked and-costumed performers, carved on plummets; *g,* owl-human hybrid, carved on bannerstone (d–g not to scale).

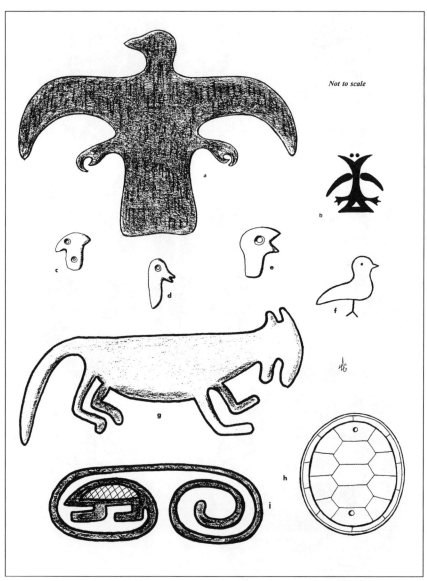

Fig. 2.4. More sacred symbols: *a*, crow carved on soapstone vessel; *b*, nestling with open beak carved on plummet; *c*, bird-head pendant, crested form; *d*, bird-head pendant, long-billed form; *e*, bird-head pendant, big-headed form; *f*, song-bird form carved on plummet; *g*, panther figure carved on soapstone vessel; *h*, gopher tortise gorget; *i*, long-tail design carved on plummet (none to scale).

1946:776). The Choctaw believed that one of a deceased person's two ghosts, the outside shadow, or *Shilombish*, changed into an owl or a fox and went around scaring people who came near the corpse. Owl feathers were believed to help Creek "doctors" see at night. Basically, birds were associated with spiritual power, death, bad luck, witchcraft, weather forecasting, advance warning, kindness, night vision, and news bringing—an impressive array of supernatural and special abilities.

If the antlered owl-plummet engravings represent masked dancers or shamans, they have general counterparts among many groups who believed that disguised performers actually became powerful spirits and that masks themselves were living supernatural helpers capable of driving away witches and curing sickness (Gill 1982:69). The case for owl masking at Poverty Point is strengthened by the occasional appearance of horizontal stripes across the whole face or just on forehead and ears (fig. 2.3 f–g), stripes that could be designs on wooden or woven masks, face painting, or tattoing.

Other Poverty Point objects with symbolic, possibly magical, significance include a panther figure cut into a soapstone vessel (C. Webb 1944) (fig. 2.4g); a periwinkle or marine gastropod figure engraved on a gorget (C. Webb 1982:fig. 28 [39]); waterfowl webbed-feet engravings on plummets (C. Webb 1982:27 [18, 26]); open clamshell pendants (C. Webb 1982:fig. 29 [3940]); musk turtle and gopher tortoise gorgets (C. Webb 1982:fig. 28 [26]) (fig. 2.4h); animal-claw or bird-talon pendants (C. Webb 1982:fig. 29 [45–46]); frog and "locust" beads (Connaway 1977:fig. 32; C. Webb 1971:fig. 1); and a "long tail" (opossum?) engraved on a plummet (C. Webb 1982:fig. 27 [19]) (fig. 2.4i).

Many of these figures are represented in tribal lore, in both heroic and sacred stories. Turtle and "Long Tail" figure in "just so" stories—how Turtle's shell came to be cracked and colored, and how Possum's tail got to be bare (Bushnell 1909:533–534). Creek hunters carried terrapin and panther bones with them as good-luck charms (Swanton 1946:774). Waterfowl and frogs figure in the Choctaw explanation of how Aba created water (Bushnell 1909:534–535), and the Cherokee believed eclipses were caused when a giant frog swallowed the sun (Hudson 1976:126). The Choctaw believe that humans were created when Aba caused them and locusts to come out of the ground together and dry out on top of a sacred mound, Nanih Waiya (Swanton 1931:5–37).

The Choctaw creation story furnishes a link among first people, locusts, and earth mounds and is an important integrative argument for the sacred nature of Poverty Point mounds and at least one of its classes of iconic objects (Blitz 1993; J. Gibson 1990). John Connaway (1977, 1991:3–4) maintains that "locust" pendants are not locusts at all but represent a variety of animals, including owls, and that their wide geographic and temporal distribution indicates they are not confined to Poverty Point contexts. He is right, of course, but they are present at Poverty Point. If only we could dig one up, we would have a much stronger case.

Sacred Place, Yes—Secular Place, Yes

These correlations convince me that Poverty Point was a sacred place, a place of ritual and rite, a place of spirits and power, a place of mystery and magic. Historical analogs and archaeological matches are just too numerous for all to be coincidental. Some may be, and I would not be inclined to press any one resemblance too strongly. It is the weight of evidence that convinces. I feel comfortable in assuming that the shared symbolism of southern historic tribes contains many elements, if not the core body, of ancient Gulf cosmic symbolism, and I do not hesitate to link Poverty Point with Gulf language speakers, if for no reason other than geography.

Was all of Poverty Point a sacred place or only certain sections of it? Was sacredness perpetually inherent or limited to certain events or periods? I find the sacred to be too enmeshed with the secular to separate at Poverty Point. Sacred and secular are rarely separated in traditional societies anyway, nor are they always in our own (Renfrew 1994:47). I think we can make a strong case that most of the small contemporary sites surrounding Poverty Point were primarily workplaces, but Poverty Point itself is a different kind of place, a special kind of place.

It may be worthwhile to continue this exercise, if for no other reason than to sharpen our archaeological skills, but I have resolved, to my satisfaction, the issue that prompted this investigation—trying to separate sacred from secular. Sacredness inheres at Poverty Point, it pervades, so I have no qualms about identifying Poverty Point as a sacred place. But Poverty Point is also a secular place. The notion that it must be one or the other is without substance. Even with perfect methods and the collective knowledge of archaeology, I do not think we can separate the inseparable.

Chapter 3

✠ Prehistoric Enclosures in Louisiana and the Marksville Site

Dennis Jones and Carl Kuttruff

Along the eastern margin of this [the Avoyelles] prairie the Red River once flowed, and upon its northeastern margin, almost within the corporate limits of Marksville, are still to be seen the well-defined lineaments of an earthwork, crescent in form, too laboriously constructed and too skillfully laid off to warrant the opinion that it was the work of any savage tribe.
(H. Skipwith 1881:110)

Skipwith's description of the earthen enclosure at the Marksville site in east central Louisiana added to a large body of speculation by nineteenth-century scientists, explorers, settlers, and ordinary citizens concerning the builders of the mounds and geometric earthworks throughout eastern North America (Willey and Sabloff 1974). Diverse groups including wandering tribes of Israel, refugees from the lost continent of Atlantis, or an extinct race of "Moundbuilders" were all considered candidates (Silverberg 1968). Skipwith's opinion that no "savage tribe" was capable of building the enclosure at Marksville was common at the time, and it was popularly believed by local residents that the enclosure had been constructed by de Soto's army in the sixteenth century (Toth 1974:13–16).

As archaeology progressed into the twentieth century and the chronology of prehistoric North America was better understood, it became evident that many of the earthen enclosures, mounds, and elaborate geometric structures were constructed during Middle Woodland times (ca. 200 B.C. to A.D. 400), and many of the most elaborate sites were found to be affiliated with the Hopewell culture that flourished in the Ohio River Valley (Squier and Davis 1848; Brose and Greber 1979). The extent of Hopewell culture, or its influence, is seen throughout much of eastern North America: from western New York State, to the upper Midwest, into Kansas, down the Mississippi River Valley, and into Florida (Griffin 1967; J. Gibson 1970; Toth 1988). Similarities in artifact styles and the plans of many of the sites suggest widespread contact and exchange. This wide area containing shared cultural traits has been called the Hopewell Interaction Sphere, and the distribution of certain types of earthen enclosures themselves may prove to be an indicator of the extent of interaction.

Archaeologically, very little is known about most of the enclosures themselves, as very few systematic investigations of these earthen structures were conducted until very recently. Most early investigations at enclosure sites focused on other features, especially burial mounds. As a result, many questions about the enclosures remain unanswered, not only in the Hopewell heartland but in other parts of eastern North America as well.

Prehistoric Louisianans built several sites of earthen construction that are noteworthy for their antiquity, complexity, and size. Recent studies demonstrate that some of the oldest earthworks in North America were constructed in the Lower Mississippi Valley (Gibson and Shenkel 1988; Russo 1994), and the extraordinary Poverty Point site in northeastern Louisiana was without peer in North America during its heyday around 1500 B.C. (J. Gibson 1980, this volume; C. Webb 1982). Over a millennium later, prehistoric peoples produced an impressive complex of mounds and earthen enclosures at the Marksville site.

Located in east-central Louisiana (see fig. 1.1), the Marksville site (16AV1) has received only sporadic scientific archaeological attention in this century. A significant portion (but not all) of the site is now a Louisiana State Commemorative Area (SCA) and is well maintained, with a small museum as part of the facility. The Marksville site has also given its name to a prehistoric culture and chronological period that is regarded as a manifestation of the Hopewell culture in the Lower Mississippi Valley. A commonly cited span for the Marksville presence in the region is A.D. 1 to A.D. 400, although recent evidence suggests that Marksville appeared by at least 100 B.C. (Toth 1988; Walling et al. 1991).

Previous Archaeological Investigations at the Marksville Site

The earliest professional investigator of the Marksville site was Gerard Fowke (1927, 1928) of the Smithsonian Institution, who reported on the mounds and earthen enclosures he found along the eastern edge of the Avoyelles Prairie terrace in Avoyelles Parish, one of several such "islands" of high ground in east central Louisiana surrounded by lower alluvial floodplains (Fisk 1940). Prairie terraces are the youngest Pleistocene surfaces in Louisiana (Autin et al. 1991). The Avoyelles Prairie terrace is covered by a mantle of fine loess. Loess soils are generally very stable until they are disturbed, but once displacement occurs, erosion proceeds rapidly. The Avoyelles Prairie terrace is the first significant high land located on the Red River upstream from its confluence with the Mississippi River. Old River, which occupies a stream course largely formed by an ancestral flow of the Mississippi River, is located at the bottom of the terrace below the Marksville site.

Fowke's map of the Marksville area (fig. 3.1), modified to show the location of the 1993 investigations, incorporated what are now recognized as three separate archaeological sites that were built and occupied along the eastern edge of the terrace during three different time periods. Fowke's Mound 1 is now the Nick Farm site (16AV22), which dates to the Plaquemine period (A.D.1200–1700). Mounds 2 through 12, along with the two earthen enclosures and the circle, are recognized as the Marksville site (16AV1). Mounds 13 through 20 are the Greenhouse site (16AV2) and date primarily to Troyville–Coles Creek times (A.D. 800–1100) (Ford 1951; Jones 1991).

Fowke (1928) reported that Enclosure A, most of which is now in the SCA, was about 3300 ft (1006 m) long, 3 to 7 ft (0.9 to 2.1 m) high, and had at least three, possibly four, gateways. Within the forty-acre interior of Enclosure A are Mounds 2 through 6. Fowke also noted a platform mound attached to the interior of Enclosure A. Enclosure B, north of A, was considerably smaller than A and encompassed Mound 7. Fowke stated that there were two gateways in Enclosure B, but his map shows only a single gateway. This enclosure was 510 ft (155 m) long, but Fowke assumed that it was once longer and had been shortened by erosion.

Fowke also reported an earthen circle about 320 ft (98 m) in diameter, just south of Enclosure A and linked to the larger enclosure by what he called a "causeway"; he did not depict this causeway on his map (Fowke 1927, 1928). Fowke's description of the circle, causeway, and southern gateway of Enclosure A, which he also photographed (fig. 3.2), is especially significant here because this area was investigated in 1993. Fowke wrote:

> Another inclosure of a different nature lies south of the large inclosure A. From the second gateway here is built up a crooked causeway 5 or 6 feet wide at the base and only a few inches higher than the water and mud on either side of it. Its general direction is south 20 west. At 170 feet from the center of the gateway it connects with an embankment which is practically circular except on the side toward A, where it extends in a straight line for several rods along the outer edge of the moat. This part, which is still covered with timber, is 20 feet wide at the base and 2 feet high, which figure would probably apply to the entire embankment as it was when completed. Most of it, however, is now entirely leveled and can be traced only by the color of the earth where it stood. The diameter is about 320 feet; the causeway joins it at the western end of the straight side, almost exactly north of the center of the circle. (1928:412–413)

The symmetrical and well-maintained portions of Enclosure A seen by visitors as they enter the Marksville SCA today are the product of a Federal

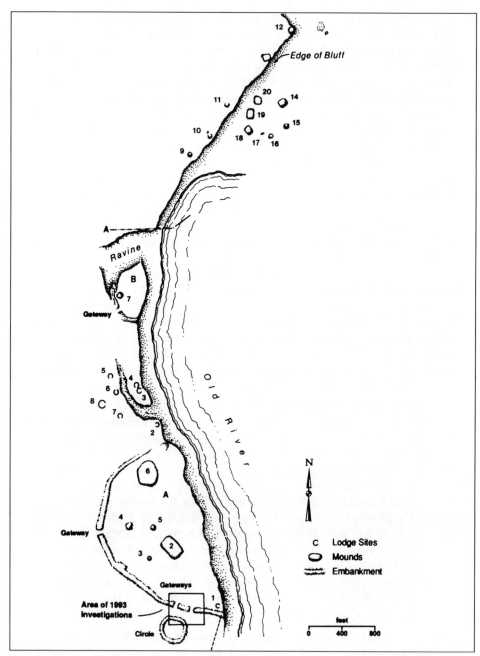

Fig. 3.1. Gerard Fowke's 1926 map of the Marksville site and environs (adapted from Fowke 1928).

Emergency Relief Administration (FERA) reconstruction project done in 1933, which presumably incorporated surviving portions of the original embankment. However, little archaeological investigation was conducted before the reconstruction, and the modern symmetry may not reflect the original shape of the embankment. The unreconstructed portions of Marksville Enclosure A are not as regular and imposing as the reconstructed sections.

In 1933 Frank Setzler of the Smithsonian Institution conducted a substantial project at Marksville under the auspices of the Federal Emergency Relief Administration. Even prior to this project, Setzler noted ceramic similarities between the Marksville site and northern Hopewell sites (Setzler 1933a, 1933b). Surprisingly, he made little mention or comparison of the enclosures at the Marksville site and those in Ohio.

Unfortunately, a complete report was never written about the 1933 work at the Marksville site (Setzler 1934; Setzler and Strong 1936). A brief description was given by Ford (1936:226–231), but location, extent, and results remained little known until a publication by Toth (1974). Toth's research also validated Seltzer's claim that the lithic and ceramic artifacts from Marksville suggested relationships with northern (Illinois) Hopewell.

In 1939, after flooding had interrupted investigations of the nearby Greenhouse site, Work Projects Administration (WPA) crews were moved to excavate portions of Marksville Mound 2 and a midden area, but again no attention was directed toward the enclosures. Data from this project remained unreported until a publication by Vescelius (1957) almost twenty years later.

Fig. 3.2. The southern gateway of Enclosure A at the Marksville site in 1926 (reproduced from Fowke 1928).

In 1971 Thomas Ryan (1975) did focus on the enclosures at Marksville. He analyzed a 1935 aerial photograph and interpreted visible features as evidence of three additional crescent-shaped earthen enclosures at the site. As Ryan was conducting fieldwork, one of the authors (Kuttruff) assisted him in mapping an elevation profile across the southern embankment and adjacent borrow pit or moat. That profile crossed the embankment in the area where investigations were conducted in 1993. Figure 3.3 is Ryan's interpretive map of the aerial photograph, which shows the locations of the additional enclosures and other features that were evident. Most of the area shown on this map, except that within the SCA and some other densely wooded sections, has now been developed for modern residences or has experienced continued cultivation. Archaeological verification of Ryan's interpretation of additional enclosures has never been performed.

Dennis Jones and Malcolm Shuman produced a contour map of Enclosure A at the Marksville site in 1989 (fig. 3.4). Their work demonstrated that Fowke's map of the large enclosure was generally accurate, except for his depiction of the southern portion. Where Fowke showed this section trending southward to the edge of the terrace, Jones and Shuman (1989) found that it curved in a more northerly fashion, making Enclosure A more regularly crescent shaped than Fowke had indicated. Jones and Shuman also prepared a detailed map (fig. 3.5) of the double gateway shown in the southern portion of Enclosure A on Fowke's map. By scaling from Fowke's map, they inferred that the east-west extension of American Legion Road through this portion of the site passed through one of the existing "gateways." Thick vegetation covered the southern portion of Enclosure A and limited the accuracy of the map of this area made by Jones and Shuman. These researchers failed to find any evidence of the circle to the south of Enclosure A shown by Fowke (1928) (Jones and Shuman 1989).

Evidence of a later historic aboriginal occupation of the southern portion of the Marksville site was reported by Ford: "More evidence that seems to point to a former occupation of the area [near Marksville] by the Choctaw within recent times was found in 1932 by a negro tenant in the southern end of the Marksville enclosure. He found a burial a few feet under the surface in his garden. Accompanying it were iron, C-shaped bracelets, glass beads, and an undecorated hemispherical bowl very similar in shape, paste, and finish to the vessels indicated by the sherds from the Nick place" (1936:49).

Toth's (1974) detailed synthesis of previous work at the Marksville site says little about the earthen enclosures, primarily because no reported archaeological excavation of the embankments had been undertaken. Almost envisioning the future, Toth noted on the last page of his report, "The well-preserved section of the embankment at the southern end of the site offers the best chance of dating the earthworks. Cross-sectioning it and analyzing its con-

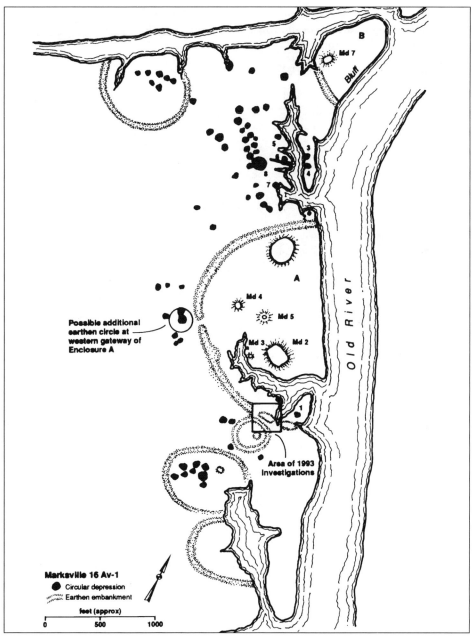

Fig. 3.3. Thomas Ryan's interpretive sketch of the Marksville site, based on a 1935 aerial photograph. Note the three additional enclosures identified by Ryan (adapted from Ryan 1975).

tents should be the first priority. . . . The mounds [and earthwork] present a formidable enterprise, but the work can be aided by the careful employment of earth moving equipment" (1974:94).

The 1993 Excavations

In 1993 the southern section of Enclosure A was partially owned by Marc Dupuy, Jr., of Marksville, who had arranged for this portion of the site to be

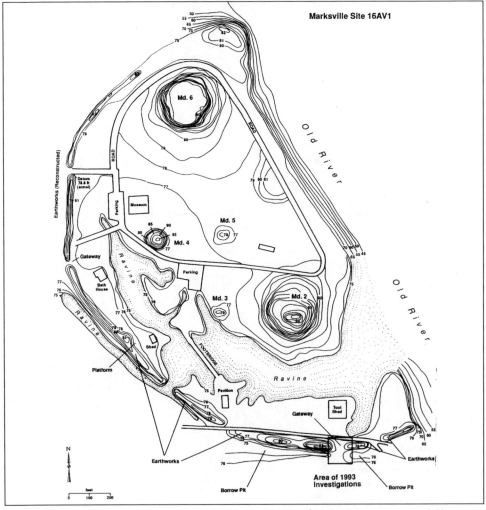

Fig. 3.4. Contour map of Enclosure A at the Marksville site (adapted from Jones and Shuman 1989).

set aside as a preservation servitude under the auspices of the Louisiana Archaeological Conservancy (LAC). The servitude provided that the earthwork was not to be cultivated or otherwise disturbed, and that the area would be available for archaeological research. In October 1993 the authors, assisted by several members of the Louisiana Archaeological Society (LAS), conducted an archaeological investigation on this servitude.

Research Questions and Initial Preparations

After reviewing the literature for excavations of prehistoric enclosures in general and the Marksville site in particular, we developed a series of research questions.

1. What were the original dimensions of Enclosure A? Was it built all at one time or in multiple episodes? Are there indications of any special construction techniques for the enclosure?

2. What was the function of Enclosure A at the Marksville site? Was this portion of the site ever occupied in a residential manner?

3. Are there any significant celestial alignments relative to the southern gateway that might relate to intrasite planning?

4. Are postmolds from palisades or other features associated with the enclosure?

5. Was this portion of the site ever occupied prior or subsequent to the Marksville period?

6. How deep were some of the borrow pits on the outside of the enclosure?

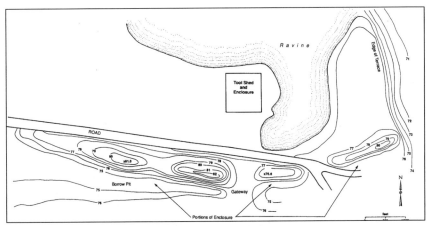

Fig. 3.5. Contour map of the southern portion of Enclosure A at the Marksville site (adapted from Jones and Shuman 1989).

The area around the southern gateways of Enclosure A was cleared of small trees and thick underbrush by a crew from the Avoyelles Parish prison, revealing that the northern section of the small circular enclosure was intact and could be traced along the southern boundary of the LAC's preservation servitude. This surviving portion of the circle was flat sided and paralleled the nearby portion of Enclosure A, as shown on Fowke's map (see fig. 3.1) and noted by Toth (1974:11). The area south of this surviving part of the circle has been plowed so extensively that no trace of the embankment as mapped by Fowke could be seen on the surface. Testing this remaining segment of the earthen circle was therefore incorporated into the 1993 project.

Clearing also revealed a distinct gap in the enclosure that had not been observed in 1989. The more accurate 1993 field project map (fig. 3.6) can be compared with Jones and Shuman's (1989) map of the same area (see fig. 3.5). Both maps generally corroborate the gateway plan shown by Fowke, but with several notable exceptions. The two gateways appear to be much closer together, separated only by a small artificial knoll that is now heavily eroded. The 1993 map also shows that the raised area that Fowke had dubbed a "causeway" spans the area between the gateways in Enclosure A and the remnant of the southern circle. This feature was not perceptible in 1989 due to its low elevation and the thick vegetation. Finally, the 1989 map shows the location of a large ravine in the southern portion of the site; Fowke (1928) mentioned the erosion in his report but did not show it on his map.

Soils in the area of the Marksville site are classified as a Calhoun-Loring-Olivier association, which forms in areas of level or gently sloping terrain and consists of acidic and silty soils (SCS 1970). Within the soils atop the Avoyelles Prairie terrace, natural soil horizons have developed as a result of geological, landform, time, climate, and biological activity. These soil horizons also have formed in the prehistoric earthworks since their construction. Therefore, it was important to recognize these horizons in the profiles of excavated earthen archaeological features such as the enclosure at Marksville in order to understand their construction and age.

If we use recognized definitions, the soil horizons encountered during 1993 consisted of A, E, and Bt horizons. An A soil horizon forms at or just below the surface and is characterized by an accumulation of humidified organic matter mixed with some mineral fractions. The main characteristic of the underlying E soil horizons are that silicate clay, iron, and aluminum, or some combination of these, have been leached out by water, leaving a concentration of sand and silt. The B horizon, which always forms below the A and E horizons, is dominated by the obliteration of all or most of the original rock structure. The Bt distinction signifies that there has been an accumulation of silicate clays on the soil horizon (SMSS 1988).

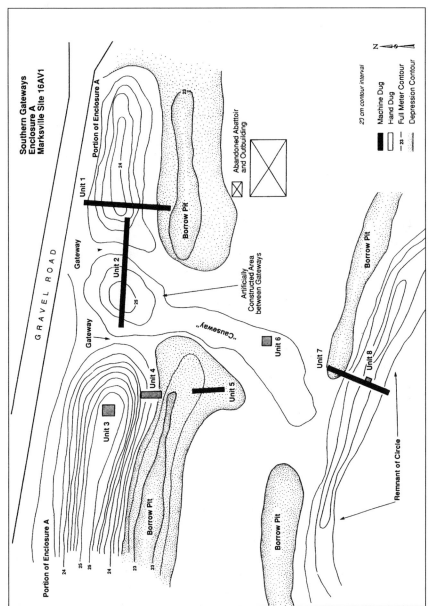

Fig. 3.6. Contour map of the 1993 Louisiana Archaeological society (LAS) project area.

Excavation Units

After the contour map of the project area had been completed, machine and hand-excavated test units were placed at eight locations to address as many of the research questions as possible (see fig. 3.6). A backhoe was judiciously used to obtain stratigraphic information in a cost- and time-effective manner. Pre-excavation soil probes showed that there was no prehistoric midden in this portion of the site.

Unit 1

This backhoe excavation was placed in the portion of Enclosure A east of the gateways to provide stratigraphic information about construction of the enclosure and to determine some of the enclosure's original dimensions (figs. 3.7 and 3.8). The unit was over 14 m long and reached a depth below the buried surface upon which the embankment fill was placed; the base of the excavation was 1.3 m below the highest part of the enclosure.

The uppermost level, Zone 1, was weathered (and perhaps partially disturbed) construction fill and slope wash. Zone 4, beneath Zone 1 and on either side of Zone 2, also was slope wash from upper portions of the original embankment, but is less leached and weathered than Zone 1. An undisturbed portion of the original earthwork structure, Zone 2, contained some evidence of loading and was sealed beneath Zone 1 and between the two sections of Zone 4. The embankment fill is a mixture of materials from old A and E soil horizons. The lateral base of Zone 2, representing the original width of the base of the embankment, was 5.3 m wide with a maximum thickness of 70 cm. The interior and exterior slopes of the embankment probably sloped inward at an angle about 40 degrees off vertical. The original embankment height in this area remains unknown, but the excavations document a minimum height of 1.05 m near the center, as measured from the top of the original ground surface to the top of the existing earthwork. A 2–3 cm remnant of the old A horizon atop the undisturbed and underlying soil horizon (Zone 5) was preserved beneath the basal width of the embankment fill. It had been truncated to some degree, perhaps by aboriginal clearing, and was missing to the north and south of the base of the embankment, where it had probably been scraped up and included in the construction fill.

A preconstruction post hole, originating from the top of the remaining old A horizon, showed clearly in the western profile of the unit (fig. 3.9). It had a maximum diameter at the top of 20 cm and was exposed to a depth of 25 cm. Zone 3 in figure 3.7 may represent soil removed during the original excavation of the post hole. A portion of the undisturbed Bt soil horizon was exposed in the deeper portion of the excavation at the northern end of the profile.

Two possible prehistoric artifacts were recovered from Unit 1. A cobble

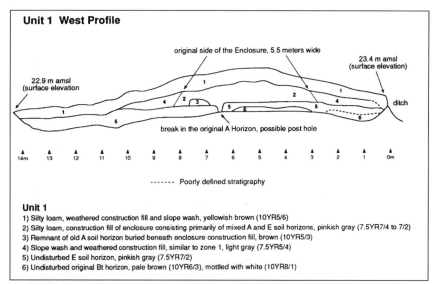

Unit 1 West Profile

original side of the Enclosure, 5.5 meters wide

23.4 m amsl
(surface elevation)

22.9 m amsl
(surface elevation

ditch

break in the original A Horizon, possible post hole

14m 13 12 11 10 9 8 7 6 5 4 3 2 1 0m

------- Poorly defined stratigraphy

Unit 1
1) Silty loam, weathered construction fill and slope wash, yellowish brown (10YR5/6)
2) Silty loam, construction fill of enclosure consisting primarily of mixed A and E soil horizons, pinkish gray (7.5YR7/4 to 7/2)
3) Remnant of old A soil horizon buried beneath enclosure construction fill, brown (10YR5/3)
4) Slope wash and weathered construction fill, similar to zone 1, light gray (7.5YR5/4)
5) Undisturbed E soil horizon, pinkish gray (7.5YR7/2)
6) Undisturbed original Bt horizon, pale brown (10YR6/3), mottled with white (10YR8/1)

Fig. 3.7 West profile of Unit 1, 1993 LAS project

Fig. 3.8. Unit 1, 1993 LAS project. This unit was machine-excavated through the embankment in the southern portion of Enclosure A.

of chert recovered from the excavation backdirt has a single conchoidal fracture that may be the product of prehistoric lithic production, although the fracture could have been produced by modern traffic on the nearby gravel road. Collected from the surface near the southern end of Unit 1 was a large broken cobble of quartzite that may be a portion of a grinding stone. It exhibits what appear to be two flaking scars, and a portion of its surface seems smoothed by grinding.

Unit 2

Another machine-excavated unit, Unit 2 measured over 18 m long (fig. 3.10). It was placed to investigate construction of the gaps at the southern gateway in Enclosure A, testing the base of the enclosure on the east side of the gateway, the artificial rise or knoll that formed the double gateway, and the two gaps between the knoll and the rest of the enclosure.

In this unit, Zone 1 was weathered and slope-washed fill that extended along the upper portion of the entire profile. In the eastern part of the profile, this zone represents fill for the eastern portion of the embankment and the middle knoll of the gateway area, which was centered at about meter 13 on the profile.

Zone 2 consisted of redeposited A, E and Bt soil horizons that were weathered fill, but that still preserved faint indications of basketloading. Like

Fig. 3.9. Western profile of Enclosure A embankment showing possible postmold.

Zone 1, Zone 2 was continuous across the entire profile, varying in thickness from 15 to nearly 75 cm. In the eastern part of the unit, this zone is a continuation of Zone 2 in Unit 1. The remainder of the zone consisted of fill placed in the gateway areas to create the central rise of the gateway. It is apparent that there was some effort to raise the level of the gateway surface, perhaps to continue the visual line of the enclosure while at the same time leaving distinct gaps between the central mound and the ends of the embankments.

A distinct zone of redeposited A horizon soil, Zone 3 was also part of the construction fill. Zones 4 and 5 were undisturbed Bt and E soil horizons, respectively. No artifacts or midden were observed in the profile of Unit 2 or in the undisturbed soil zones beneath the embankment.

The stratigraphy of this unit was very informative about the construction of the gateway in the southern portion of Enclosure A. The western (right) portion of the profile showed conclusively that there was an artificially constructed knoll that divided the space between the two more extensive portions of the enclosure into two gaps. The construction fill of this mound reached a maximum thickness of 1.6 m at meter 16 in the unit, and a maximum height above the level of the original grade at meter 13.

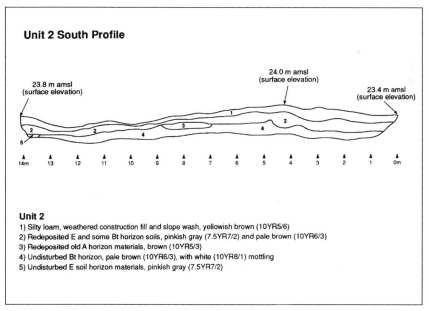

Fig. 3.10 South profile of Unit 2, 1993 LAS project

Unit 3

Unit 3 was hand excavated and began as a 2 x 2 m square on the summit of the highest surviving portion of Enclosure A. The unit was placed to determine if postmolds (evidence of a palisade) or any other structure were associated with the top of the embankment. The unit was excavated to 30 cm below the surface, but failed to reveal postmolds or any other features. The soil matrix between 0–30 cm consisted of weathered mound fill; weathering had completely leached out any evidence of basketloading.

As excavations were being conducted in Unit 4 (discussed below), Unit 3 was excavated to a greater depth to compare the stratigraphy of the two units. The 2 x 1 m eastern half of Unit 3 was excavated to a depth of 2 m

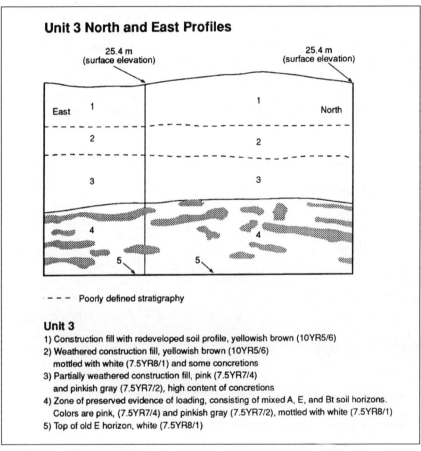

Unit 3 North and East Profiles

25.4 m
(surface elevation)

25.4 m
(surface elevation)

East   1   1   North

2   2

3   3

4   4

5   5

- - -   Poorly defined stratigraphy

Unit 3

1) Construction fill with redeveloped soil profile, yellowish brown (10YR5/6)
2) Weathered construction fill, yellowish brown (10YR5/6)
   mottled with white (7.5YR8/1) and some concretions
3) Partially weathered construction fill, pink (7.5YR7/4)
   and pinkish gray (7.5YR7/2), high content of concretions
4) Zone of preserved evidence of loading, consisting of mixed A, E, and Bt soil horizons.
   Colors are pink, (7.5YR7/4) and pinkish gray (7.5YR7/2), mottled with white (7.5YR8/1)
5) Top of old E horizon, white (7.5YR8/1)

Fig. 3.11. North and east profiles of Unit 3, 1993 LAS project. Boundary definitions between stratigraphic zones are estimated because the differences are very subtle.

below the current summit of the embankment. Excavations were terminated when the top of the old E horizon, or original ground surface, was encountered (figs. 3.11 and 3.12). All the upper strata of Unit 3 consisted of embankment fill. The upper three zones in the profile graded from completely weathered soils at the top to less weathered soils at the base of Level 3. At 1.25 m below surface, the weathering appeared to have terminated, and Zone 4 contained well preserved basketloaded materials consisting of a mixed A, E, and Bt soil horizons. The undisturbed E horizon upon which the enclosure was built was encountered at exactly 2 m below the surface of Unit 3.

Unit 4 and Unit 5

These two units provided profiles to investigate the relationship of the base of the outside of Enclosure A with its associated borrow pit (fig. 3.13). Unit 4, measuring 2 x 1 m, was hand excavated, while Unit 5 was excavated with a backhoe to a length of 6 m. A 4 m gap was left between the units because of large trees.

Zones 2 and 6 are the undisturbed old E horizon and underlying undisturbed Bt horizon, respectively. The breaks between Zone 6 and Zone 5 and between Zones 4 and 2 serve to define the original northern edge of the borrow pit and the basal depth of the northern part of that feature.

In Unit 4, Zone 3 represents the beginning of unweathered basketloaded

Fig. 3.12. Eastern profile of Unit 3, 1993 LAS project. Note basketloading in lower portions of the profile.

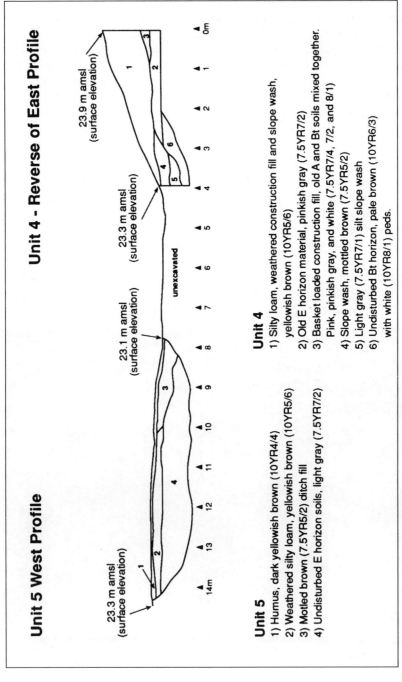

Unit 5 West Profile

23.3 m amsl (surface elevation)

23.1 m amsl (surface elevation)

unexcavated

Unit 4 - Reverse of East Profile

23.9 m amsl (surface elevation)

23.3 m amsl (surface elevation)

Unit 5
1) Humus, dark yellowish brown (10YR4/4)
2) Weathered silty loam, yellowish brown (10YR5/6)
3) Mottled brown (7.5YR5/2) ditch fill
4) Undisturbed E horizon soils, light gray (7.5YR7/2)

Unit 4
1) Silty loam, weathered construction fill and slope wash, yellowish brown (10YR5/6)
2) Old E horizon material, pinkish gray (7.5YR7/2)
3) Basket loaded construction fill, old A and Bt soils mixed together. Pink, pinkish gray, and white (7.5YR7/4, 7/2, and 8/1)
4) Slope wash, mottled brown (7.5YR5/2)
5) Light gray (7.5YR7/1) silt slope wash
6) Undisturbed Bt horizon, pale brown (10YR6/3) with white (10YR8/1) peds.

Fig. 3.13. Reverse of east profile of Unit 4 and west profile of Unit 5, 1993 LAS project.

fill corresponding to the basketloaded zone (Zone 4) defined in Unit 3; the bases of the two zones in the two units were at the same elevation. Zone 1, in the northern part of the unit, represents embankment fill, while the southern part of this zone, overlying the northern edge of the borrow pit, was slope wash. Weathering had completely removed any traces of basketloading and obscured indications of the original location and configuration of the slope of the embankment. We assume, however, that the base of the earthwork would have corresponded with the northern edge of the borrow pit, as shown by the break between Zones 2 and 4. Zones 4 and 5 in Unit 4 contained weathered slope wash that had eroded into the original borrow pit. Zone 5 represents the first wash into the borrow pit from the slope of the embankment and was distinguished from slope wash in Zone 4 by differential weathering caused by ponding in the borrow pit.

Unit 5 also provided information about the original dimensions of the borrow pit associated with Enclosure A. The southern boundary of the ditch (or "moat") is defined by the breaks separating Zones 3 and 4 and Zones 2 and 3. Zone 1 was the present humus in Unit 5, while Zone 2 was the E horizon and Zone 4 was the underlying Bt horizon. Zone 3 within this unit is comparable to Zones 4 and 5 in Unit 4 and consisted of soil accumulation in the original moat. The derivation of this material is uncertain, but some of the lower portions may have come from the erosion of the embankment.

From the stratigraphy revealed in Units 4 and 5, we determined that the borrow pit for the enclosure was originally about 7.5 m wide. Its original

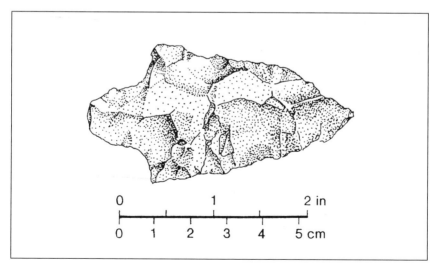

Fig. 3.14   Gary Stemmed, *var. Maybon* point, 1993 LAS project

depth was impossible to determine exactly because of trees, but the measurements provided by the profiles suggest that a depth of less than one meter. Apparently the builders of the enclosure used only the most easily moved material, the A and E soil horizons. Upon reaching the Bt horizon with its higher clay content, the builders apparently opted to move laterally instead of downward as they dug. Archaeologists who have dug by hand into this clay material sympathize with the prehistoric builders.

Unit 6

Unit 6, a hand-dug unit on the raised portion of the project area that Fowke had dubbed a "causeway," was located to determine if this feature represented earthen construction or had been formed by lowering the surrounding area by the construction of the circle and Enclosure A. The unit was a 2 m square that was excavated in 10 cm levels to 30 cm below the surface. Beneath a thin layer of humus and A horizon was an undisturbed E horizon. A series of soil probes to a depth of one meter below the surface detected no evidence of basketloading.

No midden, postmolds, or other prehistoric features were revealed in Unit 6, but the only indisputable prehistoric artifact recovered during the 1993 project, a Gary Stemmed, *var. Maybon* projectile point made of brown chert (fig. 3.14), was found at a depth of 11 cm below surface, at the very top of the undisturbed E horizon. Williams and Brain (1983:233) regard the Gary Stemmed, *var. Maybon* as a marker for the late Marksville to early Baytown periods.

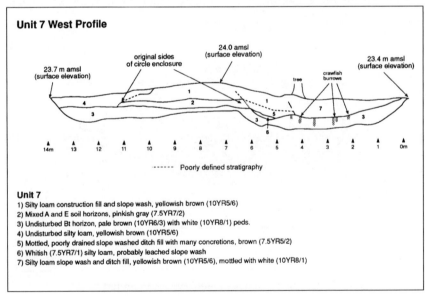

Fig. 3.15 West profile of Unit 7, 1993 LAS project

Unit 7

This mechanical excavation was placed essentially perpendicular to the northern edge of the rediscovered earthen circle and measured over 14 m long. It incorporated a segment of the circle, as well as the borrow pit on the northern side. Zone 1 was weathered construction fill; some fill from the embankment had eroded into the borrow area (fig. 3.15). Zone 2, overlying the original undisturbed Bt soil horizon, was less-weathered fill that showed evidence of basket loading. The two ends of Zone 2 and the break between Zones 1 and 4 probably represent the original basal width (approximately 5.5 m) and side slopes of the enclosure.

Strata designated Zones 5 and 6 in this unit represent slope wash from the embankment into the borrow pit. Zone 4 was slope wash from the embankment into the interior of the circle, while Zone 7 probably derived from slope wash and other sources after abandonment of the site. The upper surface of Zone 3, an undisturbed Bt soil horizon beneath the borrow pit, clearly defined the southern and northern margins, as well as the original base of the borrow area. Prehistoric crawfish burrows revealed in the profile helped to establish the original base of the borrow pit, as their openings originated at the base of the original moat and did not reach to the current surface.

Our testing suggests that the base of the circular embankment was originally 5.5 m wide, which is comparable to the original basal width of Enclosure A. The basal width was defined by Zone 2, which was undisturbed and unweathered construction fill. The slope of the circle was apparently steeper on the exterior next to the borrow pit; the inside slope was seemingly not as steep. The borrow pit was approximately 6 m wide and was originally very shallow, with a depth of no more than 50 cm. The original height of the embankment is impossible to determine, but the depth of the borrow pit and extent of the slope wash suggest that it was less than a meter high.

Unit 8

Unit 8, a hand-dug unit on the summit of the circle remnant to the east of and adjacent to Unit 7, was excavated in arbitrary 10 cm levels to look for postmolds or other features associated with the summit of the circle. Excavation reached a depth of 30 cm, but no features were encountered. A possible secondary chert flake was found in the 10–20 cm level. Several nails, brads, and other historic debris were recovered in the 0–10 cm level, and probably derived from the barbed-wire fence that once ran just south of the circle remnant along an old property line. The soil within this unit, save for the upper 5 cm of humus, was composed of the weathered silty loam construction fill that was designated Zone 1 in Unit 7.

Summary and Conclusions

Many, but not all, of the research questions proposed for the 1993 field project were answered. We learned several important new facts about Enclosure A and the Marksville site. Unfortunately, the age of the embankment remains unknown because we did not recover any material for radiometric dating. The single diagnostic artifact recovered, a Gary Stemmed, *var. Maybon* point, generally supports a Marksville-period occupation.

On the positive side, we do know how the enclosure was constructed, and we have insights into how the tested area relates to the rest of the site. For example, it appears that Enclosure A was built in a single episode. None of the profiles in Units 1, 2, 3, or 4, which exposed over 30 linear meters of the structure's interior, showed any evidence of the weathering or differences in construction-fill deposition that would suggest separate building episodes. The profile in Unit 7, which exposed the remnant of the earthen circle, also showed a single episode of construction. Likewise, the construction fill for the enclosure and the circle appeared to be solely from the adjacent borrow pits. Apparently no distinct soils from some other area were carried to this part of the site for use as embankment fill.

The soil used in the construction of the enclosure and the circle was loess mixed with E and Bt horizon soils from the upper portions of the borrow area. No other portion of the Marksville site served as a source for construction fill. The distinction between the construction fill and the slope wash that eroded over the original embankment's slopes was very subtle, but detectable. It appears that the embankment was originally about 5 m wide, with sides sloping inward. The borrow pit for the enclosure was about 7.5 m wide and less than a meter deep. The original basal dimension of the circular embankment to the south of Enclosure A appears to have been about 5 m. Excavations into the borrow pit for the circle found that it was about 6 m wide and only 50 cm deep. The borrow pit outside the circle remnant probably once circumscribed the entire outer perimeter.

It was impossible to determine precisely the original height and shape of the two embankments. They may have been level on the summit, like the reconstruction of the enclosure in the Marksville SCA, but they may have been rounded or even peaked. From the size and depths of the borrow pits, it appears that the wall of the large enclosure was significantly higher than the circle. There was no evidence of a palisade, stockade, or other structure on the summits of the embankments.

The area around the southern gateway lacks evidence of prehistoric residential occupation. Very few prehistoric artifacts were recovered, and there was no evidence of middens, houses, hearths, or any other indication of a domestic presence. In fact, only four prehistoric artifacts were recovered from eight units that contained hundreds of cubic feet of dirt. This suggests that not only was this portion of the site unoccupied by the Marksville-era people who probably built it but that prehistoric residents of this part of Avoyelles Parish also avoided it after the site's heyday. This is especially significant given that the Nick Farm site (16AV22), a mound site dating to the later Plaquemine culture, is only about 2000 ft (610 m) to the south.

The borrow pits for the circle and enclosure are on the exterior of both features and are separated by about 20 meters. Our investigations suggest that they were never very deep. Evidently, whatever digging was done by the prehistoric builders, they moved only the most easily excavated material, and these borrow pits were consistently wider rather than deeper. They would not have served as a significant impediment to anyone wishing to scale the exterior face of the enclosure, which militates against Enclosure A serving as some sort of fortification.

The postmold found in Unit 1 suggests some sort of preconstruction activity connected with Enclosure A. Perhaps posts were set at various places where the embankment was to be built in order to plan or facilitate its construction; such features have been found at Pollock Works in Ohio (Riordan 1993a and this volume). The lack of an obvious buried A horizon in the test units within the enclosure or the circle suggests that the original ground surface was prepared for these structures prior to building, as has been reported at Hopewell enclosures in the Ohio Valley (Riordan 1993b).

Perhaps the most significant contribution of the 1993 project is that we now know the configuration of the southern gateway at Enclosure A. It appears that the gateways or gaps were each at least 5 m wide and were separated by an artificial knoll that was probably not as high as the enclosure itself. Extending south of the gateways and attached to the knoll, the relatively higher area that Fowke (1928) dubbed a "causeway" is still extant and remains consistent with Fowke's description over sixty years ago. This raised area, if indeed it was a pathway, is about 5 to 7 m wide and only 20 to 30 cm higher than the surrounding surface. As Fowke reported, this feature appears to connect the earthen circle and the gateways, and curves southwesterly as it approaches the circle. All of these features together—the enclosure, the two gateways, the causeway, and the circle—apparently combined to make the entrance through the southern portion of Enclosure A unique.

The 1993 project provided data that correct earlier depictions of Enclosure A at the Marksville site. It now appears that the southern gateway and the circle were purposefully constructed to create two entrances into the interior of Enclosure A. Perhaps these two entrances had special significance for ceremonial processions that entered or exited the interior of Enclosure A. This configuration contrasts with the surviving gateway in the western portion of Enclosure A, which currently appears to be nothing more than a simple gap.

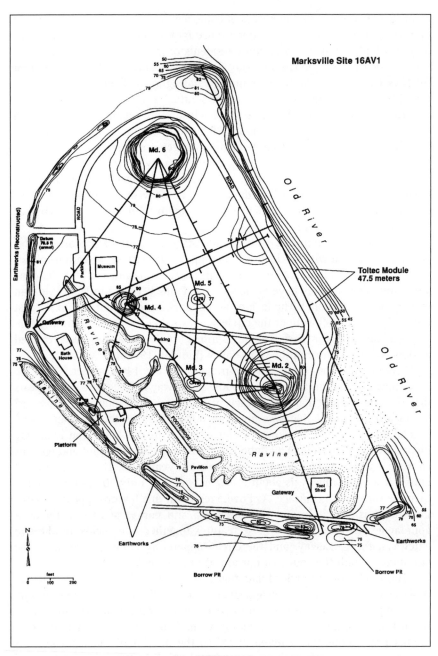

Fig. 3.16. Application of the Toltec Module at the Marksville site (adapted from Jones and Shuman 1989).

However, the 1933 aerial photograph taken for the Smithsonian and analyzed by Ryan (1975) shows the outline of an earthen circle just outside this gateway. This feature has been added to Ryan's sketch map of the aerial photo (see fig. 3.3). It does not appear to be as large as the circle at the southern gateway, but its potential similarity to the circle tested in the 1993 project is worth noting. No trace of this circle is visible today.

Intrasite planning at Marksville was addressed by Jones and Shuman (1989) in their report on mound sites in Avoyelles Parish. Sherrod and Rolingson (1987) proposed the widespread use of a spatial interval dubbed the "Toltec Module" (47.5 m or 155.8 ft) for mound spacing and intrasite planning at sites throughout the Lower Mississippi Valley. Figure 3.16 illustrates the placement of various features at Marksville relative to the Toltec Module. The distances between mounds and gateways at the Marksville site are consistent with this interval. It should be emphasized that Sherrod and Rolingson do not claim that the prehistoric builders of Marksville or any other site were using a 47.5 m module as such, but rather were probably employing multiples of some anthropocentric measure, such as numbers of paces or body lengths, to plan their sites. This spacing interval reinforces the notion that the Marksville site was created with reference to a preconceived plan. It is especially interesting to note that the eastern, open end of the enclosure fits within the Toltec Module spacing, as does the distance between Mound 2 and the southern gateways of Enclosure A.

The alignments between the mounds at Marksville, especially from the flat-topped Mounds 2 and 6, do not correspond to solstitial or equinoctial azimuths. Apparently the mounds were not arranged to mark the observation of solar phenomena, although they may have been used to commemorate other heavenly movements that have not yet been recognized. Importantly, the placement of mounds and enclosures relative to celestial phenomena can only be seriously considered when archaeological investigation has determined that all structures at the site are roughly contemporary.

Much research remains to be done at the Marksville site. Future work could focus on other parts of the site, such as additional sections of Enclosure A, especially the platform that is incorporated into the southwestern part of the embankment. Further research on Enclosure B, at both the embankment and the mound, might determine if these features are comparable to Enclosure A and its mounds. Investigations into the surviving mounds outside the enclosures, which are currently designated as part of the Marksville site (Fowke's Mounds 9, 10, and 12), might also be informative.

Marksville and other prehistoric sites along the eastern edge of the Avoyelles Prairie terrace have figured heavily in our understanding of prehistoric Louisiana. Research done in the 1930s has served as benchmark archaeology, but unfortunately this area has seen only sporadic investigation since then. With continued support from those who aided the 1993 fieldwork, as well as additional patrons, continuing research may add to our knowledge of the Marksville site and its place in Louisiana prehistory.

Note

We wish to thank several organizations and many individuals who made the 1993 work at the Marksville site possible. The project would have been impossible without Marc Dupuy, Jr., of Marksville. A practicing attorney, he has been a long-time supporter and patron of archaeology in Louisiana. Marc and the Dupuy Land Company arranged to place the portion of the site that he and his family owned into a preservation servitude with the Louisiana Archaeological Conservancy.

Exxon Corporation helped fund the 1993 project through their USA Volunteer Fund. Long-time Louisiana Archaeological Society members in Baton Rouge, Lloyd Pine and Stuart Herrmann, are employees of Exxon and helped with proposals to the fund.

Many people in the town of Marksville were happy to see "their" site get some attention and were more than eager to help. Marc Dupuy helped us with the logistics of the project in many ways, including arranging for Sheriff Bill Belt of Avoyelles Parish to provide a crew from the parish prison to clear vegetation before the work began and to backfill when the excavations were finished. Twyman Guillory was the Deputy Sheriff who supervised the crew.

Alton Coco let us use his camp on nearby Boggy Bayou for the duration of the project. Ward Zischke, the curator at the State Commemorative Area, allowed us to use the museum and park facilities while we were working at the site. Brent Scallon, who owns Scallon Contractors in Marksville, was unusually generous in letting us borrow his company's backhoe to excavate some of the units during the project. Lyle "Bubba" DeCuir deserves a special thanks for his thorough and quick repair of one of the backhoe's tires, which went flat on the very first day.

We would be remiss if we did not thank those LAS members who worked on the project. They provided days of unpaid labor above and beyond anyone's expectations (probably including their own). Those participating were: Nancy and Charles Affeltranger, Thierry Callec, Norman Davis, Ellis Denning, Ida Dodge, Katherine Dyer, Jim Fogleman, Stuart Herrmann, Harold and Lillie Jeansonne, Pat and Lloyd Pine, Theresa Rivers, David Willis, and Ward Zischke.

Chapter 4

Defining Space

An Overview of the Pinson Mounds Enclosure

Robert L. Thunen

Over the last fifteen years, Pinson Mounds (fig. 4.1) has been one of the most intensively investigated Middle Woodland ceremonial sites in eastern North America (e.g., Mainfort 1986, 1988; Mainfort and Walling 1992). Located 15 km south of Jackson, Tennessee, the site lies in the transitional area between the West Tennessee coastal plain and the West Tennessee uplands (Miller 1974). The mound complex covers over four hundred acres and extends for approximately two miles along the uplands above the Forked Deer River. Within the complex are a minimum of twelve mounds, five of which are rectangular platform mounds, ceremonial habitation areas, and a roughly circular earthen enclosure. The largest mound (Mound 9) is 22 m (72 ft) tall and is the second-tallest mound in the United States. Based on over forty radiocarbon dates, major earthwork construction dates from about 100 B.C. to A.D. 300 (Mainfort 1988; Mainfort and Walling 1992).

The Pinson Enclosure

My investigations focused on the enclosure and associated mounds. Known since William Myer's (1922) day as the "Eastern Citadel," this area was the subject of small-scale testing in the years 1986–1989. Among Hopewellian earthworks in the Midsouth, the Pinson enclosure is unusual. It is the only recorded enclosure in the region that forms a complete circle (albeit not exact), and its association with a number of large flat-topped mounds is unique for the area (Thunen 1988b).

Located on the southeastern portion of the Pinson Mounds site, the enclosure is situated on the bluff overlooking the South Fork of the Forked Deer River (fig. 4.1). The interior covers 6.7 ha, similar in size to Mound City, Ohio, but smaller than many other Ohio enclosures. For approximately 140° of its circumference, the enclosure is a perfect circle with a diameter of about 181 m (Mainfort and Thunen 1986) (fig. 4.2). On the southern and eastern sides, the embankment wall is more elliptical in shape, and the eastern section conforms to the bluff crest above a deep ravine (fig. 4.3). The embankment walls are approximately 2 m tall. Sections of the embankment have been destroyed by erosion and agricultural activities, making analysis of

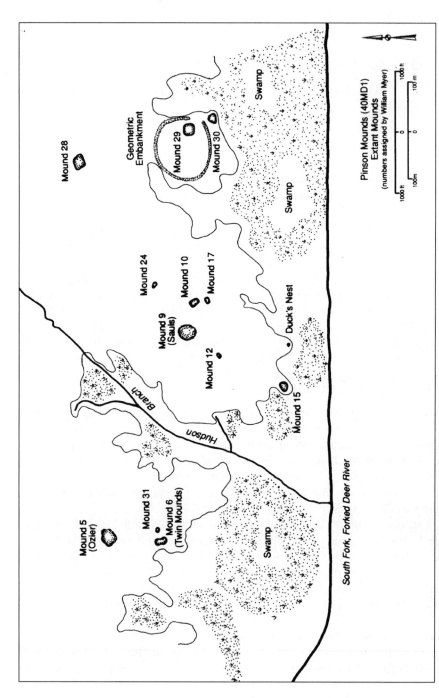

Fig. 4.1. The Pinson Mounds site (after Mainfort 1986).

entrances or culturally defined gaps difficult; in particular, little of the southern embankment section survives.

Mound 29, the fifth-largest mound at the site, is located within the southeastern quadrant of the enclosure and just due east of the enclosure's radial
center. It is a flat-topped, rectangular structure measuring 3.6 m tall and
approximately 51 x 49 m at the base. A nearby conical mound (Mound 30),
thought by Myer (1922) to be a bird effigy, is located southeast of Mound 29
and outside the projected embankment wall. From Mound 30, the topography
drops abruptly down to the bottomland swamps and wetlands.

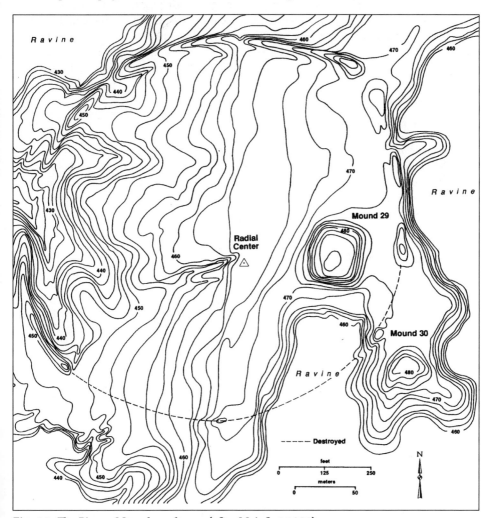

Fig. 4.2. The Pinson Mounds enclosure (after Mainfort 1986).

Previous Research

William Myer (1922) was the first professional archaeologist to map and investigate the Pinson Mounds site, including the enclosure. He recorded several gaps in the enclosure wall, including the rather large opening between Mounds 29 and 30, which he considered to be part of the original construction. Moreover, Myer felt that in prehistoric times this gap was closed off by a palisade. Like many early antiquarians, Myer saw the embankment wall and putative palisade as a defensive structure. Modern research at the Pinson enclosure began with a limited surface survey by Fischer and McNutt (1962). In 1963 Dan Morse (1986) tested several localities at Pinson Mounds, including the embankment and Mounds 29 and 30. His tests in the enclosure did not produce a substantial artifact assemblage, a situation characteristic of the site as a whole (see Mainfort 1986). Among the few artifacts recovered were sand-tempered cord and fabric marked wares that are typical for the Woodland period in western Tennessee.

Testing the Enclosure

My basic research goals were to test the enclosure's interior and associated mounds for data pertinent to the chronological development of the enclosure and mounds, and for evidence about the function of the enclosure. This chapter presents an overview of four field seasons (1986–1989) of small-scale testing, with specific emphasis on the earthworks.

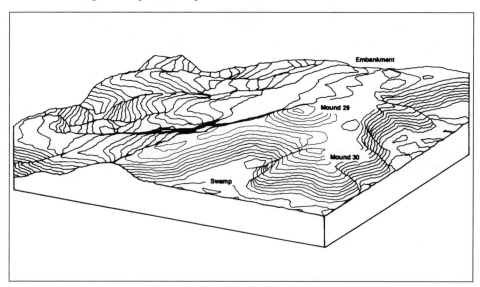

Fig. 4.3. Perspective view of the Pinson mounds enclosure looking from the southeast.

In 1986 test excavations were placed into a section of the embankment wall and the east side of Mound 29 for the purpose of linking stratigraphically the embankment and platform mound. Unfortunately, excavation revealed that the earthworks, as well as the enclosure's interior, had suffered heavy erosion from cultivation and natural processes. The embankment profiles showed no evidence of water-worn surfaces on any of the early soil zones, suggesting continuous, uninterrupted construction of the enclosure wall. This evidence correlates nicely with Morse's (1986) findings; in both tested locations, the original embankment soils were distinctive and exhibited basketloading.

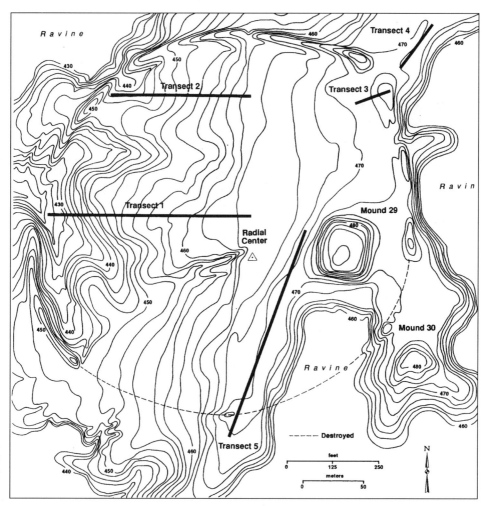

Fig. 4.4. Soil transects at Pinson Mounds in 1987 (base map adapted from Mainfort 1986).

The eastern edge of Mound 29 was tested with 1 x 2 m units to examine the outer mound stratigraphy. Profile walls demonstrated that the majority of the fill was not in a primary depositional context. However, near the western end of the excavations, undisturbed mound fill was encountered.

During the 1987 field season, research focused on understanding the soil dynamics and erosion of the enclosure interior, and searching for evidence of structures or activity areas, such as those found by Baby and Langlois (1979) at Seip. Five transects were tested with a soil probe to assess the potential for intact occupation zones and to document the depth of the sterile substratum (fig. 4.4).

Transects 1–4 revealed a shallow plow zone that extended into sterile subsoil. Transect 5 followed a raised area just to the west of Mound 29. This ridge runs southwest from the mound toward a destroyed section of the embankment wall. A sherd of Alligator Bayou Stamped pottery was found along the ridge. Here the soil probes revealed relatively thick, undisturbed soils adjacent to the southwest side of Mound 29 and thinning to the southwest along the ridge. The depth of these soils was surprising because it was assumed that the ridge was a natural feature on which erosional soils from the mound had been redeposited (Thunen 1987).

The area to the west of Mound 29 was tested in 1988 (Thunen 1988a). Excavations focused on defining the nature of the deposits found the previous year. Our initial interpretations were that the ridge was a disturbed geological or historic feature with a deep plow zone, or that the area was a prehistoric activity area or possible ramp associated with Mound 29. To test these options, ten 1 x 2 m units were excavated. Five were placed to investigate the north/south limits of the soil zone, and the others to define the east/west limits and how the soil zone articulated stratigraphically with Mound 29. The basic stratigraphy of the area consists of three distinctive zones. Zone A is the loamy plow zone, which ranged in depth from 5 to 20 cm; this zone produced plow scars and historic Euroamerican artifacts. Zone C is hard-packed reddish-brown clay subsoil. Zone B includes a series of distinctive basketloaded clays, ranging in color from dark brown to a grayish tan with pockets of diffused, sandy gray and yellow sand. This zone was defined in the westernmost test pit and extends into the mound itself. It thickened from west to east, with the top edge angling slightly up as the zone entered the mound, and it appears to articulate with and is part of the first construction phase for Mound 29. Based on this testing, the feature can confidently be interpreted as a ramp associated with the mound. Discovery of this feature cautions us about the potential for additional unidentified ramps associated with Mound 29 and the other rectangular earthworks at Pinson Mounds.

In 1989 we turned our attention to the enigmatic Mound 30, identified by Myer (1922) as a bird effigy and the subject of considerable speculation ever since. Mound 30 is located in the center of a small finger ridge that extends southward from the bluff line just outside the enclosure. The mound is roughly 2 m tall, with a diameter of 24 m. The highest point is due north of the approximate center, and slope spreads out rapidly toward the bluff edge. Limited testing by Morse (1986) disclosed three or four possible construction episodes, represented by horizontal zones of sands and clays.

We excavated a trench into the southern slope of the mound. It was placed off center to test the west "wing" and central "body" of the putative bird (fig.

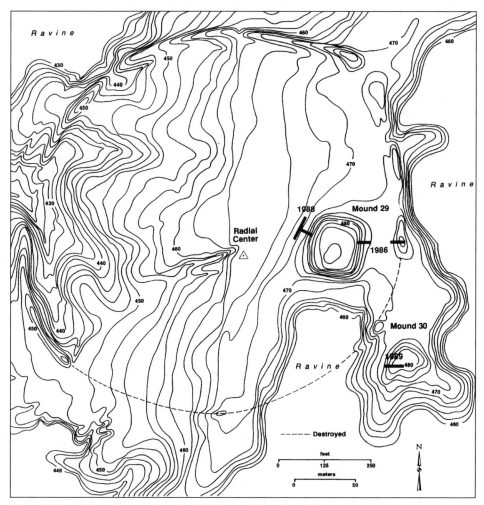

Fig. 4.5. Location of excavations in the Pinson Mounds enclosure, 1986–1989.

4.5). Consisting of eight 1 x 2 m units, this east/west trench cut extended from the western edge to the approximate center. The north and south profiles revealed a complex construction sequence with two possible focused construction areas within the stratigraphic sequence (Thunen 1990b). Although no features were observed in the mound fill, an activity area was defined at the base of one pit and a possible feature was noted in another. Stratigraphic evidence suggests a complex construction sequence that included both basketloading and undifferentiated fill in different portions of the mound. In many respects, the stratigraphy of Mound 30 is similar to that of Pinson Mound 6 (Mainfort 1986). In the westernmost unit, the bulk of the mound fill consists of distinctive soil zones, several of which have a gray ash or "powdered sugar" appearance. In general, the soil zones in this square are linearly layered, similar to basketloading observed in other earthworks at the site (Thunen 1990b).

In another of the western squares, a constructed clayey basin or curb was revealed at the base of the mound fill. This feature cut diagonally across the excavation, so complete excavation was not possible, and lack of time did not permit more extensive investigation. Although an architectural feature, it does not appear to be the edge of a burial crypt or a crematory basin. It is significant that this feature modified the initial floor. Stratigraphy in this unit revealed the apparent edge of a zone of basketloaded soils, as well as a zone of undifferentiated fill that extends some 6 m to the east. These zones may demarcate specific construction episodes and may cover discrete activity areas on the mound floor, as suggested by the curb/berm feature. As a working hypothesis, I suggest that this feature may mark the outer edge of a burial area, similar to the platform and sand cap of the south Twin Mound (see Mainfort 1986:fig. 55).

The location of Mound 30 is comparable to that of Middle Woodland mounds in the lower and middle Illinois River Valley. These latter are accretional structures that often cover mortuary crypts (Brown 1979). Until further detailed excavations provide information on the construction sequence, the function of Pinson Mound 30 remains speculative.

Conclusions: Planning and Design

I now turn to a consideration of the Pinson Enclosure as a built environment and review several important design considerations. The location of the enclosure was an interesting choice—interesting because natural features helped to emphasize the cultural construction. By using a bluff edge peninsula, about one half of the embankment wall was exaggerated, giving the illusion of a high wall from the outside. On the northwest side, where no bluff is present, the wall is located on a sloping surface, which also helped to exaggerate the wall. The peninsular location helped modify the embankment and create an effective barrier, both in a symbolic and physical sense of isolation and restriction. Further, the location lacks an ease of access except from the north.

By placing the enclosure on the peninsula, the designers also emphasized a particular direction, a sense of access to the enclosure. Although the enclosure is accessible from all directions, this would generally entail a steep climb, and the most natural approach (and one that is level) is from the north into the enclosure. Placement of the enclosure on the peninsula created an acute sense of place using both natural topography and cultural architecture.

Use of the peninsula for the enclosure is also something of a paradox because a true circle with a radius of 181 m, of which a 141–degree section was built, would not fit within the confines of peninsula. The builders could have chosen to shorten the radius or move the enclosure further to the north by utilizing the flat area north of the peninsula. The fact that the enclosure was placed on the peninsula, despite the fact that a perfect circle with a radius of 181 m would not fit in the available space, and in spite of the presence of a large, flat area to the north, suggests that the enclosure was an important boundary marker for the eastern edge of the site and is linked to Sauls Mound, to the west (see fig. 4.1).

On the southern and eastern sides, the embankment walls form a crude ellipse. They align with the bluff edge and are inside the projected path of a perfect circle. If the radial center location was the important factor in the enclosure's design, the designers knew in advance that a true circle of the desired radius would not fit on the peninsula. In fact, no matter what the radius, the southeastern bluff edge limited the building area. Using the defined radial center, a perfect circle with a radius of only 110 meters will fit on the peninsula, and the resulting enclosure would barely encompass Mound 29.

This suggests that one important design consideration was the placement of an embankment wall arc on the peninsula, rather than a complete circle. Arc embankment wall enclosures are the dominant Middle Woodland geometric form in the Midsouth. If the arc was the planned form, the associated walls to the east and south may have been the secondary parts of an accretional construction process to define the area further. The arc wall, together with the bluff line, provided a continuous edge definition for the interior area. The eastern and southern bluff edge walls may have been added later to give additional definition to the area. This suggests a two-stage planning process for completion of the embankment wall: one for the arc section, the other the bluff sections. It may be possible to test this scenario by testing the junctures of the arc and bluff edge walls, although destruction of key portions of the embankment, as well as natural erosion, would make such a task difficult. Moreover, if the embankment was constructed in two or more stages, this may have been done within a relatively short time span, further compounding interpretive difficulties. At this point, I hypothesize that the arc represents an initial construction stage, followed by the bluff edge embankment wall.

There are two striking characteristics about Mound 29 in terms of its placement. First, if the arc construction was the central feature of the design plan, the mound itself was not located within the arc. Second, and perhaps more important, Mound 29 and the radial center of the arc seem to be aligned with the centrally located Sauls Mound (see fig. 4.1). This east/west alignment appears to be planned, and not merely a case of connecting the dots between points A and B by this researcher. The ramp was associated with the first mound construction phase and was at least 8 m wide with a minimum length of 7 m. These figures must be considered a minimum estimation due to the erosion and historic plowing that have altered this feature.

Offsetting Mound 29 from the arc's radial center enhanced the focus toward the radial center and, importantly, the builders were guaranteed a larger interior space for activities that could focus both toward Mound 29 or back toward the center of the Pinson Mounds site (Mound 9). Thus, offsetting Mound 29 from the radial center created a larger area for performance or spectators. Construction of a ramp leading down to the radial center would have heightened the sense of a center, as well as added drama to the psychology of direction. The ramp created a focus for cultural definition within the enclosure. It suggests a control of movement up onto the top of the platform mound. Additionally, if Mound 29 was deliberately located with reference to Sauls Mound (Mound 9) and the arc's radial center, it represents an example of what I have defined elsewhere as projective planning (Thunen 1990a).

Can a chronology for the Eastern Citadel be derived from the information gathered to date? Unfortunately, no datable charcoal has been recovered, so there are no absolute dates for this area. The limited ceramic samples for various tested localities are rather uniform and provide no evidence of specific construction episodes associated with the enclosure.

Based on architectural construction techniques and requirements of the various planning processes, I have sufficient grounds to postulate a construction sequence that can be tested by further excavation. Construction of the Eastern Citadel began with the selection of the radial center for the arc. From that point, the arc and Mound 29 were laid out and defined. Mound 30 was started within the same time frame, with the use of gold and white sands as decoration or markers for construction stages. During construction of the arc embankment, the bluff wall sections could also have been started, although they could have been added later. To construct the latter wall sections, no reference to the radial center was required. Indeed, direct measurement from the radial center would have been impossible for the east section because Mound 29 blocked the view and use of measuring devices. The second phase of construction entailed additions to Mounds 29 and 30, as is suggested by the presence of sand layers in each (see Mainfort 1986).

If the above construction chronology is correct, or even partially correct, what can the earthworks tell us about the spatial and behavioral organization of the area? First, this peninsula is the only truly secluded area at the Pinson Mounds site. This sense of isolation was further exaggerated by the embankment, which created and enhanced the topographic qualities of the area. By creating the embankment, the builders defined the area as cultural space. What had been a natural environment became a cultural one.

Second, placement of the platform mound off-center from the radial center can be interpreted as the result of three factors: (1) alignment to the site as a whole through Sauls Mound; (2) and the intention to focus attention back to the radial center from the mound; as well as (3) to create a larger area for focused activities. Finally, the location of Mound 30 on a small finger ridge extending out from the peninsula is an excellent example of isolating an earthwork (possibly a burial mound) using the existing topography.

This analysis suggests that the builders, rather than using a single, formal planning model, utilized architectural principles to create a cultural place from a unique geographic space at the Pinson Mounds site. This suggests that location was a critical factor in the creation of the Eastern Citadel. Once the location was selected, the builders used a variety of planning principles to design and build their cultural place.

Note

All field archaeologists owe a huge debt to everyone who supports their work. Thanks go to Dr. Robert C. Mainfort, Jr., who served as West Tennessee Regional Archaeologist during my research at Pinson; his support and interest were important to this work's completion. The staff at Pinson Mounds State Archaeological Area, particularly Mary Kwas and Jerry Adams, was helpful and encouraging during my work at the park. Tennessee State Archaeologist Nick Fielder's support and cooperation is also gratefully acknowledged. Support for this research was provided by National Science Foundation Dissertation Improvement Grant BNS-8722665 and by a series of University of North Florida faculty development grants. Thanks also go to my dissertation director, Dr. James A. Brown, for his interest and patience over many years. Finally, the dedication of the students who participated in the Pinson project—Jan Murphy, Vicki Rolland, Bill Stanton, Peter Silva, and Lonnie and Nancy Taylor—is much appreciated.

Chapter 5

Boundaries, Resistance, and Control
Enclosing the Hilltops in Middle Woodland Ohio
Robert V. Riordan

During the Middle Woodland period in Ohio, when the Hopewell culture dominated the ceremonial landscape, certain places were identified as special, sacred, or both. Some were geometrically shaped earthwork enclosures located on river terraces, often surrounding mounds that frequently covered the remains of charnel houses. The mortuary remains that have been so extensively documented at these sites denote them as focal places to the scattered communities in their immediate vicinities. The extent to which other corporate activities, including craft production, economic transactions, and even residential use may have occurred at them is still a subject of some debate, largely due to a lack of much archaeological attention to the non-mound components of their interiors.

Another type of earthwork employed embankments that either partially or fully encircled the summits of hilltops, peninsulas, or other geologically isolated landforms. Southern Ohio is home to the greatest concentration of hilltop enclosures, although examples exist in other states. Since their outline forms are dictated by the naturally irregular topography of their elevated locations, hilltop enclosures lack the sense of planning so obvious in the geometric enclosures of the river valleys. Although hilltop sites have been subjected to more than a century of intermittent archaeological exploration, the fundamental purposes for which they were built still elude us.

Antiquarians and archaeologists have conducted a protracted debate over how these enclosures should be regarded, although the ideas about their use have always revolved about a secular/sacred dichotomy. Over the years many individuals have held very strong opinions concerning their possible functions, but there have also always been those, antiquarians and archaeologists alike, who have waffled in their judgment. In this chapter, I first want to sample briefly the range of opinion recorded by scholars since the early nineteenth century concerning the potential uses of Middle Woodland hilltop enclosures. The relationship between the functional nature of enclosures, the manner in which they are bounded, and the implications of different landscape settings for site interpretation will be discussed. Finally, evidence from the Pollock Works enclosure of southwest Ohio will be cited as an example of a diachronic interpretation informed by the detection of changes in the way that its boundaries were prehistorically defined.

Antiquarians and Archaeologists on Hilltop Enclosures

Authors are distinguished below with regard to their writings on hilltop enclosures as either antiquarians or archaeologists, although the distinction in reality has not always been very clearcut. Antiquarians were individuals who authored studies of hilltop enclosures derived from consideration of their outward appearances, and not from evidence obtained from any more than trial excavations. Their arguments, therefore, were without exception speculative although frequently informed either by simple logic and/or by analogies drawn from externally similar structures of other cultures and times. Individuals such as Caleb Atwater, Ephraim Squier and Edwin Davis, H. W. Overman, Alexander Kocsis, S. H. Binkley, and J. P. MacLean are among those who published antiquarian views concerning Ohio hilltop sites. Archaeological writers, on the other hand, are those whose discussions of hilltop sites have been informed by material evidence excavated either by themselves or by others. Major archaeologically informed positions have been expressed by Warren Moorehead, Frederick Putnam, Gerard Fowke, Henry Shetrone, Richard Morgan, Olaf Prufer, Charles Faulkner, Fred Fischer, Patricia Essenpreis, Willard Bacon, Robert Connolly, and this author.

Interpretations of hilltop site function have emphasized various secular as well as unspecified ceremonial uses. Since antiquarians were bound only by external data, while archaeologists were further informed by excavated data, it might be expected that antiquarian ideas would be scattered widely over the interpretive spectrum while archaeological opinion would be more narrowly focused. These expectations are not borne out by the literature.

The antiquarians as a group came down heavily on the side of hilltop enclosures as military, usually defensive, sites. In an early statement, David Drake in his 1815 *Picture of Cincinnati* stated "the hill-constructions, which are generally in the strongest military positions of the country, were designed solely for defence, in open and vigorous war" (216).

Fort Ancient, as the largest such enclosure, was frequently the starting point for hilltop site descriptions, and was generally discussed in somewhat awestruck tones (e.g., "the most celebrated . . . of all fortifications" [MacLean 1879:20]). With its walls and commanding position high above the Little Miami River, it was unanimously regarded as the fortification that logic seemed to dictate that it had been. Caleb Atwater, for example, identified it as an "ancient fortification . . . for reasons too apparent to require a recital" (1833:65–66).

In their landmark compendium of sites, Squier and Davis collectively reported hilltop and some other enclosures under the category "Works of Defence": "Occasional works are found on the hill tops, overlooking the valleys, or at a little distance from them; but these are manifestly, in most instances, works of defence or last resort, or in some way connected with warlike purposes" (1848:6). While the effect of their opinion cannot be accurately measured, expectably it was influential during the rest of the century: their work did not dispute the common wisdom concerning these sites, and it was reported in a publication bearing the imprimatur of the United States government. Squier and Davis were also echoing the stated opinion of a former general and president of the United States, William Henry Harrison, who had evaluated one hilltop enclosure (Miami Fort) as perhaps the last place of resistance of the Aztecs in their retreat toward Mexico (1839:225). J. P. MacLean, one of the last antiquarians, noted, "That there were serious invasions, and that great conflicts occurred, the number and formidable appearance of these works amply testify" (1879:30). MacLean may also have been the first to conduct an archaeological excavation when he dug in an embankment at Fort Carlisle in 1884 (1887:67), apparently finding nothing to alter his convictions.

However, antiquarian opinion was not unanimous in identifying hilltop earthworks as forts. Alexander Kocsis believed both hilltop and valley sites to have been the work of the Turtle Nation of Moundbuilders. Kocsis (1973:13–15) alleged that antiquarian scholars who believed that the Marietta works were Roman in origin were wrong; quite clearly they had been built by a "heterodox branch of the Turtles," the Seip earthwork had its "large turtle mound," and Tennessee's Old Stone Fort, the particular focus of his scholarship, was considered to have been a turtle effigy. The more orthodox Caleb Atwater, despite his identification of Fort Ancient as a fort, declined to so designate most other Great Miami Valley sites: "Few or none of them appear to have been forts. . . . Their being situated on a hill is by no means a certain indication that they were forts, or that they were ever military works, when it is recollected that most, if not all, the places of religious worship in Greece, Rome, Judea, etc., were on high hills" (1833:69). This sort of cautious analogy, embracing the possibility that hilltops were bounded for sacred purposes, was infrequently repeated during the nineteenth century.

Following the intensive work conducted at Fort Ancient by Warren Moorehead in 1888–1891, and Frederick Putnam's investigation of the Foster's enclosure (also on the Little Miami) in 1890, published archaeological data became available for the advancement of archaeologically informed opinions. Putnam and Moorehead differed in interpreting their sites, perhaps reflecting the differences in their academic backgrounds. Moorehead was not professionally trained, had been a relic collector and dealer, and was more likely to have been strongly influenced by the prevailing antiquarian opinion. He approached his work with the notion that hilltop sites were forts, and came away with that view intact. In fairness, however, his interpretation was in part based on his archaeological discoveries, particularly the burials near the Great Gateway of the South Fort. He saw these as evidence that "a battle, perhaps many battles, were fought here" (1890:41), never entertaining the possibility that they were not contemporary with the embankments; in fact, they were probably related instead to the Fort Ancient culture's residential use of the South Fort a thousand years later (R. Connolly, personal communication). With characteristic adamancy he opined, "Fort Ancient was built for defense. For no other conceivable purpose was it erected" (41), later reemphasizing, "Fort Ancient is a defensive earth-work, used at times as a refuge by a large tribe of Indians . . . our decided conviction is that it possesses nothing of a religious nature; nor was it constructed for a religious purpose" (112).

In dismissing the possibility that the fort was built for ceremonial or sacred reasons, he moved away from any archaeological basis for his reasoning, substituting instead a prejudicial argument: "The builders of this work probably cared very little about religion, recognized few religious duties, had no religious ceremonies within the enclosure, with the possible exception of the worship of the sun. It is safe to say that they thought little of the hereafter, and were probably busily engaged in hunting, fishing, and traversing the war path, instead of thinking of things higher and better" (1890:112).

This stance may be contrasted with Putnam's conclusion concerning Foster's, written after a summer's excavations into the earth, stones, and burned soil of that Little Miami River Valley hilltop site: "Should it prove possible, further explorations will be made here in order to clear up the mystery in which it is involved. It is known locally as 'The Fort,' but although well situated it does not seem at all to answer the requirements of a fortification" (1891:137).

In rejecting the outright identification of Foster's as a fortress, despite finding tremendous amounts of burned soil and carbonized material within and under the embankments, Putnam had initiated the academically respectable fence-sitting tradition with respect to the function of this and similar sites. His cautious example, however, did not bring his disciplinary descendants immediately to heel, and in comparison to Moorehead's work at Fort Ancient, his essentially unpublished discoveries at Foster's appear to have been virtually forgotten.

Gerard Fowke stated his opinion concerning hilltop sites in his massive *Archaeological History of Ohio* (1902): "To all who carefully examine their location it is evident that they were made for defensive structures" (1902:238). He also offered a new explanatory twist, suggesting that since the sites seemed to be far from the great river valley enclosures where the people must have resided, they may have been erected instead by the invaders of the country (1902:268–269).

The Old Stone Fort near Manchester, Tennessee, was first professionally examined by the Tennessee state archaeologist, P. E. Cox, in 1928. After two weeks of digging embankments with four helpers, he concluded that the enclosure had been built all at one time and for temporary protection and defensive purposes (Cox 1929:8).

In Ohio, forty years after Moorehead and Putnam had finished their work, Henry Shetrone addressed the question of hilltop enclosures. He considered Fort Ancient to occupy "an eminently strategic location" and that the high northeastern walls "afforded protection from encroaching enemies" (Shetrone 1930:225). In his discussion of Fort Hill, however, he climbed partway up Putnam's metaphorical fence and questioned whether the number of gateways might not fatally weaken its defensive potential (1930:230).

By the 1940s, Richard Morgan, curator of archaeology at the Ohio Archaeological and Historical Society, had excavated an embankment at Fort Ancient. He stated that "evidence shows that Fort Ancient was used for ceremonial as well as for supposed defensive purposes. It is possible that Fort Hill too was used to some extent for clan or tribal rituals. Its inaccessibility and remoteness would have been important for ceremonial functions as well as for defensive purposes" (Morgan and Thomas 1948:34). This opinion, printed in guidebooks sold at both sites and repeated in leaflets handed out there to this day, and repeated as well in a professional review article on Ohio archaeology (Morgan 1952:89), seems to have done more than anything else to establish credibility for a use other than defense for hilltop sites.

In the 1960s Olaf Prufer wrote his dissertation (1961) and two influential summary articles on Ohio Hopewell (1964a, 1964b). He also directed, in 1964, the excavation of an embankment at Fort Hill (1997). He proposed that the hilltop sites were among the latest major Hopewell enclosures, built as refuges for a population experiencing troubled times toward the end of the Middle Woodland period (1964a:69–70). In passing, he mentioned that defensive theories were by then unpopular (1964a:67). If this was an accurate assessment, it would appear to represent the effect of Morgan's opinion on professional hallway debate and graduate teaching. Prufer recently reiterated his position that the "primary function of the enclosures was defensive" (1997:311–327), but he admits that "some ceremonial functions were also carried out." He summarizes by stating that "good evidence can be adduced for both positions; similarly, some of the evidence does not fit either particularly well" (Prufer 1997:313).

Two larger archaeological projects examined hilltop enclosures in the mid-1960s. Fred Fischer dug for two seasons (1965–1966) at Miami Fort, and

Charles Faulkner worked at Old Stone Fort in 1966. Like Putnam and Moorehead before them, they left their fieldwork with diametrically opposed functional explanations. Fischer believed Miami Fort was defensive, while Faulkner thought Old Stone Fort was a ceremonial center. Fischer's reports (1965, 1967) languished in mimeographed form with a limited circulation while Faulkner's opinion was published (1968), thereby becoming considerably more influential in shaping subsequent professional thinking on the subject.

In 1981 I started to investigate the Pollock Works, and a year later Patricia Essenpreis began limited work at Fort Ancient. Essenpreis and Moseley published an article (1984) that persuasively interpreted Fort Ancient as a strictly ceremonial site, arguing that it was too big and violated too many tenets of military common sense to have been defensive. Essenpreis also advanced this position in several conference papers (e.g., 1986; Essenpreis and Duszynski 1989). During these same years, based upon my interpretation of what I had by then seen at Pollock, I was in full agreement with her, and similarly stated in preliminary reports and conference papers that Pollock was built for ceremonial, not defensive, reasons (e.g., Riordan 1982, 1984, 1986). By 1990 it seemed more than ever that this was the position that most researchers had adopted in their infrequent references to hilltop enclosures. Most recently, Willard Bacon has speculated that Tennessee's Old Stone Fort was built to control or defend against supernatural entities and phenomena, but not to repel human enemies (Bacon 1993:268).

Enclosures: Control and Resistance

An enclosure will be generically defined as an open space that has been physically bounded for some purpose, at least in part by architectural elements. A review of the known uses of such edifices at various times and places indicates that most can be grouped into two categories: those whose boundaries exist to exert control over the defined internal space, and those whose boundaries offer resistance to, and provide a measure of protection from, an external threat.

Controlling Enclosures

The first type of enclosure is that which exercises control over a defined internal space. The form of control can be either passive or active.

Passively controlling enclosures establish a symbolic form of control over a space, providing the members of the using culture with a way of recognizing the area involved and sometimes the nature of its designated use. Boundary markers are intended to elicit an appropriate set of behaviors on the part of the population toward the enclosed space. Examples include real property of all kinds, whether individually or corporately owned, from yards and estates to some kinds of private or public commercial and manufacturing activity areas, as well as places of public use such as plazas, dedicated religious tracts (including cemeteries), and even military bases. By means of such devices as corner pins, fences, signs, walls, embankments, ditches, and surfacings, boundaries are visually and cognitively defined. The use of the space may be identifiable from the type of marker employed, or through visual inspection of the enclosed space itself. As two examples, consider an agricultural field and a residential front yard. Understanding the use of a field might depend on its visual inspection, revealing turned furrows or some stage of crop growth; the fence that defines its edges both identifies the limits of a particular unit of a farm's production and passively implies the exclusivity of its use to its owner. The fence may also be intended, still within the concept of passive control, to keep animals from straying in and eating the crop, but its physical attributes will not be constructed so as to completely deny entrance to another human. Therefore, while the fence does not physically prevent some other farmer from planting a crop within the field's boundaries, none will because of the legal possession that it signifies, and even casual walkers may be deterred from a ramble within. A residential front yard is usually understood as the space between a public road (or the sidewalk that parallels a road) and a domicile. It is frequently denoted by a surfacing of tended grass. Even in the absence of a wall or fence, there is an implicit understanding that the use of such a space is reserved to the home-owner, and that casual trespass is discouraged.

Since the visual definition of these areas is alone expected to induce proper behavior toward them by the members of the group, boundary markers are generally not intended to physically prevent improper access by unqualified persons. Their degree of elaboration, however, may be a statement about the relative wealth and power of the owner.

According to our current limited understanding of Middle Woodland geometric enclosures, they were places of multiple use by owning corporate groups. Their designs may have reflected the worldview of these societies, and it is believed that some may have been conveniently aligned to permit observation of celestial events. Under the terms in use in this discussion, they are considered as examples of passively controlling enclosures, since their embankments defined the limits of dedicated corporate use without the creation of physically impassable barriers.

Actively controlling enclosures are different from the above in that they generate a coercive form of control over entities contained within a defined space. Examples include animal pens, corrals, zoos, prisons, and some other institutional settings. Specific behaviors or results are expected to be induced by the form of an enclosure. The boundary markers will be constructed in a manner that constitutes a direct response to the perceived characteristics of the entities whose freedom they constrain. Boundaries may take the form of ditches, fences, embankments, walls, or combinations of these elements, and may include facilities for those who monitor the behavior of those within. In some cultures, a cemetery (or burial mound, or earthwork?) may be understood not as simply a place to deposit the dead but also as the place where the spirits of the dead are symbolically incarcerated, and where they can be placated, neutralized, or simply provided with a place of proper communion with the living.

Unfortunately for interpretation, the archaeological manifestations of actively controlling enclosure architecture will not always exhibit qualitative differences from that intended only for passive control. Consideration of the wider archaeological context, however, may be helpful in sorting out difficult cases. For example, while identical types of fences could conceivably have been used to mark the borders of a residential property and an animal pen, the relationship of fence elements to other features should explicate the difference.

Resistive Enclosures

The second category of enclosure offers security to those within from something external. Examples can range from secured, but far from impregnable, places to highly elaborate fortifications. The level of resistance offered by boundary elements may reflect the severity and longevity of the external threat perceived by the builders. The enclosure boundaries will be rationally constructed in a manner capable of protecting the group by assisting in the neutralization of an external threat for at least some critical length of time.

Such places may, of course, be either defensively or offensively intentioned. Forts may be placed on a political border and designed to repel incursions from beyond it, but they can also be located across such borders, serving as secure bases from which to launch offensive operations.

Boundary features employed in functionally resistive enclosures will be typically substantial, giving evidence of rationally conceived protection from the type of onslaught that might be launched by the opposition of its time and place. Site locations may be selected with an eye to offering part of the desired protection. Boundary architectural features may be similar to those of some actively controlling enclosures (walls, embankments, ditches), but their placement may indicate the direction (internal or external) from which a threat is perceived.

Most resistive enclosures are purely functional in character. Examples from prehistoric North America likely include the stockades surrounding numerous Iroquois (e.g., Funk 1967) and Mississippian (e.g., Black 1967) sites. To be sure, most of the time such constructions probably offered the inhabitants a degree of peace of mind by making a symbolic statement of their security to outsiders, and functionally proving their worth during only relatively brief portions of their existences. On the other hand, some resistive enclosures may initially appear purely symbolic to an outsider, especially those intended to resist supernatural entities. A screen built to protect people from free-wandering ghosts is, however, made with a pragmatic purpose in mind, and will likely be regarded as serving it well; it is, therefore, considered to be a functionally resistive example. While such examples may exhibit some of the same architectural forms as other functionally resistive enclosures, their boundaries may be more ephemeral, and leave fewer (or even no) archaeological traces.

Purely symbolic resistive enclosures have been built, usually aimed at the achievement of a particular picturesque effect. Certain garden follies, sham castles, or fortifications were never intended to resist anyone and most were probably functionally incapable of doing so, but were executed as part of fashionable landscape designs or architectural movements. Ludwig of Bavaria's Neuschwanstein is an extreme example of this expensive form of symbolism.

Perceptions of Contemporary Settings

The landscapes in which sites existed have been long lost due to cultural and natural changes since their periods of use. While an accurate recovery of these settings may be beyond us in most instances, a consideration of their possible dimensions may give some deeper insights into site interpretation. Enclosures in particular, as elaborate architectural creations realized in earth and stone, were not only planned environments but were also intended to be perceived in particular ways by their using populations. Our understanding of these sites is enhanced if we can appreciate at least the range of landscape settings in which enclosures resided. Even if we cannot predict with complete accuracy their prehistoric conditions, an awareness of the implications of their potential settings may bring us closer to the vanished world we seek.

The manner in which a site's cultural features were integrated with, as well as obtruded from, its contemporary landscape setting is referred to as its *presentation*. This could be effected through the manipulation of both the built and the natural environments. A "proper" site presentation, which might be intended to create a desired visual and psychological impact without violating basic functional considerations, could involve the construction of certain architectural elements and also include various degrees of landscape modification.

The built environment includes all the construction going into the obtrusion of a site, including such features as embankments, structures, mounds, palisades, and ditches. It also includes land modifications such as grading or soil borrowing, which create both archaeological features and impacts on the setting of a site. The natural environment may also be modified to suit someone's conception of proper presentation, through such activities as planting or clearing. While certain kinds of data, such as features inherent in a site's construction, the discovery of graded areas or borrow pits, extracted pollen samples, or evidence of deforestation due to burning will all assist in defining elements of the prehistoric presentation of a site, in most instances there may be little hard data to indicate just how a site was integrated into its landscape.

It must also be realized that even a reasonably accurate reconstruction, whether scientifically or more speculatively based, still offers only limited emic insights. Successful recovery of a prehistoric presentation does not automatically carry with it an ability to understand the kind of impact that a site had upon its using population. Presentations are inextricably bound to a cultural background, which influences the perception of architecture and landscape as much as the physical components of a setting.

In much of North America, seasonal changes in vegetation bring another dimension to a site's presentation. Winter woodland vistas in Ohio, for instance, differ considerably from those in the verdant summertime; sight lines of a half or quarter mile in winter may close up to ten meters in summer. Seasonality was probably an important consideration to prehistoric builders, who knew their creations would be viewed quite differently in July and January.

Even if there is much we cannot know about a site's presentation, just the statement of its parameters, the variant ways in which a site could have been seen by a contemporary, may suggest certain things about its use. In considering how Middle Woodland enclosure architects may have wished their sites to be perceived by their contemporaries, I entertain three categories of presentation: clear, open, and closed. These correspond to gradually increasing degrees of forestation that were acceptable to the builders. A clear presentation denotes a site in a setting devoid of forest; for a Middle Woodland enclosure, this applies to the external surroundings of embankments as well as to the space within them. The current presentation of the infrequently mowed portions of Mound City is an example of this. High and dense weed growth is, however, possible, even expectable. A site like Mound City could not have been kept clear of weeds by the simple expedient of burning over the site because there were probably charnel houses in use that would have been destroyed. An open presentation is one in which a limited amount of deforestation has been done, possibly confined to certain parts of a site such as gateways or sight lines. A closed presentation signifies an absence of concern with deforestation; if construction occurred in a forested area, for instance, trees would expectably have been allowed to remain close by and within an enclosure. The implications of a certain kind of presentation are not limited to the time of construction but also extend to the period of use thereafter. The clearing and ground disturbance that would expectably have accompanied the construction of an enclosure would probably have encouraged a denser weedy and scrub growth than would usually have existed in a mature forest; unless this growth were checked, such sites could have become more closed in their presentation for a significant time after their building than would have been true of surrounding areas. Maintenance of some presentations could have entailed more work in subsequent years than did the actual construction effort.

Thus, if a clear presentation were a requirement for an Ohio Middle Woodland hilltop enclosure, giving it high visibility, not only would there have been the expense of clearing a significant acreage within and immediately below the walls of the structure in order to make it visible, but there would also have been a high annual maintenance cost to keep it so. An open presentation, wherein the builders would perhaps have cleared the embankment locus but elsewhere would not have attempted to alter the existing forest, would have carried a maintenance cost in keeping weedy growth down in the disturbed areas. A closed presentation would have been accomplished (perhaps inadvertently) if the builders disturbed the ground, built their site, and then made no effort to combat the invasion of weeds and scrub growth that would normally follow. On the other hand, if a hilltop site were to be used only in winter, the necessity of clearing would not have been as great in order for it still to have had high visual recognition.

Would the use of hilltop enclosures have conditioned their presentations? If they were forts, we would not expect that tall trees would have been tolerated directly adjacent to the embankments, but elsewhere their presence might not have mattered. Unlike European Neolithic societies with their hillforts, Ohio Middle Woodland peoples lacked effective long-range projectile weapons, and consequently would not have required open fields of fire. If such a fort were more of a refuge, with the purpose of hiding as well as protecting a population, it might have been located some distance from settlements and its setting actually enhanced by an obscuring cloak of forest.

The proper presentations for sacred or ceremonial uses are more difficult to guess at, since the range of possible specific functions is vast and the presentation demands variably dependent. If hilltop enclosures were primarily places where rituals were conducted, then an easy ability to distinguish their presence visually on the landscape could have been a consideration. Logic (admittedly Western) suggests that there might have been a preference for keeping the geometric enclosures on the river terraces relatively open, with both architecture and perhaps sightlines clearly visible. This would potentially have enhanced the perceptions of persons located both outside and within them, but would have increased their cost to their societies in the form of an annual labor bill for their maintenance.

The Pollock Works

The archaeology of the Pollock Works, located in southwest Ohio and under investigation since 1981, offers some new things to a discussion of hilltop site function. It underscores the idea that it is important to be alert to the possibility that local needs and situations changed over time, and that enclosures may have been adapted diachronically to fit different uses, or different manners of use. Archaeological data obtained from different parts of a site may therefore have pertained to distinct episodes in its use.

The Pollock Works is located in Greene County, southwest Ohio, near the town of Cedarville. A 5.5 ha limestone mesa was created and isolated from the surrounding topography by Massie's Creek. As recorded by Squier and Davis (1848) (fig. 5.1), it was embellished with earth and stone embankments

Fig. 5.1. Squier and Davis (1848) map of the Pollock Works.

on its west and north sides, where the natural vertical cliffs did not prevail. Access up the gradual western slope was successively blocked by low crescents, then by 3-meters-high embankment segments that stretched across the 90 m distance between the cliff on the south and the creek bluff on the north. This part of the enclosure, referred to as the barrier wall, is penetrated by three gateways. It is in excellent shape today, but the external mounds and crescents were destroyed by quarrying for subsurface limestone during the last hundred years. Atop the steep, 7-m-high bluff along Massie's Creek on the north, Squier and Davis mapped a low, meter-high embankment that ran from the barrier wall east for about 210 m. This portion of the earthwork I have termed the perimeter wall. Barrier and perimeter walls remain in good condition, not significantly altered from their appearance in *Ancient Monuments of the Mississippi Valley* (Squier and Davis 1848:plate XII, no. 3). The archaeological project has excavated fifteen trenches through embankment segments, and fifteen radiocarbon dates have informed the reconstruction of the site's chronology (e.g., Riordan 1995). Although the entire area was cleared in historic times until the 1950s (fig. 5.2 is an excellent low oblique aerial photograph from the Smithsonian's National

Fig. 5.2. Aerial view of the Pollock Works in 1934. Courtesy National Anthropological Archives, Smithsonian Institution, Daché Reeves, photographer.

Anthropological Archives taken by aviator Daché Reeves in 1934), a scrub forest now covers the enclosure's interior, and a more mature forest hides the approaches to it. In the terms of the discussion above, the site's modern presentation is closed.

The single most important fact discovered about Pollock is that the site plan of Squier and Davis was the mature result of a building program that probably lasted 150 years. That its plan and its constituent elements did change over time has implications for how the site may have been used both during and after that period.

Our work has shown that the first building at the site caused an embankment 1.5 m high to connect the creek bluff with the beginning of the natural cliff on the south, spanning some 90 m. This stage appears to date to the first half of the first century A.D.

In stages two and three, the height of the barrier wall was augmented by successive layers of soil. At this time the north gateway took form, preserving the original elevated surface of the first stage but leaving the space on top free of subsequent soil additions. The south gateway may have been part of this version of the site plan and, although there is no way to know with certainty, the mounds and external crescents may have also taken form. These stages represent episodic additions that probably occurred over a period of fifty to one hundred years. During this period there was no construction on the bluff edge above the creek.

The fourth construction stage constituted a major change at the site, the most interesting but also the briefest building phase in its history. A fence was built on top of the barrier wall, its vertical support timbers for the most part widely spaced and set slightly below the embankment summit toward the interior of the enclosure. The uprights were interwoven with wood, and it apparently stood about 1.5 m high. Its construction was complemented by a partially mud-plastered timber stockade that stood all along the creek bluff. Employing an estimated 600 vertical posts spaced approximately a half-meter apart, which ranged (in the observed sample) from 19 to over 40 cm in diameter, it stood 4 m high. The uprights were horizontally interwoven with light timbers and sticks up their full height, and in most places thickly plastered with mud the first two meters. A considerable amount of limestone was carried up from the creek, used both to chink the posts and to pile against the stockade's exterior. The calibrated average of a series of ten radiocarbon dates from the barrier fence and perimeter stockade dated between A.D. 130 and 228 (Riordan 1995:76).

Then, as I interpret it, the builders elected to destroy the fence and stockade, setting them afire, baking the mud plaster and burning the timbers. They collapsed inward toward the interior of the enclosure along the perimeter wall, and against the sloping surface of the barrier wall. That so much of it has been preserved indicates that the final half-meter of soil on the barrier wall, and the meter-high embankment of earth and stone on the creek bluff, were both added very soon after the destruction, and assuredly by its owners rather than by any attackers. This bluff embankment–building and barrier wall–capping episode constituted the fifth and probably final construction stage.

Discussion: Context and Function of the Pollock Works

The results of the intensive archaeological efforts undertaken at the Pollock Works allow some tentative ideas to be advanced concerning its place in the functional continuum described above, and even more tentatively concerning its original presentation. While the evidence obtained to date is still too ambiguous to permit the luxury of definitive conclusions, enough is at hand to advance some ideas about the type of enclosure that it was, and to conclude that the nature of its use did change with time.

In its earliest version, Pollock's broad and low embankment, connecting the outcropping cliff with the slope to the creek, would seem to have constituted an enclosure intended to exert passive control over the space it defined. Its focus seems to have clearly been on the acreage of the mesa, its intent being to bound the one section that lacked the natural definition of slope or cliff. The unprepossessing form of the embankment was not meant to physically deter anyone from access to the mesa, although its message may have had a subtext intelligible to those approaching it that not everyone was equally free to intrude.

In terms of its presentation, the emphasis definitely seems to have been on an approach to the enclosure from the west, up the gradual slope toward the crescents and barrier wall. If the low exterior crescents and mounds were intended to be easily seen during the warm months of the year, the presentation must either have been clear, at least in the vicinity of the earthwork, or open. If the site's use was restricted to the colder months, and its visual recognition by people was an important consideration, then expectably some degree of clearance was maintained. Alternatively, if people were not the primary intended viewers, and the enclosure operated on a more spiritual plane, then perhaps only clearing to the extent necessary to effect construction was required.

Following the earliest phase of construction until sometime late in the second century A.D., the changes at Pollock seem to have been mainly additive, slightly modifying or enlarging upon the original idea behind it. The successive soil mantles placed on the barrier wall may have been a way of periodically redefining them, renewing and underlining their separation from their surroundings (if only for a season or two). The incorporation of more than a single gateway into the plan is another of these changes. The reason for multiple entrances is not apparent, although perhaps astronomical sightlines, which have not yet been evaluated, might have constituted a rationale.

Construction of the bluff stockade quite possibly represented a radical transformation of Pollock. A very substantial physical barrier was created toward the end of the second century, where for a century or so before none had been considered necessary. In the discussion above it was mentioned that functionally coercive enclosures, aimed at controlling that which lies within, and resistive enclosures, aimed at what is without, may share similar architectural features. At Pollock, the question is against whom (or what) this sudden architectural change was directed, and whether the intent was security or control. Clearly, however, something besides the original passive definition of the mesa was being addressed.

One explanatory hypothesis is that some hostile activity had shattered the normally placid woodlands of southern Ohio, and that the Pollock stockade was a functionally resistive enclosure intended to help secure a local population (Riordan 1996). It is important to note that if this construction did constitute a military response to events, it is also viewed as having disrupted the site's traditional uses. Presumably, when more peaceful conditions returned and it was no longer needed, its builders burned it down. Its replacement by earth and stone may even have been required for the enclosure's rededication or reconsecration.

A different scenario can be envisioned, however, in which the enclosure might have shifted toward a place intended to exert an active form of control, and that the focus of the stockade builders remained firmly on the enclosed mesa rather than on a hostile external world. The building and burning of the stockade could have been an intensification of a magico-religious effort to control that which was (or was considered to be) contained within. One point in favor of this scenario is the relative flimsiness of the barrier wall fence, which was lower and supported by posts smaller in diameter and more widely spaced than those employed along the bluff. Its location on the interior slope of the embankment segments further ensured that it offered less than an optimal resistance to an external threat.

There is some evidence that stockades may also have been destroyed by fire at the Miami Fort, Foster's, and Milford Township enclosures (Riordan 1996:252). If this interpretation is correct, redundant events occurring at similar sites could alternatively betoken widespread unrest or the regional repetition of an episode important in the ritual life of local societies.

The presentation of the site may not have been altered if it was converted to a fort during its fourth construction stage, since its setting would have been dictated by the requirements of its prior use. If the presence of the stockade means that its use shifted to a more active form of internal control, perhaps over contained spiritual entities, instead of offering external resistance, then maintenance of a clear or open presentation may not have been considered necessary. The fire that engulfed the stockade, if not simply part of a natural event such as a forest fire (which its possible repetition at other enclosures may render less likely), could have been a visual spectacle (and an ephemeral aspect of its presentation) intended to be witnessed by the members of an assembled group, heightening whatever spiritual or other benefits the act may have conferred on them.

Whatever the truth concerning these events, it appears that the focus of concern of the fifth construction stage, and for whatever period the enclosure was subsequently used thereafter without apparent further modification, was again on the enclosed mesa. The plastered timber stockade, an unnatural and obviously cultural element that was intruded onto the scene, was replaced as a boundary by a low embankment whose form closely mimicked nature. Pollock was thereby restored to a passively controlling enclosure, resuming the ancient purpose for which its embankments had been originally built.

Chapter 6

Architectural Grammar Rules at the
Fort Ancient Hilltop Enclosure

Robert P. Connolly

The Fort Ancient site (fig. 6.1) is located on a bluff 80 meters above the Little Miami River drainage (see fig. 1.1) in Warren County, Ohio. The earthwork's multiple construction events are bracketed by the Middle Woodland period (200 B.C.–A.D. 400). Fort Ancient's 5.7 km of embankment walls encompass approximately 51 ha of an upland plateau that is surrounded by precipitous ravines. On the basis of this geographic setting, the complex is considered a hilltop enclosure. The earthwork incorporates a multitude of earthen mounds and crescents, stone circles, flagstone pavements, and two parallel walls extending 0.7 km northeast of the enclosure's embankment walls. Although most of the architectural elements at Fort Ancient remain intact, by the mid-nineteenth century the two parallel walls had been destroyed by historic-period farming (fig. 6.2).

Extensive research projects, beginning with those of Warren King Moorehead (1890), William C. Mills (1908), Richard Morgan (1939, 1940), and Patricia Essenpreis (Essenpreis 1986; Essenpreis and Moseley 1984) have individually addressed multiple aspects of the earthwork. Current field research has focused on the patterned distribution of architectural elements centered on the 67 gateways at the Fort Ancient site. Drawing on previous and current investigations, this chapter examines evidence for the rule-governed nature of earthwork construction at Fort Ancient. Field research demonstrates that while the extent of construction at hilltop enclosures is inherently restricted by their physically circumscribed locations, Middle Woodland populations extensively modified the upland plateau to accommodate the specific placement of embankment walls and other architectural features (Connolly 1996a). In addition, the construction of these features is more precise and elaborate than previously thought.

Building on the recognition of the precise construction of the Fort Ancient complex, I elaborate on the canons of construction or the architectural grammar that governed site growth. Essenpreis originally noted the planned and evolutionary nature of the rules governing the construction of Fort Ancient. She wrote (1986:8–9) that the "earthworks are explained as agglutinative and sequentially built, from south to north, with different enclosures drawing on architectural canons that shifted from irregular to standardized forms. During

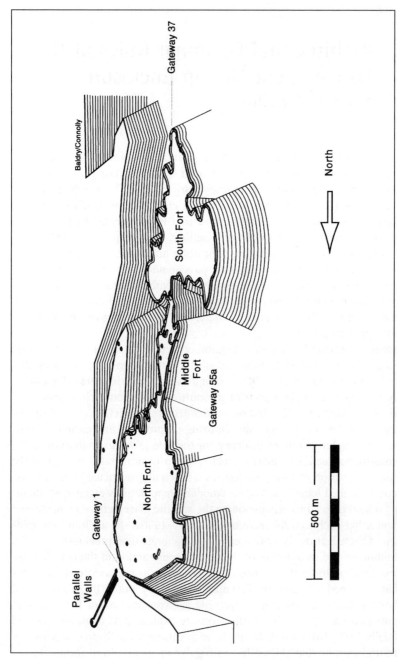

Fig. 6.1. Location of primary gateways at the Fort Ancient site (drawing by Susan Baldry and Robert Connolly).

this period, primary gateway form at Fort Ancient shifted from being demarcated by two 'conjoined' mounds, which were connected both to each other and to adjacent embankments, to utilization of free-standing mounds, independent from each other, although attached to the embankments of the Parallel Walled Enclosure."

Essenpreis's research focused on embankment wall form and the three primary gateways. After reviewing and expanding on her discussion of primary gateways, I will focus here on secondary gateway complexes and their constituent elements.

Architectural Grammar

The goal of this study is to examine the distribution of architectural elements for the purpose of eliciting construction rules of the built environment at hilltop enclosures. Based on these rules I have constructed an architectural grammar. Such a grammar can be used as a heuristic device to organize and elicit meaning from the rule-governed construction and use of hilltop enclosures. I use the term *rule* to identify the patterned distribution or association of architectural elements that occur without exception throughout the earthwork complex and the term *trend* where the distribution or association is predominant but either exceptions occur or there are insufficient data to definitively consider the occurrence a rule. That is, rules are absolutely true statements, and trends minimally are statements that are true most of the time.

Two sets of grammatical rules may be constructed for the built environment: rules of a design grammar for the actual construction of the built environment at hilltop enclosures, and rules of an interpretive grammar that provide meaning and cue correct behavior at hilltop enclosures. Here I focus on rules of a design grammar. Although the two sets of rules are interrelated, a clear explication and understanding of a design grammar must precede the consideration of an interpretive grammar. That is, a thorough examination of the patterns and distribution of the architectural elements at earthwork complexes is necessary prior to consideration of meaning in the built form. Otherwise, meaning will be necessarily surficial in terms of the actual physical form of the built environment and consequently not able to move beyond abstract theoretical models for the meaning of monumental constructions. A design grammar is therefore a descriptive grammar that provides the basis for recapitulating the generative process of earthwork construction. The goal of a design grammar is to recognize the patterns and distribution of elements at hilltop enclosures. The point is that, through determining the design rules, architectural patterns can be delimited and made intelligible as part of a system.

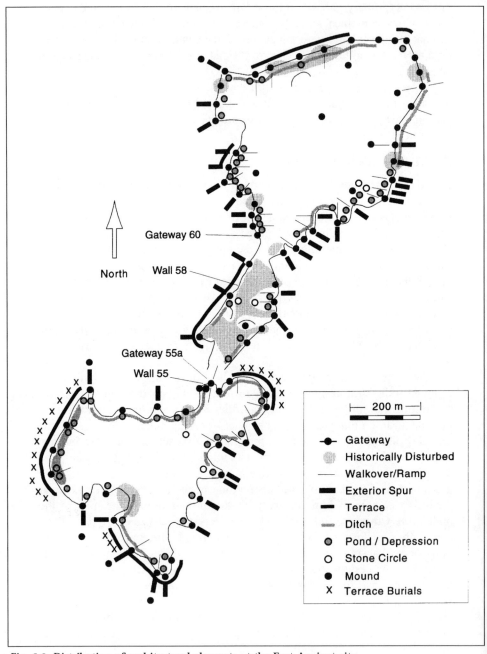

Fig. 6.2. Distribution of architectural elements at the Fort Ancient site.

Gateway Complexes as Units of Analysis

In common usage, a gateway at Woodland-period earthworks is defined as a marked depression in an otherwise level section of embankment wall. The use of the term gateway to describe these architectural elements is somewhat unfortunate because the name implies that gateways functioned only as means of egress and ingress at an earthwork complex. While service as a passage is apparent in many cases, this function is not universal for all gateway features. In addition, the type of passage needs to be evaluated. Further, at Fort Ancient several gateway exteriors lead to precipitous drops into adjacent ravines, thus providing no physical access to the enclosure. Gateway openings are also suggested to function as the foresights from the centers of nearby mounds for observing astronomical alignments at Fort Ancient (Essenpreis and Duszynski 1989). The proposed alignments include maximum northern moonrise, minimum northern moonrise, and summer solstice. Similar gateway opening and mound configurations are proposed to manifest the same alignments at other Middle Woodland earthworks (Hively and Horn 1982). Therefore, gateways are not functionally identical to or used solely as expedient passageways into an enclosure. Essenpreis divided gateways at Fort Ancient into two types: secondary gateways that are marked as simple depressions in embankment walls, and primary gateways that are formed by raised sections of embankment walls, usually referred to as conjoined mounds and also occurring as free-standing twin mounds.

Elements most often associated with gateways include embankment walls, limestone pavements, ditches, ponds, walkovers, ramps, exterior spurs, and exterior terraces. Combinations of these elements around a single gateway constitute a gateway complex. The architectural elements of embankment walls, except within the gateway openings, are not discussed in this chapter. The physical constituents and construction of embankment walls are well documented at only three locations in the Fort Ancient complex (Essenpreis 1986, 1990). The significant amount of variation documented at the three locations precludes meaningful discussion in this chapter. For the purposes of this study, walls are defined as the level sections of embankment between gateway openings.

The numbering system used in this chapter for denoting specific gateways and embankment walls was developed by Moorehead (1890). The numbering system moves clockwise from the Gateway 1 designation shown in figure 6.3. The embankment wall section occurring immediately before the gateway in the clockwise pattern is designated with the same number as the gateway. That is, the section of embankment wall between Gateway 1 and Gateway 2 is numbered Wall 2. The numbers assigned by Moorehead included not only gateway openings but irregularities or breaks in the embankment wall, many of which resulted from natural erosion. Based on extensive archive research and pedestrian surveys, today the true number of gateways is set at sixty-seven (Connolly 1996b). All figures in this chapter reflect current estimates of gateway placement but retain the Moorehead numbering system. Numbers assigned by Moorehead that are not considered true gateways are simply ignored in this chapter (fig. 6.3).

Primary Gateway Complexes

As noted by Essenpreis (1986:9), the three primary gateway complexes at Fort Ancient exhibit a regularity in constituent architectural elements. Because these complexes are located in portions of the enclosure that span the total earthwork construction period, an evolution in the grammar rules of the complexes is seen through time. In the South Fort, Gateway 37 (fig. 6.1) is considered a primary gateway because of the conjoined mound or raised sections of embankment wall that form the gateway opening. The architectural elements associated with Gateway 37 are an exterior spur containing a stone mound and a limestone slab pavement that extends 80 vertical m to the banks of the Little Miami River and, on the interior, an elevated walkover that leads to the central plateau and is flanked by depressions on either side. Of the three primary gateways at Fort Ancient, Gateway 37 is the least elaborate and contains the fewest associated architectural elements. Based on the sequence of earthwork construction first proposed by Moorehead (1890), Gateway 37 is the oldest of the three complexes.

The Gateway 55a complex includes a ramp on the north side of the gateway that leads to the isthmus of the Middle Fort. The ramp on the south side of the gateway contains an ossuary-type burial deposit and serves as a walkover between lateral ponds or ditches. A burial mound of indeterminate size is located immediately west of the south ramp. A limestone slab pavement lines the ditch that follows the interior of Wall 55 for approximately 46 m. A second pavement, possibly of the same approximate length, originates near the conical mound and continues on a straight line south into the South Fort. Finally, the two crescent embankments north of Gateway 55a function as a funnel device for the complex. A small stone mound containing the parts of two burials is recorded on the interior curve of the east crescent embankment.

The Gateway 1 complex includes Gateway 1, from which extends a ramp to the interior and exterior of the enclosure. The interior ramp leads to a small conical mound that is covered with burnt limestone and contains one possible human burial. The trajectory of the exterior ramp leads to the opening between two twin conical mounds. Two parallel walls extend from the mounds to the northeast for 0.85 km and encircle a small earthen conical mound. A limestone pavement of indeterminate dimensions is enclosed by the parallel

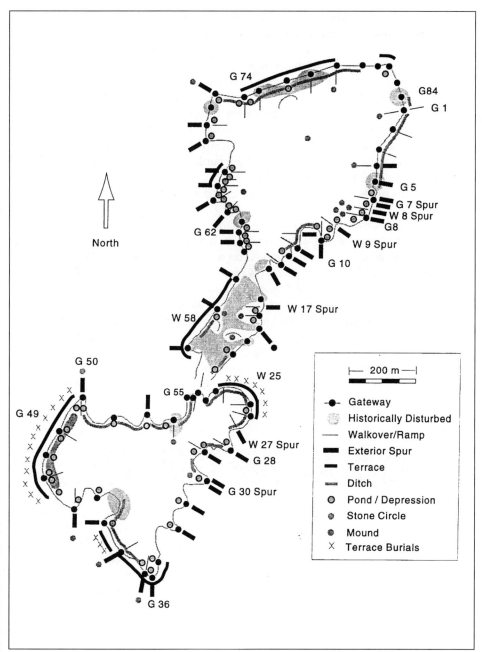

Fig. 6.3. Distribution of ponds, spurs, terraces, and walkovers at Fort Ancient.

walls near their point of origin at the twin mounds. From the two twin mounds ditches extend to the northwest and southwest and connect with adjacent ravines. At least one spring head is located within the space between the twin mounds and Gateway 1.

Table 6.1 lists the architectural elements associated with each of the three primary gateways identified at the Fort Ancient site. However, it is important to emphasize that these are the only elements either currently visible or reported in the literature. A plausible assumption is that additional elements were in place at the original construction of the enclosure or periodically in place over the use-life of the earthwork for specific activities or cyclic events. These latter elements likely included features referred to by Rapoport (1990) as semifixed feature elements such as perishable screens, structures, or banners.

A comparison of elements beginning with Gateway 37, moving to Gateway 55a, and ending with Gateway 1 confirms the shifts of "construction canons" through time that Essenpreis conjectured. Similar sets of elements are used in the construction of primary gateways at all three locations. However, the arrangement and physical manifestation of the elements becomes more elaborate moving from south to north. For example, the arrangement and expression of conjoined mounds and funnel devices demonstrate the modifications. At Gateway 37, the conjoined mounds are low and symmetrical. An exterior funnel device is absent or at best expressed as the limestone pavement extending 80 vertical meters to the banks of the Little Miami River at the base of the enclosure. At Gateway 55a, the conjoined mounds are significantly larger, asymmetrical, and capped with limestone. The exterior crescents funnel

Table 6.1 Architectural elements at Fort Ancient site primary gateways

	GATEWAY		
	37	55a	1
Location	South Fort	South/Middle Ft.	North Fort
Form	Conjoined mounds	Conjoined mounds	Twin mounds
Gate symmetry		Right larger	Right larger
Ramp/walkover	Interior	Interior/exterior	Interior/exterior
Pavement	Exterior	Interior/exterior	Exterior
Ditch/pond	Interior	Interior	Exterior
Water Source	?	Interior	Exterior
Exterior funnel		Crescent	Parallel walls
Assoc. mound	Exterior	Interior/exterior	Interior/exterior
Human burial		Interior/exterior	

earthwork users into the gateway opening. At Gateway 1, the conjoined mound form is not located on the embankment wall but instead is set in front of the North Fort enclosure, presumably as two unattached and asymmetrical twin mounds, although they may have been connected at the base. The parallel walls are the exterior funnel at Gateway 1, replacing the crescents at Gateway 55a. (A linear funnel device in the North Fort is also consistent with the more linear embankment wall forms of the North Fort when compared to the Middle and South Fort.) Therefore, an elaboration and consistent evolution in architectural elements of primary gateways is apparent.

Secondary Gateway Complex Architectural Elements

As with primary gateways, secondary gateways contain associated architectural elements that, along with the gateway opening, form a gateway complex. Following is a brief discussion of the individual types of architectural elements composing secondary gateway complexes. Distinctions are made between the element types occurring at secondary gateway complexes and their expression at primary gateway complexes. No single ideal or model of a secondary gateway complex is apparent as in the case of primary gateway complexes (see table 6.1).

Ponds, Ditches, and Walkovers

Three types of ground-surface depressions are associated with secondary gateways. Ponds are defined as distinct, well-formed, oval to round ground-surface depressions. Simple surface depressions are defined as oval to round but shallower and less well formed than ponds. Ditches are defined as distinct linear depressions that are placed parallel to the interior or exterior of embankment walls. Traditionally, ponds and ditches on the interior of embankment walls are interpreted as expedient sources for soils in embankment-wall construction. However, the precise construction, morphology, and function of these features at two excavated gateway complexes (Connolly 1996a) contradict the traditional thinking.

Walkovers are defined by the presence of interior ditches or ponds in association with secondary gateway openings. If a gateway opening leads directly into a pond or ditch, no walkover is present. If a gateway leads to a flat interior or exterior surface, no walkover is present. Only if a gateway leads to a level section of land that is flanked by ground-surface depressions is a walkover present. Unlike ramps, walkovers do not fan out from the gateway opening. Walkovers are no wider, and often are narrower, than the gateway opening. Unlike ramps, walkovers do not provide a gradual descent from the gateway opening but simply provide level access from the embankment wall base across ground-surface depressions.

The distinction between ponds and ground-surface depressions visible today may simply be a result of modifications by the Civilian Conservation

Corps (CCC) in the 1930s. Simple ground-surface depressions are most often located where evidence of CCC activity is found. Fieldwork conducted to date has not attempted to reconstruct the prehistoric form of all ground-surface depressions. Therefore, while the distinction between simple ground-surface depressions and ponds currently visible at Fort Ancient is recognized, assessing the integrity or significance, if any, of the two varying forms is not a focus of this study.

Many ditches are also altered from their prehistoric forms. Approximate reconstructions are possible by consulting original field notes from the pre-1930 period. For example, today the interior of Wall 55 (fig. 6.2) is completely flat except between Gateway 55 and Gateway 55a. However, Mills (1908) reports and provides photographs of a distinct ditch running the entire length of Wall 55. Therefore, this study may confidently assume the existence of the ditch feature as part of the original earthwork construction. Similar certainty is not warranted, however, for the placement of ditches and ponds in the Middle Fort. For example, from Wall 58 to Gateway 60 the inte-rior along the embankment wall is flat, although a single excavation unit bisecting the wall at this location (R. Morgan 1940; Essenpreis 1990) recorded a distinct ditch feature lined with limestone slabs. No pre-1930 record reports the presence of the ditch. The actual extent of the ditch at this location is unknown.

The distribution of pond and ditch features shown in figure 6.3 is conservative. Features are not assigned in areas containing evidence of historic disturbance unless they have been unambiguously documented by a pre-1930 field observation. Therefore, anomalies must be anticipated in any patterned distribution of ground-surface depression forms at Fort Ancient. However, as discussed later, reliable trends and patterns in the distribution of these architectural elements are readily demonstrated.

No obvious differences exist between the pond and ditch features associated with primary and secondary gateway complexes. The sole exception to this statement is the unique set of ditches extending from the Twin Mounds (Connolly 1996b; Essenpreis and Moseley 1984).

Exterior Spurs and Terraces

In his sequential description of survey stations along the length of the Fort Ancient embankment walls, Moorehead (e.g., 1890:11–13) refers to exterior spurs as "bastions." He hypothesized wooden blockhouses were placed at these locations as defensive lookouts. However, no empirical evidence of any blockhouse structure is known. Moorehead further argued that exterior spurs were entirely natural formations. Based on limited excavation data and extensive pedestrian surveys, qualification of this assertion is necessary. Although the spurs are natural features of the landscape, their uppermost surfaces often were modified culturally to accommodate a variety of prehistoric activities.

Exterior spurs at Fort Ancient are extensions of the interior plateau placed outside the enclosure by the construction of embankment walls. The width, length, and relative elevation of the exterior spurs vary throughout the site. No systematic topographic survey of the exterior spurs has yet been conducted to quantify the extent of the variation. For the purpose of this study, simply the presence or absence of exterior spurs at secondary gateways is noted.

The placement of secondary gateways relative to exterior spurs is highly patterned throughout the Fort Ancient complex. As demonstrated below, exterior spurs are arguably the architectural elements at Fort Ancient that best predict the locations of gateways and interior walkovers.

Exterior terraces, like exterior spurs, are most often extensions of the interior plateau placed outside the enclosure by the construction of embankment walls, and are significantly modified from their natural state. For example, terraces exterior to the South Fort were widened by the prehistoric quarrying of limestone on their margins. The length, width, and relative elevation of exterior terraces also vary throughout the enclosure.

Mounds and Stone Circles

All mounds on the interior of the Fort Ancient complex, whether constructed of stone, earth, or stone and earth, and all mounds on exterior spurs are elements of gateway openings. No morphological distinction between mounds associated with primary and secondary gateway complexes is readily apparent. However, the mounds on exterior spurs associated with secondary gateways tend to contain more evidence of human burials.

All stone circles documented within the Fort Ancient embankment walls are elements of secondary gateway complexes. A typical stone circle is composed of a 4–6 m circle of limestone stacked one to three courses high. The interiors of the circles contain the identical soil matrix as the surrounding exterior areas. No prepared floors or ancillary architectural elements are known. In addition, no evidence of prehistoric activity is recorded from within stone circles. Field notes from Mills (1908) contain the only documentation of a stone circle excavated at Fort Ancient. Four stone circles are visible on the ground surface today, and the approximate locations of several others are documented in the reports of Moorehead and Mills.

Summary of Architectural Elements

The architectural elements associated with secondary gateways include walkovers, limestone pavements and retaining walls, ponds and ditches, exterior spurs and terraces, stone circles, mounds, and unknown ancillary structures. The latter structures are represented by postmolds excavated in the immediate proximity of gateway openings (Connolly 1996b). All of these features except stone circles and terraces are also found in association with primary gateway complexes at Fort Ancient. The difference in comparable elements at the two gateway complex types is expressed more in degree than in kind. That is, primary gateway complex elements are often more expansive than their secondary counterparts. An example of this trend is the distinction between the primary gateway ramp and the secondary gateway walkover. The conjoined mound form of primary gateways is the most visible qualitative distinction between the two types of gateways. A further distinction between primary and secondary gateway complexes is our inability to propose an ideal model for the constituent elements of the latter type.

Distribution of Secondary Gateway Complex Elements

Figure 6.2 shows the distribution of secondary gateways and associated architectural elements at the Fort Ancient site. Several clarifications are necessary to establish the level of accuracy of the distributions shown. First, the locations of all elements illustrated are approximate. Second, symbols for various elements are standardized and do not reflect intra-element size variation. In most cases, the assessment of element size variation is beyond the scope of this study. For example, as discussed above, simply the presence or absence of spurs is recorded. Third, primarily historic but also natural formation processes have dramatically altered many secondary gateways at Fort Ancient. Figure 6.2 notes locations where no documentation exists to provide a reliable estimate of the earthwork's prehistoric form. These locations are labeled "historically disturbed." Finally, the "X" symbols on figure 6.2 that mark terrace burials are meant only to indicate approximate location and not numbers of individuals or discrete burial concentrations. The terrace burial locations illustrated are based on Moorehead's published map (1890:plate 2) and present-day evidence of limestone slab concentrations. Moorehead's field notes and published accounts are particularly vague in quantifying the terrace burials. Apparently, no Middle Woodland skeletal remains from Moorehead's excavations at Fort Ancient were curated at any institution, or if curated, they were later deaccessioned and destroyed. For example, in the 1930s the Field Museum in Chicago deaccessioned and "consigned to waste" all nonwhole artifacts excavated from Fort Ancient by Moorehead (Janice Klein, registrar of collections, personal communication, 1994). Based on Moorehead's published accounts, the burials consisted of irregularly formed piles of limestone less than 1 m in height. Burials recovered from the terraces most often were fragmented and contained few if any grave goods. Even a reasonable estimate of the number of burials is not possible. However, the real significance to this study of the terrace burials and their association with secondary gateways is that they occur only in South Fort, as I will discuss.

Following is a report and discussion of the association of architectural elements at secondary gateways and their distribution throughout the Fort

Ancient site. This section also presents the initial statements that describe the patterned distribution of architectural elements at secondary gateway complexes.

Secondary Gateways and Exterior Spurs

The most visible and consistently represented architectural element at secondary gateways is the exterior spur. The number of exterior spurs illustrated in figure 6.3 is likely an underestimate. The map does not include small protrusions outside the embankment walls that were possibly larger at the time of the original construction of the earthwork but may since have been diminished by 2000 years of erosion. Thirty-two of the sixty-four secondary gateway complexes at Fort Ancient contain an exterior spur as an architectural element of their gateway complex. Exterior spurs are distributed proportionately throughout the enclosure. Although a strong correlation between gateway placement and exterior spurs is visible, exceptions are noted. For example, f igure 6.3 shows the locations of four exterior spurs not in association with a gateway (Walls 8, 9, 17, 27).

All exterior spurs, whether associated with a gateway or located on a section of embankment wall between two gateways, are marked by an architectural element on the interior of the earthwork. That is, whether an exterior spur is centered on a gateway or between two gateways, an additional architectural element must be placed on the interior of the earthwork at the spur location. The only secondary gateway complexes that contradict this statement are those altered historically or by natural erosion to such an extent that reliable reconstruction of the original earthwork form is not possible.

Besides gateway openings, there is no readily visible pattern of other architectural elements that marks the locations of exterior spurs. The elements that mark exterior spurs include either a walkover with lateral ponds, a walkover with lateral ditches, or a pond centered on the gateway opening. Perhaps fortuitously, the four examples of exterior spurs that occur between two gateway openings are all marked by walkovers with either lateral ponds or ditches.

The occurrence of walkovers with exterior spurs does not simply result from the spur extending to the interior of the earthwork. While this does occur in some instances, several lines of evidence argue against this reasoning to explain all, or even most, interior walkovers and lateral surface depressions. First, Essenpreis's (1985) examination of the Gateway 44 walkover demonstrated the surface of the feature was constructed culturally and is not part of the natural topography. Second, in most instances walkovers and spurs are not at the same approximate elevation, as would be expected if the two elements were actually contiguous. Third, the coring and excavation of ponds, walkover elements, and spurs demonstrate the land modification associated with their construction (Connolly 1996a). Fourth, the tendency, discussed below, for secondary gateways with multiple or offset spurs to contain interior walkovers that, in effect, center the gateway either between the multiple spurs or the offset demonstrates the modification of the interior plateau to accommodate walkover, spur, and pond placement.

Based on this discussion of exterior spurs, the first rule of association of the architectural elements composing secondary gateway complexes states that *all exterior spurs must be associated with either a pond or walkover at the corresponding interior location of the earthwork.*

An apparent trend exists that when two exterior spurs are in close proximity to each other, a single gateway and walkover is centered between them. This arrangement is illustrated at Gateways 7 and 30 (fig. 6.3). Similarly, a visible trend exists that when an exterior spur is offset to the right or left of the gateway opening, the interior walkover is offset in the opposite direction to center the gateway opening between the walkover and the spur. This arrangement is demonstrated at Gateways 28 and 62. At all other locations throughout the enclosure, exterior spurs and interior walkovers are centered on their associated gateway openings. The two trends of centering gateways, spurs, and walkovers are not considered rules of association simply because erosion and historic modification at some of the locations exhibiting these characteristics obscure and have possibly altered the original construction form. Therefore, instead of a rule, the centering phenomenon is stated as a trend that *in general, if exterior spurs and interior walkovers are not centered on the gateway opening, then the exterior and interior elements are offset in opposite directions to center the gateway opening.*

Ditches

The most visible difference in the distribution of ditches and ponds at Fort Ancient is that ditches must occur along the entire length of an embankment wall with a corresponding exterior terrace or flat plateau surface. Ponds also may be interspersed along the length of these ditches. The exterior terrace and interior ditch association is illustrated in figure 6.3 in the South Fort along Wall 25 and north from Gateway 36, in the Middle Fort along Wall 58, and in the North Fort east of Gateway 74. Also in the North Fort an exterior ditch extended south between Gateway 84 and Gateway 5. This space marks the only portion of the Fort Ancient enclosure with an exterior plateau.

At several locations throughout the Fort Ancient complex, ditches are formed, in part, by the placement of embankment walls at a lower elevation on the down-slope edge of the plateau. However, ditch construction and distribution patterns are not simply the fortuitous results of such embankment wall placement. This statement is supported by several lines of evidence. First, as documented by the excavations of R. Morgan (1940) and Essenpreis (1990) at Wall 58, ditches adjacent to exterior terraces were crafted features often containing evidence of limestone pavements to mark their original construction form. Second, the general morphology of interior ditch features at locations containing exterior terraces and exterior spurs is markedly similar, suggesting a preconceived template of appropriate ditch form. Third, the interior ditch and embankment wall placement at the arc of Wall 25 specifically does not follow the natural land contour. Therefore, the natural landform did not restrict the ability of the prehistoric builders to construct the ditch and wall forms in the desired arc pattern.

Based on the above, an additional rule of association of architectural elements at secondary gateway complexes states that *at secondary gateways whose exterior leads to a terrace or flat plateau, a ditch must mark the location.*

Interior Walkovers

As discussed above, although interior walkovers most often are associated with exterior spurs, several lines of evidence demonstrate the walkovers are not simply artifacts of the extensions of the exterior spur on the interior of the enclosure. Interior walkovers also are associated with exterior terraces where no spur is present. Interior walkovers never are associated with exteriors that drop to precipitous ravines. By definition, interior walkovers always are associated with adjacent ground surface depressions. A rule of association for interior walkovers states that *at secondary gateway complexes, interior walkovers mark the presence of an exterior spur or exterior terrace.*

Symmetry of Architectural Element Distribution

Although highly patterned, most of the remaining architectural elements composing secondary gateway complexes at Fort Ancient are not explained readily by specific, universally applied rules. Instead, the distribution of elements is explained best by an overriding theme of symmetry in their arrangement. For example, although no single rule explains the grouping of secondary gateways with interior walkovers, exterior spurs, and lateral ponds, where this grouping of elements occurs, a symmetrical counterpart is also present, as discussed next. The total symmetry in the distribution of elements is illustrated for the North Fort in figure 6.4. The upper half of the figure divides the North Fort along an approximate center line, while the bottom half provides a mirror image of the eastern half of the North Fort to better illustrate the symmetry. Several symmetrical arrangements are visible.

First, the general morphology of the embankment walls corresponds between the two halves of the North Fort. The portions of figure 6.4 labeled A protrude out with straight sections of embankment wall of equal length in both halves, followed by the B sections that incurve, followed by C sections that form a rough S shape. In all of section A and most of section B the east wall does not follow the contour of the plateau edge. Virtually any wall trajectory was physically possible in sections A and B of the east half of the North Fort. That the earthwork builders chose a form on the east half that mimicked the form on the west half demonstrates the intentionality of the symmetrical arrangement.

Gateway placement between the two halves of the North Fort is also symmetrical. Each half of section A contains four gateways that are approximately equidistant. The correspondence is not predicted by the presence of exterior spurs. As I discuss later in this chapter, the gateways in the east half of section A accommodate the sighting lines for astronomical alignments and correspond directly to the octagon form at the High Bank earthwork in Ross County, Ohio.

Gateway and pond placement at section C is an excellent demonstration that the location of architectural elements is not dictated by the constraints of the natural topography, including the occurrence of exterior spurs. Within both halves of section C, all exterior spurs are marked by lateral ponds and walkovers. This statement is true even where gateways do not occur on the east half of the enclosure. This symmetrical relationship is significant for two reasons. First, if exterior spurs solely predicted gateway placement, then two additional gateways should be located on the east half of the earthwork at section C. In the east half, two sets of exterior spurs, lateral ponds, and interior walkovers occur without gateways. The section of embankment wall on the east half of the North Fort below section C contains a similar cluster of exterior spurs in section C, yet no lateral ponds are present. This finding demonstrates that the placement of architectural elements in section C is not constrained by natural topography. Further, the overall symmetry in the element organization between the east and west halves demonstrates precise and meaningful placement of site architecture. Section C in figure 6.4 contains the greatest number and most tightly clustered set of secondary gateway complexes composed of exterior spurs, lateral ponds, and interior walkovers for the entire Fort Ancient enclosure. Where gateways are not present, the clustering of ponds is maintained because of the rule reported above that all exterior spurs must be marked by an architectural element on their corresponding interior location.

An additional set of architectural elements in the east half of section C includes stone circles, a mound, and a free-standing pond, all symmetrically arranged along the axis of the interior walkover at Gateway 8. This group of architectural elements is placed within a curved section of embankment walls that forms a segmented space. Similar pond, spur, interior walkover, and gateway organization is repeated in segments of section C in both the east and west halves of the enclosure.

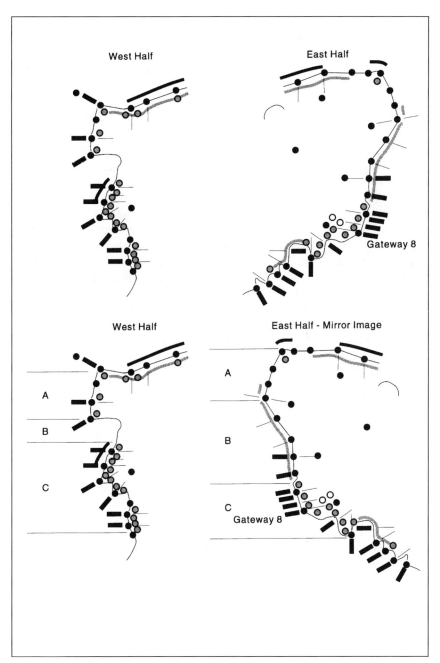

West Half

East Half

Gateway 8

West Half

East Half - Mirror Image

A

B

C

A

B

C

Gateway 8

Fig. 6.4. Architectural symmetry of North Fort, Fort Ancient.

The symmetry in distribution of architectural elements in the South Fort is even more demonstrable than in the North Fort. Figure 6.5 illustrates the South Fort divided into two approximate halves along an axis of 57 degrees, the overall landform azimuth at most hilltop enclosures in southwest Ohio (Connolly 1996b).

The symmetrical shape of the two embankment wall halves in the South Fort is readily apparent and does not require additional comment. At point A on both the west and east halves, the exterior terrace and embankment wall arc are divided equally. At point B, both halves contain interior approaches with ditches running to the south. Point B on the west half is the Great Gateway. At Points C, D, and E, three protuberances of the interior plateau are placed within the embankment walls. On the east side, these extensions continue to exterior spurs. On the west side, only Point D contains an exterior spur. All six gateways front directly onto interior ponds. For two reasons, this finding demonstrates the intentional or forced symmetry of the two halves of the South Fort at Points C, D, and E. First, a well-defined ditch is present on the west half of the enclosure. However, ponds are also placed on the west half to complement the ponds on the eastern half. A second consideration is that ponds fronting gateways without exterior spurs or terraces only occur at Fort Ancient where symmetry results. This example of symmetry is also demonstrated on the western half of the South Fort at Point H.

At Point C on both the east and west halves of the South Fort, stone circles are reported on the immediate interior of the respective ponds. Mills (1908) provides imprecise reference to additional stone circles on both the east and west halves of the enclosure, approximately between Points C and E, but does not document their number or exact location. At Point F, on the two southern corners of the South Fort, stone mounds are present on the exterior spurs. The gateways at both points lead to interior walkovers and lateral ponds. Point F on the east half is the South Gateway. Figure 6.5 shows a similar arrangement of architectural elements at Point G as recorded at Point F.

In the comparison of secondary gateway complexes between the east and west halves of the North and South Forts, a clear pattern of symmetry emerges. For several reasons, the symmetry is judged as intentional and not coincidental or the result of natural topography. First, the sheer abundance of the correlations between the two halves of the earthwork argues against chance occurrence of the noted symmetrical arrangements. Second, natural features are utilized to enhance the symmetry but do not predict how the symmetry is expressed. This statement is perhaps supported best at section C in the North Fort, where ponds and walkovers focused on exterior spurs, but without the expected gateway elements. Finally, exceptions to apparent patterns of architectural element distributions are used to enhance overall site symmetry. For example, this statement is supported by the occurrence of pond features fronting gateways at locations without exterior spurs or terraces at Points C, E, and H on the west half of the South Fort.

Symmetry is the overriding theme in the patterned distribution of architectural elements at Fort Ancient, although a direct one-to-one symmetrical correspondence of all architectural elements is not demonstrated. This lack of total congruence does not negate the significance of the symmetry noted for two reasons. First, a one-to-one correspondence is not necessary, or perhaps even expected, to demonstrate the overall intentionality of symmetry in the construction of the Fort Ancient earthworks. That a substantial portion of the architectural elements composing the enclosure are shown empirically to be in a symmetrical arrangement is sufficient to support the legitimacy of the statement. Second, discussion of the symmetry of elements is

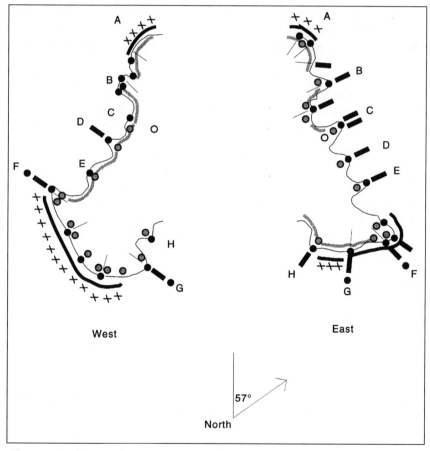

Fig. 6.5. Architectural symmetry of South Fort, Fort Ancient.

necessarily conservative and is hampered by natural and historic alterations to the earthwork complex. Additional archival research, examination of pre-1900 photographs, and further field research will likely demonstrate additional symmetrical arrangements of site architecture.

Discussion in this section has focused on the horizontal distribution of architectural elements throughout the site. Research also demonstrates examples of patterned vertical symmetry or asymmetry in some architectural elements. For example, asymmetry is argued as a characteristic of primary gateway complexes at Old Stone Fort and Fort Ancient (Connolly 1996b; Faulkner 1968). Vertical patterning is also evident at secondary gateway complexes. For example, figure 6.6 illustrates the asymmetrical pattern in the elevations of embankment walls at secondary gateway openings on the east and west halves of Fort Ancient. The distribution shown indicates the potential for this area of research. However, demonstrating additional vertical patterning will necessitate additional fieldwork, such as systematic soil coring and surveying to gauge accurately natural and historic alterations of embankment wall height.

Based on the above discussion, symmetry of archaeological elements at Fort Ancient is summarized as follows: *The patterning of secondary gateway complexes and their constituent elements is based on an overriding theme of symmetry between the eastern and western halves of the Fort Ancient enclosure.*

Gateway Spacing on Embankment Walls

Embankment wall lengths are determined by establishing the distance between adjacent gateway openings. The measurement used in this study is based on tracing the wall contour and, therefore, is not necessarily the minimum distance that would be possible if one simply drew a straight line connecting two adjacent gateway openings. However, neither method of determining gateway spacing yielded evidence of greater or lesser patterning in the distribution of embankment wall lengths. Therefore, only the contour distances are discussed below.

Figure 6.7 shows the distribution of embankment wall lengths throughout the Fort Ancient enclosure. The data presented were derived from multiple sources, including Little's (1891) survey log and Moorehead's (1890) survey data, both of which were checked against Marshall's 1985 resurvey of the site. All of these sources were field checked for overall accuracy in gateway and embankment wall placement and form, but the actual distances were not remeasured. A reasonable estimate of the maximum error for embankment wall length presented in figure 6.7 is ± 5 m.

Figure 6.8 demonstrates a lack of any highly consistent patterning in the embankment wall lengths throughout the enclosure. Figure 6.7 illustrates the

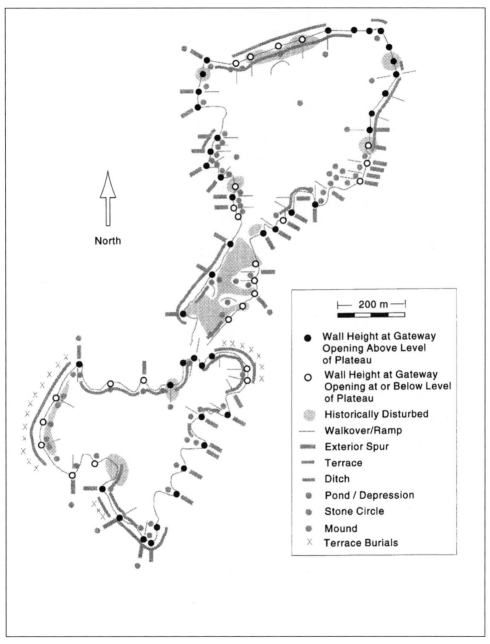

Fig. 6.6. Asymmetry of gateway opening height, Fort Ancient.

grouping of embankment walls into three averaged lengths based on the clusters detected in figure 6.8. Figure 6.7 also clearly shows that embankment wall length is consistently greater in the South Fort; median length in the South Fort is double that of the North Fort. The length is reduced only in the vicinity of the two primary gateway complexes.

In the North Fort, embankment wall lengths are grouped more by area. The only highly standardized lengths are located between Gateway 80 and Gateway 1 in the northeast corner of the North Fort. This section of the enclosure accounts for the clustering of embankment wall lengths between 40 and 50 m shown in figure 6.8. At this location, Marshall (1986) notes the embankment walls are of the same length and angle as a section of the High Bank Octagon in Ross County, Ohio. Essenpreis and Duszynski (1989) report the gateway openings in the northeast section of the North Fort at Fort Ancient accommodate sighting lines for solar and lunar alignments. Similar alignments are proposed through the corresponding gateway openings at the High Bank Octagon (Hively and Horn 1984). Marshall (1986) also notes that the distance between each side of the four mounds forming the square in North Fort (160.325 m) corresponds to the radius of the circular earthwork attached to the octagon at the High Bank complex. Finally, the sections of embankment including Walls 75, 77, 78, 79, and 80 have a median length of 79 m with a standard deviation of 6.05 m, significantly less than either the North or South Fort total values. All evidence for standardized embankment wall lengths in the North Fort is located in sections containing straight embankment walls with exteriors that, for the most part, are either flat or extend along terraces.

In summary, the northern section of the North Fort contains standardized embankment wall lengths that correspond to a similar layout of architectural elements at the High Bank earthwork in south-central Ohio. A standard embankment wall length is not apparent at other portions of either the North or South Forts. As initially proposed by Essenpreis and Moseley (1984), the greater standardization in wall form in the North Fort reflects aspects of the temporal development of the Fort Ancient earthwork complex.

Two additional trends in the grouped embankment wall lengths are visible at Fort Ancient. As noted above, wall lengths in the South Fort are greater than those in the North Fort. This disparity is not simply a result of differing topography in the two sections of the enclosure. For example, even though similar exterior terraces are present between Gateways 46 and 50, Gateways 57 and 59, and Gateways 75 and 79, there is no corresponding regularity in the embankment wall lengths of the three sections. A second visible trend is that near primary gateway complexes, secondary gateway complexes are placed more closely together. This finding is reinforced by the clustering of gateways in the section of the North Fort that leads to the isthmus forming the Middle Fort. That is, at the more constricted locations of the

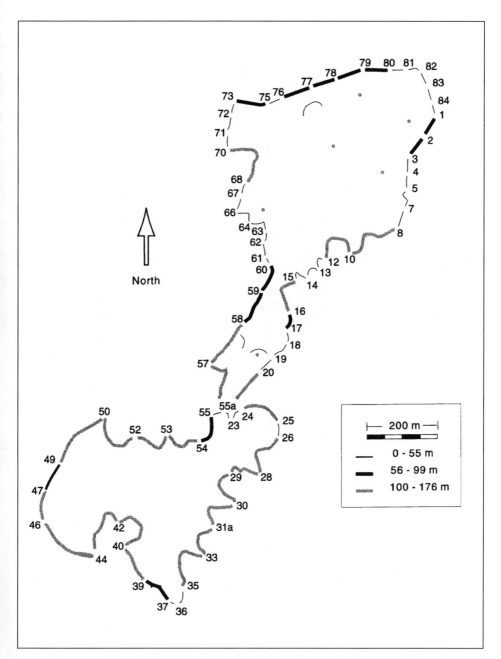

Fig. 6.7. Distribution of embankment wall lengths in meters, Fort Ancient.

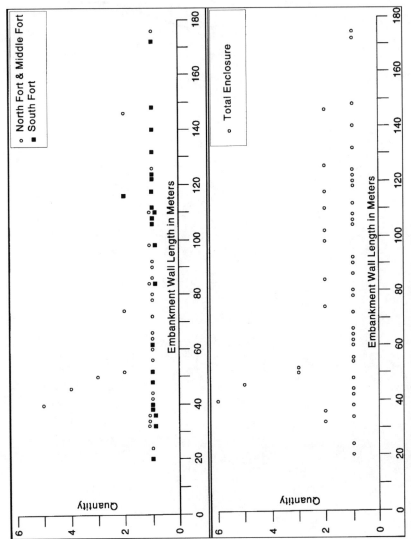

Fig. 6.8. Distribution of embankment wall lengths, Fort Ancient.

earthwork that funnel pedestrian traffic, gateways are more numerous and the distance between gateways is less than at other locations.

More accurate estimates of embankment wall lengths may demonstrate additional patterning. The margin of error assumed here (± 5 m) does not negate the validity of any of the patterns discussed above. Two rules of gateway distribution based on embankment wall lengths state that (1) secondary gateways tend to cluster more closely in the vicinity of primary gateways or other constricted areas of pedestrian traffic, and (2) the standardized placement of secondary gateways at specific portions of the enclosure enhances other aspects of site function, such as astronomical sighting lines.

Location of Free-Standing Features

A final set of architectural elements composing secondary gateway complexes includes mounds and stone circles. A very strong tendency (likely a rule) exists that mounds and stone circles on the interior and immediate exterior of the Fort Ancient enclosure must be centered on a gateway. In most instances, this centering is carried out at a secondary gateway, as shown in figure 6.9. Centering is marked by the trajectory of an interior walkover, with two possible exceptions. First, the portion of the interior plateau between Gateway 19 and the mound on the interior of the crescent is altered historically, and no pre–1930 field notes report the original ground-surface condition at this location. Whether a walkover extended toward the mound is unknown. Second, although the trajectory of the walkover at Gateway 78 leads to the southwest mound of the group forming a square in the North Fort, the distance is too great to assume a relationship between the two elements.

The consistent relationship of mounds and stone circles to interior walkovers at secondary gateways is supported by an additional observation. A poorly formed ramp leads from Gateway 4 to the southeast mound of the group forming a square in the North Fort. Gateway 4 is the only secondary gateway complex containing a ramp. Since no interior ditch was constructed adjacent to Gateway 4, a simple walkover could not mark the association of the interior mound with the gateway. Therefore, the earthwork builders were forced to decide how to tie the mound to the gateway complex. The decision was to construct a ramp visibly different from those at primary gateway complexes. Moorehead (1887) noted and contrasted the diminutive size of the Gateway 4 ramp with the Gateway 1 interior ramp. The location of the Gateway 4 ramp was altered less by historic farming activities than the Gateway 1 ramp at the time of Moorehead's investigations. If the original construction of the two ramps was comparable, Moorehead should have reported the Gateway 4 ramp as the larger of the two. He reported the oppo-

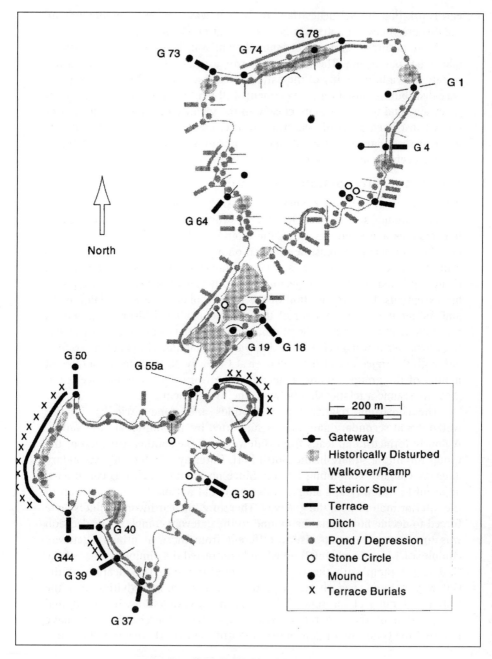

Fig. 6.9. Distribution of free-standing architectural elements Fort Ancient.

site, thus suggesting the ramp at Gateway 4 was intentionally built smaller in size than the Gateway 1 counterpart.

For the mounds on exterior spurs, the assumption is made that because of their location on gateway-centered spurs, these mounds also center on secondary gateways. This type of alignment was noted previously at primary gateway complexes.

The locations of several additional stone circles are reported imprecisely as occurring within the earthwork embankment walls, and their exact locations have not been determined. Assuming these additional architectural elements also are centered on secondary gateway openings, a rule of association for mounds, stone circles, and gateway openings states that *freestanding architectural elements, such as mounds and stone circles, must be centered on gateway openings.*

Summary of Secondary Gateway Complexes

Because of the sheer quantity of secondary gateway complexes, patterns in their distribution throughout the Fort Ancient enclosure are readily apparent. The architectural elements composing secondary gateway complexes for the most part mimic those at primary gateway complexes. These elements include the actual gateway opening, walkovers, limestone pavements, ponds, ditches, exterior spurs, exterior terraces, mounds, and stone circles. The most distinct difference in the two gateway complex types is the form of the actual gateway opening.

Given the lack of a consistent pattern in the constituent architectural elements composing secondary gateway complexes, numerous subgroups may be formed. For example, seventeen of the sixty-four secondary gateway complexes at Fort Ancient are composed of gateway openings, exterior spurs, interior walkovers, and lateral ponds. Of these seventeen gateway complexes, additional subgroups may be formed of those containing exterior mounds, interior mounds, and stone circles. Alternately, secondary gateway complexes may be grouped by those containing exterior spurs, with a similar plethora of additional subgroupings possible. In any attempt to establish mutually exclusive subgroups, over 50 percent of the secondary gateway complexes would end up in their own individual category. Research beyond that included in this study may provide the basis for a more meaningful arrangement of secondary gateway complex subgroups.

Conclusion

Middle Woodland hilltop enclosures, best exemplified by Fort Ancient, were constructed with at least the same precision and planning as all other types of Middle Woodland earthworks. The best evidence for the precision of construction is the architectural grammar rules discussed in this article. All architectural elements, such as ponds, gateways, mounds, and stone circles, were shown to be placed nonrandomly. Symmetry of elements was demonstrated to be an overriding theme.

The Fort Ancient site architecture contains the same architectural complexity in planning and construction as the classic Hopewell sites of the Scioto Valley. For example, Marshall's surveys at Fort Ancient show that aspects of Scioto Valley octagon, square, and circular forms are present at Fort Ancient in the North Fort embankment walls and mound arrangements. Although standard geometric forms, such as squares and circles, are the more readily recognized components of the Scioto Valley Middle Woodland earthworks, analysis of the earthen architecture at Fort Ancient demonstrates that sole reliance on geometric shapes is an inadequate gauge of architectural precision or the application of standardized forms.

The research at Fort Ancient also demonstrates that etic estimates of geometric precision and consideration of only final forms provide a limited estimate of the significance of Middle Woodland earthwork construction on at least two counts. First, a ranking based on embankment wall geometric form does not take into account the design grammar rules identified at Fort Ancient, nor can it account for the land modifications necessary to apply those rules. In such a scheme, a single circle and square enclosure would inherently be more complex than the embankment walls at Fort Ancient that roughly approximate the natural hilltop location. However, an alternate interpretation is that Fort Ancient, in fact, is more complex in that it incorporates portions of such geometric forms as the octagon in the northeastern embankment walls, the square in the arrangement of mounds in the North Fort, and the circle in the arc formed by the plateau extension at Wall 25. Second, interpretations based on final form exclude initial and intermediate forms. The archaeology of Fort Ancient architecture demonstrates that it was a systematically planned, dynamic earthwork, the construction of which spanned at least three hundred years (Connolly 1996b:295–300).

The identification of the architectural grammar rules that guided construction of Fort Ancient supports the assertion by Essenpreis and Moseley (1984) that Fort Ancient is a cultural manifestation similar to the classic Hopewell sites of the Scioto tradition. This assertion does not mean that Fort Ancient or other hilltop enclosures are the cultural manifestation of Scioto Hopewell; rather, as a built environment, Fort Ancient was able to, and likely did, represent the same manifestations of worldview and function for its users as did those earthworks considered "classic" Hopewell.

Fort Ancient was a multipurpose site. Just as the Scioto sites cannot be called solely mortuary sites, Fort Ancient cannot be called solely a defensive site. The full range of activities reported at most earthwork centers are also recorded at Fort Ancient (Connolly 1996b). This observation suggests that the significance of hilltop enclosures as a site type has more to do with physiographic location than actual function. Therefore, it will be useful to assess the site functions of Fort Ancient within the broader sphere of regional manifestations of the Hopewell culture.

Note

I am indebted to R. Barry Lewis for his insights into developing a framework within which to organize the Fort Ancient architecture. I also wish to thank N'omi Greber, Robert Mainfort, Helaine Silverman, Lynne Sullivan, and anonymous reviewers for their comments on preliminary drafts of this chapter.

Chapter 7

The Archaeology of the Newark Earthworks

Bradley T. Lepper

They are rapidly passing away by the sacrilegious hands of civilization. This is all wrong. It is a species of vandalism that should not be allowed. They ought to be protected by state authority, as sacredly as the Pyramids of Egypt. But as this will not be done, let us as far as possible preserve them in written records, and faithfully transmit each successive ray of light that may break forth from them. (Park 1870:56)

The Newark Earthworks are the foremost example of that class of monumental earthworks termed "sacred enclosures" by Squier and Davis in their pathbreaking *Ancient Monuments of the Mississippi Valley* (1848). In spite of the acknowledged preeminence of the Newark Works, remarkably few archaeological investigations have been conducted there. One reason for this is the devastation of the site by agricultural and urban development beginning early in the nineteenth century. Indeed, Squier and Davis remarked upon this destruction in their description of the site: "The ancient lines can now be traced only at intervals among gardens and outhouses. . . . A few years hence, the residents upon the spot will be compelled to resort to this map, to ascertain the character of the works which occupied the very ground upon which they stand" (1848:71).

The scholarly world was made aware of the existence of the Newark Works by at least 1805, when the first accounts of this mysterious monumental architecture appeared in travelogues of excursions through the Northwest Territory (e.g., Harris 1805:155–156; S. Brown 1817:305). There is a claim that Daniel Webster made an effort to preserve the Newark Earthworks as what would have been the nation's first national park (Haven 1870:41). Sadly, the site was not preserved intact, although it was not completely destroyed.

In this chapter I present the results of nearly two centuries of archaeological investigations at Newark—which, though few and far between, are important and have been neglected. I summarize the nineteenth- and early twentieth-century documentation and use it as a lens for viewing the Hopewellian achievement at Newark. I call particular attention to elements of the site that are overlooked or forgotten in most modern accounts of the site. This chapter is a substantive revision and expansion of an earlier paper that covered some of the same topics (Lepper 1989).

The Newark Earthworks in Plan View

The earliest documented attempt to survey and map the Newark Works was in 1813. John Poage Campbell, an early antiquarian, made what seems to be the first "concerted effort to collect accurate data on the mounds and earthworks of the midwest" (Murphy 1986:28). Campbell's manuscript on the "Antiquities of the Western Country" was never published, although some of his work appeared posthumously in *The Port Folio* (Campbell 1816a and 1816b). James Murphy (1995) recently drew renewed and overdue attention to Campbell's contribution. Campbell's (1813) map of "The Antiquity near Newark" is incomplete and highly schematic, but is significant because it is the earliest known plan of the Newark Works.

In 1815 author and journalist Robert Walsh, Jr., passed through Ohio and stayed just long enough to produce his own, or copy another's, map of the

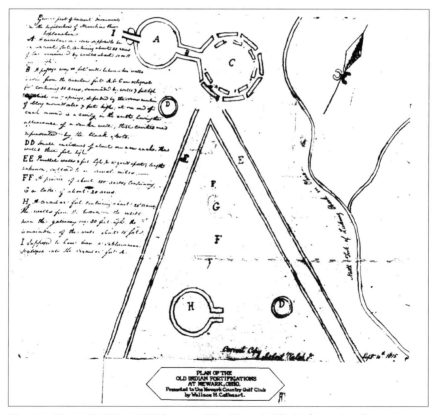

Fig. 7.1. The 1815 Robert Walsh map of the Newark Works (reproduced courtesy of the Licking County Historical Society).

Newark Earthworks (fig. 7.1). Although an improvement on Campbell's sketch, this plan also is rather schematic and was not published (Lepper 1992a). Walsh's map likely is based on an even earlier map of uncertain attribution that is in the collections of the Wisconsin Historical Society (see J. Murphy 1995).

The earliest published map of the Newark Works is based on a survey by Alexander Holmes, the surveyor for Licking County from 1812 to 1820 (Smucker 1881:262; see also Atwater 1833:6). Caleb Atwater published this map in his 1820 "Description of the Antiquities Discovered in the State of Ohio and Other Western States," and it served as the basic portrayal of the Newark Earthworks for a generation of scholars.

The Atwater map was superseded by the Squier and Davis (1848) map (based on a survey made by Charles Whittlesey in 1838) in their *Ancient Monuments of the Mississippi Valley*. The Whittlesey, Squier, and Davis map is still regarded as the standard reference, although two later maps show more detail.

The David Wyrick map of the Newark Earthworks (fig. 7.2) was published in the *Licking County Atlas* for 1866. A copy of Wyrick's map

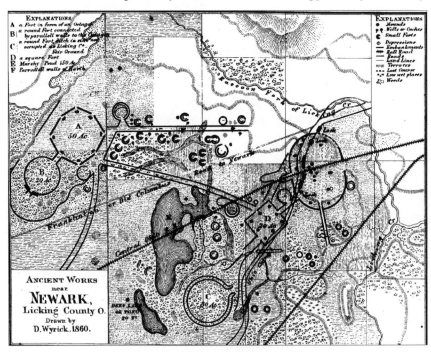

Fig. 7.2. The 1860 David Wyrick map published in Beers's 1866 *Atlas of Licking County, Ohio.*

appeared in Daniel Wilson's influential *Prehistoric Man* in 1862, but, strangely, Wilson did not credit Wyrick as the author of the map (D. Wilson 1862:335). While Wyrick's map shows many more of the smaller mounds and enclosures, it has been largely dismissed, presumably because of Wyrick's prominent role in the Newark "Holy Stones" fraud (Lepper 1992b). The tacit conclusion that appears to have been drawn was that since Wyrick falsified the "Holy Stones," his elaborations of the Newark Works also probably were fanciful. Wilson, however, visited Newark in person in 1854, and he observed firsthand that the structures documented by Wyrick were not fanciful. He then used Wyrick's map as the basis for his illustration of the Newark Works. Nevertheless, his failure to credit Wyrick as the surveyor suggests an uncharitable reticence to bring further notoriety to a character he and others regarded as disreputable. There is now compelling evidence that Wyrick was an innocent victim of the forgers of the "Holy Stones" and that he was actually a dedicated antiquarian and a competent surveyor (Applebaum 1996).

In 1862 James and Charles Salisbury produced the most detailed and accurate map of the entire Newark Earthworks (fig. 7.3). Although accepted for publication by the American Antiquarian Society, it—along with their manuscript describing the site in detail—was shelved and forgotten during the years of the Civil War. The rediscovery of the Salisbury map and manuscript revolutionizes our knowledge of this monumental complex of earthworks.

Cyrus Thomas (1889; 1894:458–468, plates XXI and XXII) presents detailed maps of major elements of the Newark Earthworks, including plans (executed by Middleton [1887]) and contour maps (produced under the direction of Holmes [1892]). Figure 7.4 is Holmes's contour map of the Great Circle. These surveys show that the geometry of the earthworks was more accurate and precise than previous surveys indicated (Thomas 1889:12–14, 18–20), but they did not attempt to update the overall plan of the entire complex of earthworks. Although the survey data presented by Thomas are by far the best, the Thomas map of the Newark Works is not equivalent in coverage to those of Atwater, Squier and Davis, and Wyrick.

A cursory examination of these maps of the Newark Works does not readily show the sophisticated understanding of geometry and astronomy that is reflected in the organization of the various architectural elements (see, for example, Hively and Horn 1982; Marshall 1987; Romain 1996). For example, the distance between the center points of the two large circular enclosures is six times the diameter of the smaller of the two, or 1920 m; the distance between the center of the octagonal enclosure and the center of the square also is 1920 m (Hively and Horn 1982). More remarkably, the area of the larger circle is equal to the area of the square to which it is connected by converging walls (Hively and Horn 1982).

The earthen enclosures and walled corridors of Newark and related sites

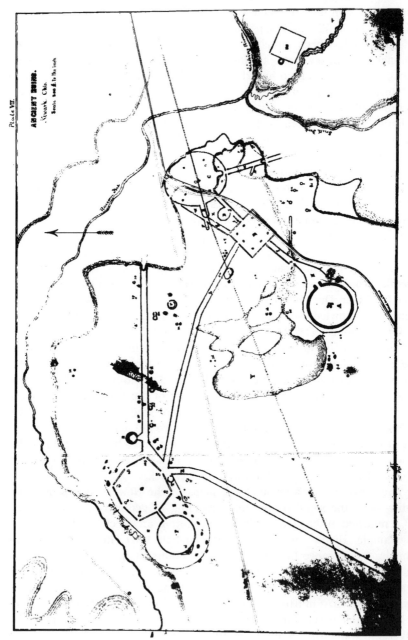

Fig. 7.3. The 1862 Salisbury map of the Newark Earthworks (courtesy, American Antiquarian Society).

were designed to contain and channel the movement of visitors. The use of this site during Hopewell times likely involved an elaborate choreography based upon the geometrically defined spaces of the earthworks at astronomically determined times. Without clambering over walls—and one does not erect such walls with the idea of violating their boundaries willy-nilly—there are only three ways of entering the Newark complex (see fig. 7.3): from the Raccoon Creek floodplain westward along the northernmost walled roadway into the octagon; from the floodplain of the Licking River's South Fork along a short, walled road into the Cherry Valley Mounds enclosure; and from the direction of Chillicothe along the walled roadway that extends southwestward beyond the margins of every map of the Newark Works.

Inside the complex, movement is further constrained by geometry. Circles are culs-de-sac; one must enter and exit through the same portal. Angular structures, the squares and octagon, have alternative routes of access and egress. In addition, the squares and octagon are associated with small circular and semicircular enclosures often located near the entrances. The main exceptions are the walled roads leading directly from each of the large circles. These patterns indicate a highly ritualized use of the architecture of Hopewellian Newark. Although the early maps of the Newark complex provide the basis for our understanding of the site structure, the earthen figures are not giant hieroglyphs that can be deciphered and read with the help of some yet-to-be-discovered Rosetta stone. They are more like abandoned machines that fulfilled (or, ultimately, failed to fulfill) their role in the societies that built them. Therefore, an understanding of their use more likely will be gleaned from evidence of the activities that took place at the earthworks, rather than from an interpretation of iconography. Nonetheless, as Fowke (1893:9) has cautioned, "No one who visits this place can fail to be impressed with the thought that he is viewing the results of a vast amount of labor intelligently performed for a definite purpose; and few can avoid the temptation of endeavoring to interpret this purpose, to fathom the motives which would impel men thus to labor, or to frame a theory that will clear away the obscurity impending as a cloud over these mysterious tokens of an unknown people. Many have tried; none has succeeded."

The following review of investigations of the Newark Works is organized around several major elements of the earthwork complex: the Cherry Valley Mounds surrounded by an oval enclosure; the Great Circle; the Observatory Circle and Octagon; a previously unreported square enclosure; and the long series of parallel walls that I refer to as the Great Hopewell Road. As Fowke suggests, avoiding the temptation to explain the purpose of "these mysterious tokens" is difficult. I offer some tentative ideas to further the discussion.

The Cherry Valley Mounds

The city of Newark originated across Raccoon Creek, east of the Newark Earthworks. As it grew through the nineteenth century, a succession of increasingly destructive land-use practices encroached upon the ancient monumental architecture, generally in an east-to-west direction. The Cherry Valley cluster of mounds was the first component of the Newark Works to be impacted. The cluster included about a dozen mounds of various shapes and sizes. According to James and Charles Salisbury, who observed the site in 1862, there were eleven mounds ranging in size "from 40 to 60 ft. [12–18 m] in diameter and from 3 to 5 ft." [1–1.5 m] in height (1862:8). Like Mound City in Chillicothe, these mounds were completely surrounded by a low embankment. At Newark the enclosure was an oval about 550 m in largest diameter. No evidence indicates that antiquarians or archaeologists excavated any of the mounds of the Cherry Valley cluster. Indeed, everything we know about their structure and content we know because of observations recorded more or less incidentally to their destruction.

When the Ohio Canal was built in 1827, a lock was dug through one mound. Israel Dille, a local antiquarian, reported to Squier and Davis (1848:72) that "In excavating the lock pit, *fourteen* human skeletons were found about four feet beneath the surface. . . . Over these skeletons, and carefully and regularly disposed, was laid a large quantity of mica in sheets or plates. Some of these were eight and ten inches long by four and five wide, and all from half an inch to an inch thick. It was estimated that *fifteen or twenty bushels of this material* were thrown out to form the walls or supports of the lock" (emphasis added).

This account can be compared with a more obscure contemporary newspaper account of the same excavations:

> In excavating the earth for a lock pit, west of the Raccoon Creek, a large number of human bones were disturbed by the plough, deposited in a manner, I believe, altogether peculiar to this cemetry [*sic*]. The bones were deposited, or at least found not more than two feet below the surface of the earth, in a place where there was a slight elevation of the ground, of about thirty inches, but not sufficient to entitle it to the name of a Mound. They were all carbonized, or burnt, were of different sizes, and amounted to the number of ten or fifteen. What was peculiar in their mode of burial, was, they were all covered with a greater or lesser quantity of very beautiful transparent mica. One of the skeletons was completely covered with the mica, and was, it seems by way of distinction, buried a short distance from the remainder. This was a large frame, and like the rest,

was carbonized. The quantity of mica would amount, according to the statement of a gentlemen who was present at the time of the discovery, to eight or ten bushels. The pieces were of various sizes and shapes, tho' generally triangular; the bases of some were four or five inches in length. Several specimens of this beautiful mineral substance may be seen in this town. To what race did this people belong. When did they exist? And why were the tenants of this cemetery [sic] buried with such marked distinction?" (*The Advocate*, Newark, Ohio, 29 March 1827).

The central mound of the Cherry Valley cluster (actually a group of conjoined mounds similar to other Hopewellian conjoined mounds, such as Tremper) was largely obliterated between 1852 and 1855, when the Central Ohio Railroad was built through it. The conjoined mounds together were approximately 43 m long by about 12 m wide and were surrounded by a "cobblestone way" or pavement about 2.5 m wide (J. N. Wilson 1868:69). The largest of the conjoined mounds, the northernmost, stood about 6 m tall and survived relatively intact until a rolling mill was built on the site sometime before 1875.

Sketchy descriptions of the structure and content of these mounds can be drawn from the Salisbury manuscript and from a paper by local antiquarian J. N. Wilson (1868). At the base of the largest mound there was a "tier of skeletons"—their heads placed together with their feet radiating outward (Salisbury and Salisbury 1862:12). Wilson observed several postmolds indicating the former presence of some sort of substantial structure, or structures. One postmold in particular "on the east side was filled with fine charcoal and ashes, and extended fully four feet below the surface of the earth" (J. N. Wilson 1868:69). The mound itself was composed of alternating layers of black loam, blue clay, sand, and cobblestone punctuated by periodic episodes of burning and burial. Artifacts found in association with numerous fragmentary burials included mica sheets, a copper "hatchet" and "quivers," large shells, beads, and "other trinkets" (J. N. Wilson 1868:69). Charles Whittlesey viewed Wilson's collection in 1868 and described additional artifacts from the "mound at rolling mill" (1868:41–43). Whittlesey sketched a "copper axe," one of "3 copper fluted ornaments," and a drilled bear canine (1868:41–42). In addition, he referred to "numerous copper studs . . . copper beads . . . whelks" (1868:43). He mentioned that the beads were "strung on hemp—or nettles" (1868:43).

Years later, after the rolling mill was torn down, another burial was encountered. Excavators recovered a remarkable "stone image" representing a Hopewell shaman (Dragoo and Wray 1964; Mason 1882). This figure is the only artifact in the collections of the Ohio Historical Society known to have come from Newark's Cherry Valley mounds. Wilson's artifact collection is lost, and no other collections are known to exist.

The other mounds in the Cherry Valley cluster were leveled for use as fill in the railroad embankment, or they vanished under equally ignominious circumstances. The brothers Salisbury stated that railroad workers uncovered "many skeletons" (1862:9) in the area between the railroad tracks and the two mounds in the southeastern end of the elliptical enclosure, suggesting that other mounds had been located here. They also noted that the soil near these two mounds was "as red as brick dust, presenting a striking contrast to that of the surrounding surface" (1862:9).

Hopewell Habitations at the Northern Edge of the Newark Earthworks

Just outside the elliptical embankment that enclosed the Cherry Valley mounds, cultural resource management (CRM) investigations conducted in 1980 recovered evidence for Hopewellian habitations (Hale 1980; Lepper and Yerkes 1997). Hale's house site is a cluster of 23 features including postmolds, a hearth, an earth oven, other pits and basins, and one "hour-glass shaped" basin lined with pebbles and containing mica sheets (Hale 1980:40). This last feature produced a radiocarbon date of 1640 ± 90 years B.P. (Beta-58450). Two other features produced dates of 2670 ± 70 years (Beta-27446) and 1845 ± 60 years B.P. (Beta-28062/ETH-4593) (Lepper and Yerkes 1997). This range of dates suggests the site is a palimpsest of occupations extending from the Early through the Middle Woodland, but the vast majority of the diagnostic artifacts are of Middle Woodland affiliation.

The CRM excavators recovered numerous artifacts including ceramic sherds, projectile points, cores and bladelets, scrapers, debitage, and numerous fragments of mica. Yerkes's microwear analysis of the lithic assemblage reveals that the tools were used briefly for a variety of general-purpose domestic tasks and then discarded (Lepper and Yerkes 1997). The ceramics from the site included a few specimens of southeastern series simple-stamped pottery. James Stoltman determined that the grit temper is composed of finely ground granite from an unidentified source in North Carolina (cited in Lepper and Yerkes 1997). There are severe limitations to these data, but they do suggest that Newark was not a "vacant" ceremonial center. People were living in close proximity to the earthworks for some period of time (see Greber 1997). Converse (1993:5) alleges that Hale's house site is only a small part of a much larger zone of Hopewell habitation that subsequently was destroyed, but he offers little data in support of this claim.

The Great Circle

The Great Circle is one of the few large elements of the Newark Earthworks to escape extensive destruction (see fig. 7.4). As Thomas (1894:461) noted, "It is undoubtedly one of the best preserved ancient monuments of our country; it is uninjured by the plow and trees of the original forest are still standing on it." The Great Circle is 366 m in diameter with walls about 5 m high. There is an interior ditch approximately 3 m deep. This enclosure was preserved because the site was used as the Licking County Fairgrounds from 1854 until about 1933 (see fig. 7.5): "From the time when the unconfined Indian ruled the region, climbed its hills, waded its rivers, and pursued its game, the popularity of this grand fort has been constantly growing. . . . One can scarcely picture a more delightful spot wherein to while away the sultry days of summer. Its superb mounds, its accessibility, its superior conveniences, its inspiring surroundings, and the many facilities afforded for perfect restful contentment and exhilarating diversion, at once commend this favorite retreat as an ideal and unsurpassed pleasure resort" (Lingafelter 1899).

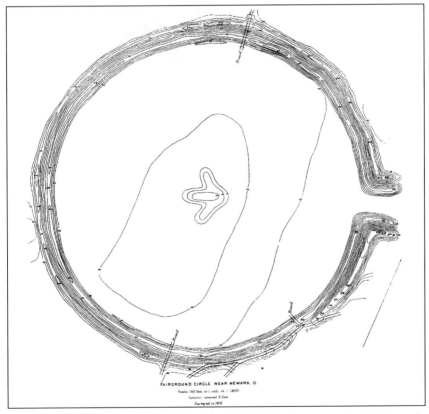

FAIRGROUND CIRCLE NEAR NEWARK. O.
Scale, 150 feet to 1 inch, or 1 : 1800
Contour Interval 2 feet
Surveyed in 1891

Fig. 7.4. The 1892 Holmes map of the Great Circle, also known as the Fairgrounds Circle since the Licking County Fair was held here between 1854 and 1933 (courtesy, Ohio Historical Society).

Eagle Mound Excavations

A group of conjoined mounds at the center of the circle (see fig. 7.4), popularly referred to as Eagle Mound—though lacking any signal attributes of that particular, or indeed any, bird—was dug into on numerous occasions (e.g., Licking 1834). Squier and Davis reported that an "altar," but little else, had been found in an excavation into the body of the bird (1848:68). Altars, as Squier and Davis (1848:143–144) used the term, referred to symmetrical, burned-clay basins considered by Mills (1922:438) to be crematories, but which likely served other functions as well (Greber and Ruhl 1989:75–88).

J. N. Wilson (1865) argued that any interpretation of the function of Eagle Mound must be regarded as tentative since it only had been "examined by digging down in one place about six feet." On the other hand, further details of these, or perhaps subsequent, excavations provided by Isaac Smucker (1873, 1881) support the idea that at least one "altar" under Eagle

Fig. 7.5. Aerial photograph of Newark, circa 1930. Note the race track and other fairground attractions visible at the Great Circle. Courtesy Facilities Planning Division, Ohio Historical Society.

Mound was a crematory basin. Smucker writes, "Excavations made many years ago into the center of the earthen figure, where the elevation is greatest, developed an altar built of stone, upon which were found *ashes, charcoal, and calcined bones*" (Smucker 1881:266, emphasis added).

Emerson Greenman excavated Eagle Mound for the Ohio State Museum in 1928. At the base of the mound he found a generally rectangular pattern of 59 postmolds defining a large structure, or perhaps two adjacent structures, 30 m long by about 7 m wide. In the center of this postmold pattern was a large (3 m x 1.5 m) rectangular "depression of the floor" (Greenman 1928:13). It was built into a prepared floor of red clay to a depth of about 13 cm. Below the red clay floor was another prepared floor of yellow clay and below that a layer of what Greenman (1928:6) described as "black well packed muck." Fires in the basin had hardened and reddened the clay lining to a depth of about 2.5 cm. The basin was filled with sand, and the only artifacts recovered from it were a fragment of a projectile point and a few pieces of white flint "cracked by fire" (1928:13).

Greenman documents more than fifty artifacts from the excavations, but only a handful were collected and curated. The most abundant artifact class noted is mica fragments. Small bits of mica, many exhibiting cut edges, were recovered from the mound floor, from numerous features, and from the mound fill. Lithic debitage was relatively abundant and several projectile points and point fragments were collected. Greenman noted charred woven matting in two features, both of which also contained small bone fragments. A single potsherd was recovered from a postmold. Finally, two copper artifacts were discovered on the northeastern side of the mound floor. One of these is a simple crescent; the other is more problematic (see Lepper 1989 for illustrations).

None of the mica fragments referenced in the excavation notes were recovered in the northeastern part of the structure where both copper pieces were found, suggesting a separation in the places in which the copper and mica were used or, at least, deposited (see Greber 1996).

During the same summer of 1928, Greenman and his crew also excavated the three mounds of the Wells Mound group. Squier and Davis incorrectly depict four mounds in this location due to a drafting error (see C. Thomas 1894:490). These mounds occupied a central position relative to the entire Newark complex but were not directly associated with any particular enclosure. All three mounds were extensively disturbed prior to their excavation. Nevertheless, Greenman uncovered a few Middle Woodland artifacts, some poorly preserved human skeletal remains, and several large mammal bones. A Smithsonian zoologist subsequently identified these as modern horse. Shetrone attributed these remains to an intrusive horse burial (note appended to Greenman 1928:4). Curiously, Smucker reported the discovery of horse bones in another mound in neighboring Franklin County (Smucker 1875:30).

Great Circle Excavations

In the summer of 1992, Dee Anne Wymer and I directed excavations into the Great Circle itself (Lepper 1996; Wymer, Lepper, and Pickard 1992). These excavations established that the enclosure was constructed in two principal stages beginning no earlier than 2,110 ± 80 years B.P. (Beta-58449). This date derives from soil humates from the intact paleosol preserved beneath the embankment. The buried A horizon also yielded pollen and phytoliths indicating that the vegetation in the area at the time the earthwork was constructed consisted of prairie grasses with a few scattered oak trees.

The two main stages of construction were preceded by the building of small clay mounds to mark the perimeter of the circle. Our trench bisected one such mound; we infer the presence of a circular arrangement of many others (cf. Fowke 1902:160). Next, the interior ditch was dug and the earth was piled onto the mounds and the intervening spaces, leaving a gap between the ditch and the resulting enclosure. Finally, deep borrow pits were dug nearby, and bright yellow-brown loamy gravels were used to fill in the gap between the ditch and the dark brown wall. The completed Great Circle would have appeared dark brown to an observer outside the circle and bright yellow-brown to an observer inside. These colors likely were an important factor in the original presentation of this architecture.

Wymer and I also conducted excavations outside the Great Circle to establish whether an outer polygonal wall depicted on the Salisbury map actually existed (see fig. 7.3). We succeeded in finding buried remnants of this outer wall, but virtually no surface indications survive. The confirmation of the existence of the outer wall documented only by the Salisburys reinforces their reliability and establishes their map as the best representation of the Newark Earthworks.

The Observatory Circle and Octagon

The Observatory Circle is a circular enclosure 320 m in diameter with walls between 1.5 and 2.5 m high. It is connected by parallel walls to an octagonal enclosure with constituent walls approximately 186 m in length and 1.5 m high.

Calliopean Society Excavations

An elevated platform mound along the southeastern perimeter of the so-called Observatory Circle (named for this very observation platform) was the site of early and remarkably sophisticated archaeological explorations. In 1836 the Calliopean Society of the Granville Literary and Theological Institution conducted excavations here explicitly to test a hypothesis originally put forward by Atwater: that this mound represented a collapsed arch or former entranceway into the circle. They found no evidence to support Atwater's claim. The mound was composed of earth and rough stones overlying a stone pavement (Lepper 1991).[1]

The Walsh Map and "Sunken Wells"

The most recent excavations conducted at the Octagon also tested an early claim about the site. The Robert Walsh map, which dates to 1815, includes the only documented reference to "cavities" or depressions located adjacent to the "oblong mounds" that are located at each opening to the octagonal enclosure (fig. 7.1). Walsh referred to them as "sunken wells" and noted that one is situated to the left of each mound when viewed from outside the enclosure.

In 1994, Moundbuilders Country Club renovated and enlarged their maintenance building inside the Octagon. Because the proposed construction was so close to the site of one of Walsh's "sunken wells," a primary goal of the test excavations that preceded construction was to locate and identify the phenomenon he had observed. Discouraging initial test pits revealed the great extent of recent cutting and filling in the area, but eventually the excavations yielded the remains of a prehistoric feature that is likely one of Walsh's "sunken wells" (fig. 7.6).

This feature (Feature 3) is an egg-shaped basin 1.7 m long, 70 cm wide, and 40 cm deep. It was filled with coarse gravel and, near the center of the narrow end, there was a postmold 8 cm in diameter (Feature 2). These fea-

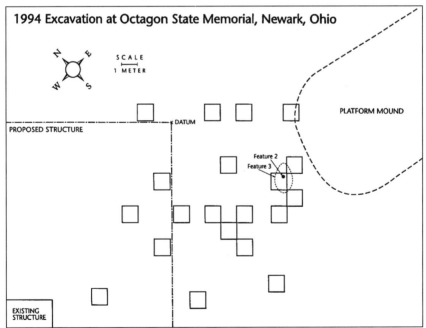

Fig. 7.6. Plan of the 1994 excavations at Octagon State Memorial showing the features encountered during the testing.

tures are truncated by a mid-nineteenth-century plow zone and buried by recent fill. Flotation samples from both the gravel-filled basin and the postmold produced no charred botanical material (Dee Anne Wymer 1994, personal communication). Soil humate samples submitted for radiocarbon dating yielded the following dates: for the postmold, 1650 ± 80 years B.P. (Beta-76908), and for the gravel-filled basin, 1770 ± 80 years B.P. (Beta-76909).

These meager data are difficult to interpret. Perhaps this post, and the others that we may infer to have been set in the other "sunken wells," were used in making the original astronomical observations that resulted in the alignments of the Octagon's embankments (Hively and Horn 1982). An alternate use would be for signposts erected to bear some identifying standard significant to each opening of the Octagon (see Greber and Ruhl 1989:61–62).

The Salisbury Square

Another of the many surprises in the Salisbury data is the appearance of a previously undocumented square enclosure across the South Fork of the Licking River on a remnant of the same glacial terrace occupied by the Newark Earthworks proper. This structure was originally about 226 m by 232 m, and its western wall was interrupted by a small circular enclosure (see fig. 7.3).

During the gradual demolition of this enclosure, the proprietor of a brickyard discovered, according to the Salisburys, "a stack of flint spears, numbering 194, about two feet below the surface" of the wall at the southeastern corner of the square (Salisbury and Salisbury 1862:27). The Salisburys report that the leaf-shaped bifaces of Flint Ridge flint were "placed points upwards in a conical pile like stacked arms, resting upon a large flat stone" (1862:19). The careful arrangement of these artifacts and their placement beneath the corner of an earthen enclosure suggest that they represent a ceremonial deposit.

Finding the exact location of the Salisbury Square is at least difficult and may be impossible, but another cache of Hopewellian artifacts was discovered recently in this general vicinity. In 1970, Marie Sunkle, while digging for worms in her backyard, uncovered a pit feature that was filled with more than 551 artifacts, including 157 Hopewell cores and core fragments, 150 bladelets and bladelet fragments, 22 projectile points (including several Adena and Archaic forms), 8 ground stone artifacts (including an unfinished Adena gorget), 2 pieces of fossil coral, and other flakes and bifaces.

Sunkle described the discovery to me in 1988, and she recalled that the artifacts were concentrated in a circle 1–2 m in diameter. She also said that she had not found the artifacts in a haphazard jumble. Instead, they appeared to be layered with cores at the top, bladelets next, and projectile points at the bottom. Subsequent to Sunkle's discovery, Raymond Baby tested the area extensively and did not recover any additional artifacts.

According to Barbara Harkness (1982), who analyzed the cache for her dissertation, the majority of the artifacts in the Sunkle cache are broken, discarded, used, and used-up tools. Nevertheless, the care evident in their placement in a pit feature unassociated with a habitation or manufacturing site, and their proximity to an earthen enclosure, suggest that this too was a ceremonial deposit.

The Great Hopewell Road

Perhaps the biggest surprise of the Salisbury manuscript is the new information on the extent of the parallel walls that projected from the octagon to the southwest. In 1820 Caleb Atwater suggested that these walls might be as much as thirty miles long and might connect the Newark Works with another so-called "work of defense" on the Hocking River (Atwater 1820:17). Squier and Davis appeared to dismiss this claim with their marginal notation that these walls were only two and a half miles long (Squier and Davis 1848:plate XXV, facing p. 67).

James and Charles Salisbury traced these walls two and a half miles and came to Ramp Creek. They found that the walls continued on the opposite bank and traced them for six miles over fields and through "tangled swamps and across streams." The walls kept to an undeviating course. The extent of this "great . . . high way; & what other ancient strong hold or place of importance it connects with, is as yet unknown—but its course if continued would lead near Circleville & Chilicothe [*sic*], where are extensive ancient ruins" (Salisbury and Salisbury 1862:15). Samuel Park attempted to trace the extent of these parallel walls just a few years after the Salisburys' survey. In 1870 he reported that the landscape in this area was so "improved" by cultivation that, if such a road ever had existed, no traces survived (Park 1870:41).

In 1930 Warren Weiant, Jr., brought aerial reconnaissance to bear on the archaeology of Licking County and independently confirmed what the Salisburys had reported. From the air he could see what was no longer visible on the ground. He discovered evidence for a previously undocumented small circular enclosure at the Licking County Airport. This circle was connected to traces of the Great Hopewell Road that he still could see from the air. In a 1931 letter to the Ohio Historical Society, Weiant wrote that he had followed the remnants of the parallel walls beyond Ramp Creek "southwestward in a straight line for Millersport." He observed additional circles, like the airport circle, branching off the road at regular intervals of one to one and a half miles. Weiant flippantly speculated that these enclosures might be "some sort of filling station or hot-dog stand" (Weiant 1931).

The Road to Chillicothe

Based upon the primary observations of James and Charles Salisbury and Warren Weiant, Jr., and the secondary observations reported by Atwater, I conclude that "the Great Hopewell Road" was a set of parallel walls that extended in a straight line from Newark's octagonal enclosure for more than ten kilometers to the southwest. Small circular earthworks with openings oriented toward the east are associated with the road and perhaps were located at regular intervals along it.

There is a surprising degree of correspondence between these observations of the proposed Hopewellian road and the Anasazi roads of Chaco Canyon (e.g., Kincaid 1983; Sofaer et al. 1989), as well as with the Mayan *sacbeob* (e.g., Folan 1991; Freidel and Sabloff 1984). How similar are these various roads? Given similar levels of technology, one might suppose that the Great Hopewell Road could have a length comparable to those of Chaco Canyon—which extend as far as fifty kilometers. This is the length Atwater originally suggested for the road from Newark.

In order to test the hypothesis that the Great Hopewell Road extended well beyond the generally accepted distance of four kilometers, I projected the lines mapped by the Salisburys and photographed by Warren Weiant across a set of U.S. Geological Survey topographic maps. The parallel walls, which began at the southeastern entrance to Newark's octagon, extend southward, but within half a kilometer the walls make two angular turns and assume a bearing of 31° west of south. They maintain that bearing as far as they have been traced. On this bearing, the road would, if extended, lead to the heart of modern Chillicothe—90 kilometers distant.

Is Chillicothe a plausible destination for a Hopewell Road beginning in Newark? The Scioto Valley, surrounding the site of modern Chillicothe, is filled with dozens of ancient mounds and earthworks (fig. 7.7). The quantity and quality of these sites confirm that present-day Ross County was an important Hopewell center. One earthwork, in particular, would have looked familiar to residents of ancient Newark. High Bank Works is a circular embankment connected to an octagonal enclosure. The Ohio Hopewell built only two such combinations, one in Chillicothe, one in Newark. Although the circles are identical in size, Newark's octagon is considerably larger. Hively and Horn (1982 and 1984) determined that these sites, though located more than 90 kilometers apart, are oriented at 90 degrees to each other. Moreover, they demonstrate that both sites encode consistent and complementary information about the 18.6-year lunar cycle.

Hopewellian Newark and Chillicothe appear to be connected in some very specific ways. They were connected in terms of geometry—each place had a circular enclosure connected to an octagon. They were also connected in terms of astronomy—each circle and octagon was aligned to important risings and settings of the moon. Were they also connected by a formal roadway, a set of straight, parallel walls nearly 90 kilometers long?

Extrapolating from the known extent and orientation of Newark's parallel walls and working with various individuals, agencies, and private com-

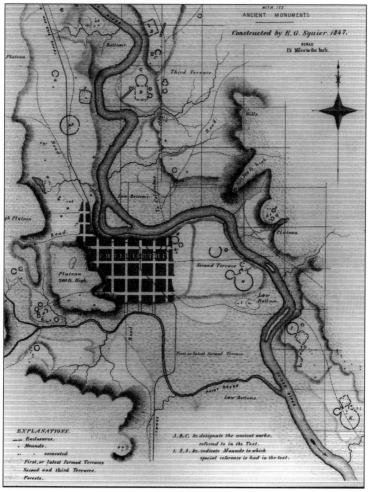

Fig. 7.7. The 1848 Squier and Davis map of a section of twelve miles of the Scioto Valley showing the high density of mound and earthwork sites in this area. The projected route of the Great Hopewell Road would bring it down the valley from the northeast corner of the map on a line beginning approximately at the P in MAP . . . to the first L in CHILLICOTHE (courtesy, Ohio Historical Society).

panies, I obtained a variety of aerial images of the projected corridor of the Great Hopewell Road. To date I have identified four locations along that corridor where there is evidence suggestive of road remnants (Lepper 1995). This evidence consists of parallel linear discolorations in the soil observed within the corridor at the predicted compass bearing. This evidence must be regarded as tentative. Only excavation at these localities will establish whether they are earthwork remnants or some unrelated phenomenon. To date there have been no such excavations.

These data suggest a great roadway of low, parallel walls extending from Newark to Chillicothe in a remarkably straight line. But what was the purpose of such a road? We may never know for sure. The Hopewell way of life changed dramatically by A.D. 500, too early for there to be surviving traditions that can reliably be attributed to that era. We can only make speculations, based on existing information and analogies with other cultures.

Over a thousand years later, when the Spanish encountered the Mayan people of the Yucatán and asked of them the purpose of the long, straight highways that connected their grandest cities, they were told that these were sacred roads. They were routes of pilgrimage, and the Mayan name for them was *sacbe*, which means "white road." This also is a Mayan term for the Milky Way. The people who used the Hopewellian earthworks did not emigrate to the Yucatán Peninsula and become the Mayas, but perhaps they shared certain beliefs with their Mesoamerican cousins (e.g., Hall 1989). And perhaps faint echoes of those beliefs still resonate within the woodlands of eastern North America.

Daniel Brinton, a nineteenth-century anthropologist, recorded an obscure tradition of the Lenni Lenape, or Delaware Indians, that may be of some relevance. The Reverend Albert Seqaqknind Anthony, a Delaware, told Brinton that, "in the good old times," before any white man had landed on their shores, the Lenape had "a string of white wampum beads . . . which stretched from the Atlantic to the Pacific, and on this *white road* their envoys traveled from one great ocean to the other, safe from attack" (Brinton 1890:188) (emphasis added). Speck (1931:23) noted that the Lenape referred to life's journey as the "Beautiful White Path," and he argued that this term could also refer to the Milky Way—"the 'Spirit or Ghost Path' over which the soul of the deceased passes to the realm above."

There are intriguing correspondences here between the Mayan "white roads," possibly metaphorical "white roads" in Algonquian traditions, and the proposed Hopewellian road. These correspondences suggest to me that the Great Hopewell Road was the functional equivalent of a Mayan *sacbe*. It was a sacred road along which pilgrims came from across eastern North America to touch the mystery and to leave offerings of rare and precious items—the exotica of the Hopewell Interaction Sphere (Struever and Houart

1972). This interaction would have been facilitated by the use of formal, sacred roadways, roadways that may have been called, in the lost or forgotten language of the Hopewell, "white roads" (Lepper 1995).

Summary

The Newark Earthworks were so imposing and elaborate that it is difficult to describe them in terms other than grandiose. Squier and Davis candidly admitted that it was "impossible to give anything like a comprehensible description of them" (1848:67). In spite of their grandeur, much of this magnificent site was destroyed, and, as Squier and Davis (1848:71) predicted, today it is possible to walk through large areas of modern Newark and not know that the monumental Hopewellian geometric earthworks ever existed.

This brief review of the archaeology of the Newark Earthworks provides only the barest glimpse into the workings of this complex Hopewellian machine; but, when so little is known, even a glimpse can provide useful insights. Mortuary activity seems to be restricted to only a few locations— most notably the Cherry Valley cluster of mounds. The largely anecdotal descriptions of the Cherry Valley mounds and the more systematic excavations at Eagle Mound suggest that episodic ritual events took place within walled structures at these locations. The caches of artifacts, unassociated with burials, uncovered at the Salisbury Square confirm that some of the ritual activity at Newark was not concerned with mortuary ceremonialism.

Habitation sites are present, but since no systematic effort has been made to locate and study them, meaningful generalizations about their frequency and organization are not possible. Nevertheless, we do know that some domestic activity took place in close proximity to the earthworks (e.g., Greber 1997).

The Great Hopewell Road, whatever its ultimate extent proves to be, is evidence for a degree of formalized interaction between distant regions that is without precedent for such an early period in the Americas. The scale of the road and its straightness over such a great distance bespeaks a ritual function (cf. Sofaer et al. 1989:368). This interpretation is supported by a few shreds and patches of ethnohistoric data, but as Folan (1991:227–228) suggests in his discussion of Mayan *sacbeob*, the function of such "sophisticated linear features" may not be easy to discern. Earle (1991:12) observed that the development of a formal road system often accompanies the rise of chiefdoms, and although the primary function of such early roads relates to socioeconomic and political integration, their form "is characteristically ritual, emphasizing the sacred charter that legitimizes the political system of regional and group domination."

The Newark Earthworks represent one of the preeminent expressions of the Hopewell florescence. The Hopewell community centered on the Raccoon Creek Valley may have constituted the most significant potential rival to the aggregate of communities in the Scioto Valley. Perhaps the Great Hopewell Road symbolically represented—and in its very construction and use would have helped to create and solidify—the bonds between these regions and their respective earthworks. Ultimately, however, the relatively weak power of Hopewell leaders could not withstand the centrifugal forces that sundered their precocious attempts at political integration.

Note

1. Charles Whittlesey, who surveyed the Newark Works in 1838, resurrected Atwater's claim but offered a novel interpretation of the feature. He proposed that there "had been a stone culvert or passage through the mound at the natural surface & it would seem to have been a covered drain for the discharge of water from the circle which has no other outlet" (Whittlesey 1838:276–277).

Chapter 8

Is the Newark Circle-Octagon the Ohio Hopewell "Rosetta Stone"?

A Question of Archaeological Interpretation

A. Martin Byers

As I will define it, to interpret the Hopewell embankment earthworks is to postulate and empirically ground models of their public meanings and the purposes that they manifest. Interpretation always involves an inferential circle that by confirmatory feedback transforms into a spiral of expanding understanding. But interpreting the works of others does not involve entering into their minds and thoughts—an impossible task even in regard to one's contemporaries. Rather, it is a matter of discovering the public codes that are embedded in the patterned residue of the past material culture, codes on which those responsible for the material culture regularly drew in performing the actions that this same material culture made possible, thereby realizing and apparently satisfying their social purposes and intentions.

For archaeologists who seek to interpret Hopewell earthworks, then, the first theoretical goal is to construct a model of these codes, and the first empirical task is to find and confirm a possible "Rosetta stone" or material clue by which to initiate an interpretive hermeneutic spiral (Bhaskar 1979). To treat an interpretive model as part of a hermeneutic spiral is to claim that, as with any scientific account, it is open to correction and modification—both in terms of its theoretical coherence and its empirical confirmation. All this is a difficult scientific task, but one that I think cannot be shirked by archaeology since, in the view from which I operate, part of what is entailed in explaining the human past is to acknowledge that, although humans are subject like other animals to objective constraints and natural laws, in virtue of our capacity to act meaningfully, the understanding we have of ourselves and the world around us is always a causal condition in the way we share our material lifeways (Bhaskar 1979; Giddens 1976, 1979, 1981, 1984; Harrè 1979; Hodder 1985, 1989).

In this regard I have argued (Byers 1987, 1992) that Newark (fig. 8.1) is the Rosetta stone by which we can enter into the action meaning that the earthworks held for the Central Ohio Valley peoples of the Early and Middle Woodland. My claim is that the Observatory Mound of the Circle and the two low embankments jutting out at its base, what I term Feature A (fig. 8.2), were the result of a sudden change of plan occurring during the initial construction of the Circle. This change required avoiding destroying Feature A, and I explain this avoidance as the outcome of a general proscription underwriting the canons or rules governing their construction practices. This proscription logically entails a world-belief paradigm informing the builders in their labor. The core of this paradigm I have termed the *sacred-earth principle*, and it characterized the world as an immanently sacred cosmos.

Recently Lepper (1993) has challenged this claim by presenting two nineteenth-century survey maps that he has recovered, one made by D. Wyrick (1866) (fig. 7.2) and the other by the Salisbury brothers (1862) (fig. 7.3). He argues that both include empirical details not noted in the earlier Whittlesey survey, on which I based much of my analysis, that disprove the sacred-earth principle and, by extension, discount my "Rosetta stone" claim. In the spirit of scientific debate, I will show how these new data not only are accommodated to the sacred-earth principle but that the credibility of Lepper's own "Great Hopewell Road" postulate is dependent on the validity of this model. All this opens up the possibility of constructing and empirically confirming models of the social structural forces that were at work underwriting these monumental endeavors.

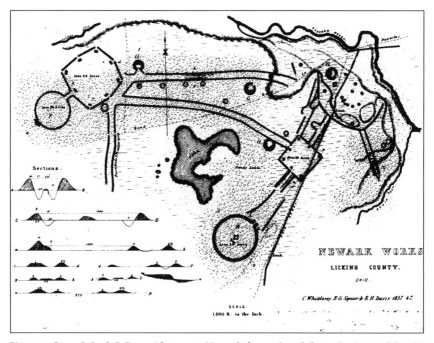

Fig. 8.1. Sacred dual C-R motif type at Newark (reproduced from Squier and Davis 1848:Plate XXV).

Material Culture as Warrants of Action

Only when particular beliefs and views conform to the validation standards of a society are they warranted as part of its collective knowledge; that is, they must fall within prescribed limits set by a society to be considered legitimate. I will extend this constitutive notion of warranting to social behaviors and argue that only when doings are warranted are they the types of social activities characteristic of the society. A warrant issued by a court jurisdiction can be used analogically to characterize the role that material culture plays in realizing this creative, transformative process. The warrant is a cultural artifact, a document that conventionally expresses and manifests the authority of the court, thereby endowing its legitimate bearer with this authority and constituting her or him as an officer of the court—for example, a bailiff or a sheriff (Taylor 1985; Searle 1983). In using the warrant, the bailiff conventionally makes her or his action intentions and social position manifest to relevant others in the very instance of behaving, thereby eliciting reciprocal behavioral expressions of recognition and participation. It is this dual expressive-elicitative use of the warrant that makes up its action-constitutive warranting moment and transforms the behavior it mediates into the type of social activity it is.

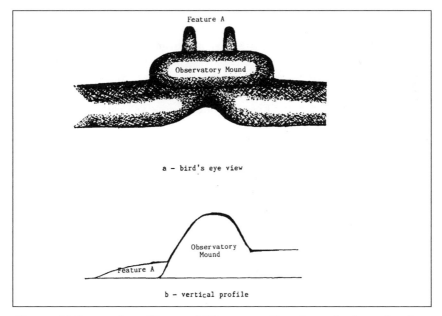

Fig. 8.2. Bird's-eye view of Feature A/Observatory Mound complex (reproduced from Byers 1987).

The action-constitutive nature of a court warrant is not unique. Rather, its transformative property is generic to a whole range of formal documents characteristic of literate societies, and by which members warrant their everyday and not so everyday behavioral interventions to constitute them as the types of social activities they are and that the doers intend. The license that gives its possessor the right to drive a vehicle on public roads, the coupons that ration basic goods in an emergency, passports and visas that permit legal crossing of boundaries and residing in countries, money and tickets, and so on are typical textual documentary artifacts that have warranting power. But this means that warranting, as a generic process, cannot be unique to literate societies. In nonliterate societies, warranting regular behaviors so that they count as felicitous passage and boundary crossing or rightful resource allocation and so on is no less necessary; all these activities require jurisdictional authorization characteristic of each society.

Douglas (1982) has spoken of primitive moneys in what I am calling warranting terms, arguing that their production and use are fully conventional, and that in most cases they are "non-inscriptive" licenses that in warranting selected behaviors constitute them as the elite social activities they are. In these terms, warranting as the rule-governed expressive/elicitative moment of activity is generically constitutive of all social life. In nonliterate societies, material culture is one of the primary modes by which this moment can be realized. This entails treating material cultural style—as realized in both artifacts and features—as action-constitutive or pragmatic conventions, and the realization of style in distinctive patterning mediates the warranting moment of behaviors. I call this theoretical characterization of material cultural style the *warranting model*, and it is the basis of my interpretation of the Hopewell embankment earthworks (Byers 1991, 1992). I will now turn to my claim that Newark is the Rosetta stone of Hopewell earthworks.

The World Renewal Model

In an earlier discussion (1987), I empirically demonstrated that the Observatory Mound of the Circle and the two low embankments jutting out at its base, what I will now call the Feature A/Observatory Mound Complex (fig. 8.2), were the product of an avoidance rule proscribing secondary disturbance of the embankment fill. I concluded that an emic principle of knowledge about the nature of the world must be underwriting this avoidance rule, and as I stated, I called it the sacred-earth principle. By drawing on this principle and the belief paradigm it entailed, the builders constituted their perception of the world as an immanently sacred cosmos ordered into at least three sacred strata, the heavens, the middle world, and the underworld, and as having at least two sacred temporal phases, the lunar and the solar.

In applying the warranting-model perspective, I can conclude that the earthworks were constructed in the form we see them so as to constitute them as monumental warrants, expressive warrants that participated in that which they represent, namely, the sacred cosmos. When material cultural items are believed to derive their warranting powers by participating in the essential nature of what they conventionally express, they can be termed icons or iconic warrants (Douglas 1966, 1970, 1975). As iconic warrants, the earthworks were built and used by the community to invoke and make present the sacred authority of the cosmos, manifest action intentions, and elicit appropriate expressive participation, thereby warranting the material behaviors community members collectively performed in their material context so as to constitute these behaviors as the type of social ritual activities community members intended them to be, namely, world renewal rites (G. Wright 1990). For this reason, I call it the *world-renewal model* of the Hopewell earthworks. I will now empirically confirm this model.

The C-R Motif Analysis

In my view, the patterning of the geometrical earthworks is based on a simple configuration I call the *C-R motif*.[1] The "C-R" designation stipulates three related elements: the circle element (C), the rectilinear element (R), and the hyphen (-) as the linking element. I postulate that there are two types of geometrical C-R motifs: the High Bank type and the Paint Creek type. The former, modeled after the High Bank site (fig. 8.3), has the circle and rectilinear elements either linked directly or connected by short parallel embankments, which I term the aggregation neck. Symmetry is an important property. If a line were drawn parallel to and through the aggregation neck and extended in both directions, it would form the axis of symmetry.

The Paint Creek type derives its name from the five "classic" examples of it found in the Paint Creek drainage: Liberty Works (fig. 8.4), Seip (fig. 8.5), Baum (fig. 8.6), Works East (fig. 8.7), and Frankfort (fig. 8.8). Adding Hopewell (fig. 8.9) brings the total to six (Byers 1987). Greber (1976, 1979) has commented on the tripartite patterning of the Paint Creek type, this being made up of the small circle, which I define as the circle element (C), the rectilinear element (R), which I call the Paint Creek Square, and the linking element (-), which I consider to be the large inner circle; I call it the infix element. In contrast to the symmetry of the High Bank, the Paint Creek type is skewed and off center.[2] These two types are usually found in relatively close proximity to each other (e.g., Liberty Works and High Bank being about 2 km apart), and in my view they must be understood as constituting a single monumental complex, which I call the *dual C-R motif*.

Construction Scenarios

The Feature A/Observatory Mound Complex (fig. 8.2) is tangent to the southwest perimeter of the circle element of the Newark Circle-Octagon (fig. 8.1). This latter, of course, is a High Bank C-R type. Its anomalous nature grounds my Rosetta Stone claim. According to the C-R motif analysis given above, this complex should not exist. I postulate that if the Observatory Mound were

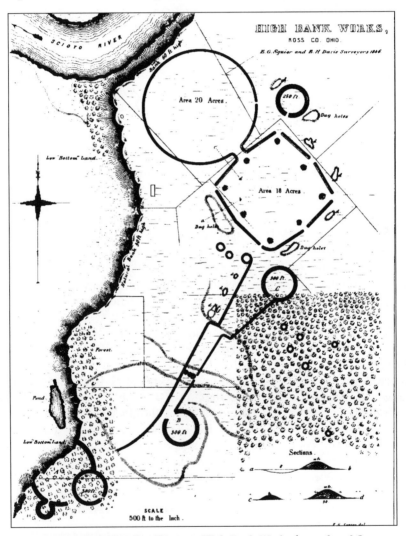

Fig. 8.3. High Bank C-R motif type at High Bank Works (reproduced from Squier and Davis 1848:Plate XVI).

removed without disturbing the parallel embankments (Feature A) under it, the latter would be revealed as an aggregation neck. The Newark Circle-Octagon, then, has two anomalies, the Observatory Mound and two aggregation necks, Feature A, and diametrically opposite what I will call Feature B, the neck that now connects the Octagon to the northeast sector of the Circle.

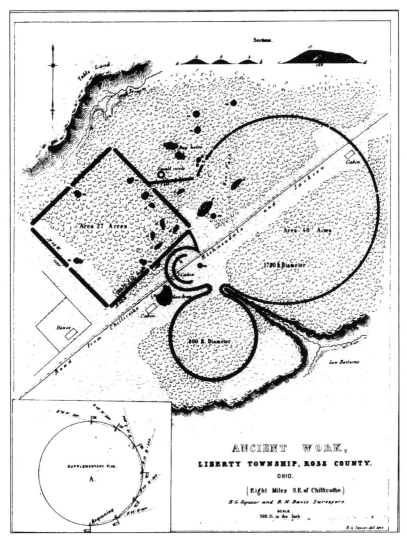

Fig. 8.4. Paint Creek C-R motif type at Liberty Works (reproduced from Squier and Davis 1848:Plate XX).

Scenario 1

The most reasonable account of Feature A is to treat it as the first step in the construction of the Newark Circle-Octagon. If so, the builders started at the southwest end of this feature. With it completed, they extended two semicircular embankments, intending to join them together at a point more or less diametrically opposite Feature A. With the Circle completed, they would have then built the Octagon onto the southwest end of Feature A, thereby completing a standard High Bank C-R motif earthwork. However, in terms of the C-R motif analysis, I can postulate that while partway through building the Circle as described above, and before finishing it, the builders changed their original plan by covering Feature A with a mounding of earth and then building Feature B as an aggregation neck as we see it now. On completing this neck they built the Octagon to it.[3]

Scenario 2

I have reconstructed other possible scenarios working logically from the empirical data but, given the C-R motif analysis, none can be rationally sustained. For example, assume the reverse of the above scenario with the Circle being

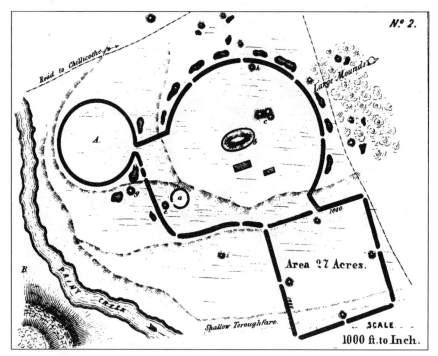

Fig. 8.5. Paint Creek C-R motif type at Seip (reproduced from Squier and Davis 1848:Plate XXI, no. 2).

built first, starting in the northeast sector, and being terminated with Feature A, at which point the change of plan occurred. This would have required covering Feature A in the manner described above. Then the builders would have removed the fill in the embankment of the Circle diametrically opposite it, added on Feature B, and finally they would have completed the earthwork by building the Octagon, as we now see it. The problem with this scenario is that if removing earth from the Circle was a viable method of construction, then the builders could also have removed all of Feature A and filled the gap in the Circle. In this way they would have saved on labor and they would have achieved greater symmetry, which, according to the C-R motif analysis, was an important property of the High Bank type.

Scenario 3

An alternative scenario that would appear to get around these problems while accounting for two aggregation necks is to reverse the whole construction process, with the construction of the Octagon being the first step and the building of the Observatory Mound being the final step. This scenario, however, would have required two changes of plan. Having finished the Octagon and Feature B, the builders would have been on the point of

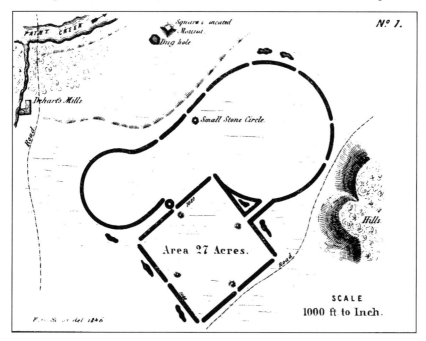

Fig. 8.6. Paint Creek C-R motif type at Baum (reproduced from Squier and Davis 1848:Plate XXI, no. 1).

completing the Circle to form a normal High Bank type when they decided to add Feature A. But having partially completed Feature A, they changed their plan again by covering it, thereby completing the Circle-Octagon as we now see it. This is actually the scenario given by Squier and Davis (1973), but it also has problems. Like the second scenario, this one does not account for the asymmetry of the Feature A/Observatory Mound Complex and, an even more glaring problem, in terms of the C-R motif analysis this scenario makes no sense, for it means that just as the builders were completing a normal High Bank feature, they drastically deviated from the pattern by adding a second aggregation neck.

No doubt other scenarios could be developed, but because all of them would be variations on the three discussed, variants of Scenario 2 and Scenario 3 would be faulted on the same grounds that I have given. From this I conclude that the Scenario 1–along with any of its possible variants– is the most plausible construction sequence. It follows then that the Feature A/Observatory Mound Complex evidences an avoidance practice, and the proscriptive rule it realizes can be expressed as: Do not modify an earthwork by disturbing its embankment fill.

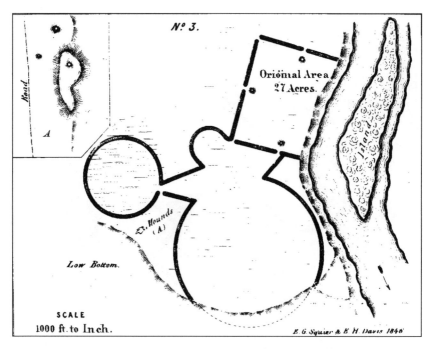

Fig. 8.7. Paint Creek C-R motif type at Works East (reproduced from Squier and Davis 1848:Plate XXI, no. 3).

I can confirm this interpretive hypothesis by demonstrating how it makes a number of other anomalies coherent. For example, at Liberty Works (fig. 8.4) there is the anomalous "lobed" circle located between the square and the small circle. Inside there is another apparent anomaly, a semicircular embankment, which I can justifiably claim is an incomplete circle since at Seip (fig. 8.5) there is also an asymmetry in the equivalent position of the infix embankment whereby a small complete circle is incorporated. Both pre-existed the later and larger earthworks in which they were incorporated, and elaborate care was taken to build around them, thereby ensuring that they were left undisturbed. As at Newark, it appears that construction plans were changed, requiring abandonment of earlier features while avoiding disturbing them (Byers 1987).[4]

In all these cases, there would have been no objective impediments to removing pre-existing earth fill. Also, the removal of earth fill would have been less costly in labor than the techniques of addition and circumvention that were used. In each case, the same avoidance was practiced, implicating a rule presupposing impediments that existed only in the shared understanding of the builders—and these were common to the peoples of both Newark and

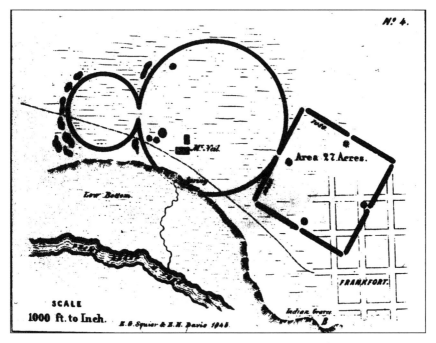

Fig. 8.8. Paint Creek C-R Motif type at Frankfort (reproduced from Squier and Davis 1848:Plate XXI, no. 4).

Chillicothe. I am warranted to conclude that such a pervasive, immanent, intangible, and dangerous property is described by the term sacredness.

Astronomical Alignments

An important line of evidence supporting the world-renewal model is the empirical analysis by Hively and Horn (1982) of the Newark Octagon, establishing that its embankments were intentionally laid out to manifest alignments that embodied the 18.6-year lunar cycle. Similarly, it has been established that the Wright Square is aligned with the solstices and the equinoxes of the solar cycle (Greber 1989; Hively and Horn 1982, 1984). The world-renewal model can interpret these lunar and solar alignments as constituting the Octagon and the Wright Square as working together to make present the sacred powers that animated the lunar and solar cycles and to transform behaviors performed in their construction and use as world-renewal ritual activity. Finally, Hively and Horn have demonstrated that the Octagon is based on a transformed square the sides of which are the same length as the 322 m diameter of the Circle, so that the Circle and Octagon form a complementary opposition.

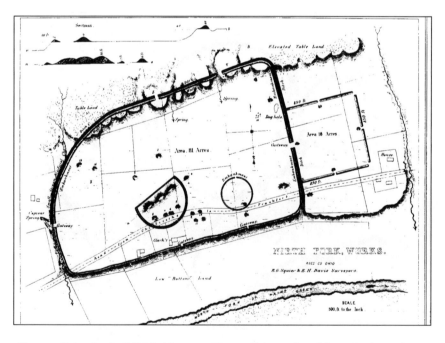

Fig. 8.9. Paint Creek C-R Motif type at Hopewell (reproduced from Squier and Davis 1848:Plate X).

Summary of Evidence

At least three rule-governed warranting expressions of material form are manifested in the construction practices of Newark: astronomical alignments, C-R complementary oppositions, and the earth procurement practices. Since the Feature A/Observatory Mound Complex and the Circle were built and completed before the rest of the earthwork, it logically follows that the earth procurement was a sacred practice in its own right and that the Feature A embankments were constituted as sacred from the very beginning of construction. For this reason, in my dissertation (1987) I postulated that the selection and procurement of embankment fill would be rule governed and that these rules would presuppose the same beliefs about the sacredness of the world as underwrote the C-R motif.

According to the description of the Newark Circle-Octagon in Squier and Davis (1973), as well as the descriptions given by Fowke (1902) and Thomas (1889), the Octagon had borrow pitting spatially associated with it while the Circle had no directly discernible pitting. On this and some further argumentation based on the particular location of these borrow pits with respect to the total earthwork, I postulated two emic earth categories correlated with the Circle and Octagon, the surface stratum and deep stratum earths, respectively. Further, noting that the alignments marking the turning points of the moon and the sun rising from below the horizon and setting back under it were embedded in the rectilinear elements of the C-R motif, not the circle elements, I concluded that the latter participate in the heavenly powers and the former in the underworld powers. Hence, the tripartite configuration of the C-R motif manifests a real emic conceptual scheme that stratified the world into three levels: the heavens (C), the middle world (R), and the underworld (-), and by being constructed according to rules, Newark, as the expression of the dual C-R motif integrating both the High Bank and Paint Creek types, embodied the sacred powers of the total cosmos, thereby constituting this site as a monumental iconic warrant.

Of course other substantive, content-based interpretations of these earthworks as iconic warrants are possible. For example, it has been argued that the Circle might manifest the powers of the world rim (G. Wright 1990). But it is a secondary concern of the world-renewal model to postulate which particular elements and categories of the world are the objects of their expressive meaning. Rather, in warranting terms, what is critical is that whatever these were, they were understood by the population to be the real source of the warranting power that the earthworks expressively embodied and manifested, and thereby constituted the behavioral interventions of the community as the types of ceremonial activities they were.

Empirical Challenge

I pointed out in my dissertation that evidence for surface stratum earth, surface-scraping, would be more difficult to discern than the evidence for deep stratum earth, this latter being borrow pitting in the local area. In this regard, Lepper points out that according to the Salisburys' map (fig. 7.3) and their commentary (1862), not only are borrow pits associated with the Octagon, confirming Fowke's data, but also extensive pitting depressions occur in the zone outside the southeastern half of the Circle. From this he concludes that Byers's "initial inference, and the intricate web of speculation he spins from it, are without foundation" (1993:9).

As I see it, any evidence that will fatally undermine the sacred-earth principle must demonstrate that no rule-governed categorical distinction in earth-fill procurements was operating. In short, in the absence of any objective constraints, and given that the Circle and the Octagon required the same type of brute labor, the patternings of the procurement residue should be equivalent for both features. But they are not, and the most interesting aspect is how they systematically differ from each other. According to the Salisburys' mapping, the "borrow pittings" associated with the Circle are multiple, apparently shallow, and symmetrically distributed outside the embankment, roughly parallel to its southern and southeastern periphery. Those associated with the Octagon are quite deep, and they are tightly grouped outside its northern sector. According to Fowke, there are only two, while according to the Salisburys there are four or five. Hence, the two spatially distinct sets are different forms of material disturbance, justifying treating the Octagon procurement residue as a deep, focused pitting pattern and that of the Circle as a shallow, dispersed pitting pattern.

The simplest explanation of this variation is that in the understanding of the builders, they were procuring two different kinds of fill. In short, the procurement aspect of the construction fulfills the complementary-oppositional interpretation of the C-R motif. But does this variation support my original view that categorically different types of fill were being used, surface and deep-stratum earths? The evidence appears to favor my original thesis. An important deduction from the sacred-earth principle is that to the builders, disturbing the natural order was serious because it entailed intervening in the sacred powers themselves. Hence, a minimizing strategy would be used. The dispersed patterning is most reasonably explained in terms of minimizing the degree of material intervention caused by shallow scraping of the earth to procure surface-stratum fill, while the focused patterning minimizes disturbance caused by deep borrow pitting required to procure deep-stratum fill.

What all this highlights is the need to confirm the construction Scenario 1 by means of direct empirical verification. A two-pronged, minimally invasive excavation could be directed at demonstrating the construction sequence and illuminating both our knowledge of the nature of the earth-fill practices and the complexity of the emic categories of earth types. The first would be achieved by verifying that Feature A extends under the Mound as a continuous part of the Circle. The second would be accomplished by revealing the internal patterning of the earth fills for both the Octagon and Circle, much along the lines reported by Lepper (1993) with regard to controlled excavation of the Fairground Circle and by Connolly and Sieg (1993) at Fort Ancient.

Hence, rather than Lepper's new data being grounds for denying that Newark is the Rosetta stone of the Hopewell earthworks, the world-renewal model and its sacred-earth principle can comfortably account for them while, in positive fashion, these new data reveal more complex rules than I originally suggested, thereby expanding our understanding of this worldview. It now becomes more pressing to explore the question: What precisely is going to count as appropriate earth fill for different elements of a complex earthwork if this feature is going to be a proper warrant? Greber, in her analysis of the Harness Mound (1983), was first to raise the issue of material symboling as a credible problem. Wymer, Lepper, and Pickard (1992) extended this to the earth fill, showing it was categorized according to color and texture. The warranting model grounds this material symbolism as action-constitutive in nature.

Discussion

A test of any interpretive theory is to assess it in terms of how it contributes to our understanding of the data. I believe the world-renewal model, adequately understood and applied, supports Lepper's (1993:23) claims that the peoples of Newark and Chillicothe constructed a great ceremonial way connecting their locales: "Based on several interwoven lines of evidence . . . I conclude that the Great Hopewell Road was a virtually straight set of parallel walls 60 m apart and extending from the Newark Earthworks to the cluster of earthworks in the Scioto Valley centered at modern Chillicothe, a distance of 90 km."

Drawing on Schele and Freidel's (1990) work, Lepper points to the great *sacbeob* of the classic Mayas for analogical support of the rationality of the Great Hopewell Road, suggesting that since the Mayas built their roads as "monumental expressions of politico-religious connections between centers" (Lepper 1993:24), then it seems reasonable to assume that the Hopewell did so also. But invoking Schele and Freidel's interpretation of Mayan monumental sacbeob cannot be done piecemeal, so that in accepting that these roads realized "political-religious" alliance, Lepper is committed to the position that monumental construction presupposes Mayan beliefs that stipulate the world as being an immanently sacred cosmos. Hence, in treating

Hopewell earthworks in similar terms, he is committed to an equivalent notion, namely, the sacred-earth principle of the world-renewal model.

But establishing that monumental construction entails beliefs about the world as a sacred cosmos is not sufficient to explain why it would make sense for a people to express these beliefs in this costly manner; and claiming that they were really using this construction to express a political commitment begs the question. That is, even though monumental features presuppose beliefs about the sacredness of the world, why should monumental construction, as such, be part of what it takes to constitute a political alliance? What is the connection between religious beliefs and political alliance that makes monument construction a rational means of constituting the latter? Is it not possible that the very same beliefs could be held by communities involved in political alliances without monumental construction figuring in at all? Indeed, would it not be more rational to use this surplus labor for constructing defense locales or storage depots?

Invoking Schele and Freidel's work will not help much here. In my view, they use the Mayan glyphs and art as evidence to postulate models about Mayan cosmic beliefs. But it does not follow that the Mayas used their monumental constructions as mere referential devices by which they could "speak" about their beliefs. Rather, these must be understood as action-constitutive devices, as monumental iconic warrants, expressive media by which the sacred powers of nature were literally invoked, i.e., presenced, thereby transforming the behavioral interventions performed therein as fully felicitous ritual acts. In these terms, the action-constitutive intelligibility of the Mayas' monumental construction is the basis of their political rationale. These served—in Mayan terms—as fully practical and, therefore, as essential expressive material media by which the Mayas constituted human-sacred interaction, thereby discharging their sacred duties and constituting and reconstituting their collective reputation and position in the human world.

Hence, we can see the significance of empirically establishing the sacred-earth principle as central to Hopewell construction practice. In terms of the warranting model of material culture, the sacred-earth principle grounds the interpretive postulate that the earthworks are monumental iconic warrants. By being elements of a practical political strategy, they would be monumental warranting features by which the responsible communities invoked cosmic authority so that in their context they transformed their behavioral interventions into human-sacred cosmic social interaction. Seen in these terms, I can accept Lepper's claim that the Great Hopewell Road had political-strategic relevance, and it is only in these terms that it made sense to construct it. This and similar constructions would have been taken by their builders to be essential warrants by which the allied communities integrated their material capacities, so as to produce warranted interventions as major and fully felicitous ceremonial acts, thereby discharging collective duties to the sacred cosmos and constituting and reconstituting their reputation as honorable societies that had to be heeded.

Since we are speaking about material warrants, the regular usage of which had cosmic implications, then variation in form and manner of construction had sacred and therefore political implication. Whereas mutual emulation realized alliances, intentional mutual deviations among neighboring communities might be best interpreted as expressions of mutual hostility, making construction part of a political process of mutual exclusion. Political posturing would be mediated through material manifestations of mutually exclusive and alternative canons of construction. These contrasting earthworks would not stand as merely alternative ways of achieving equivalent cosmic benefits. They would be mutually perceived as deviant and, therefore, constitute challenges to the validity and the very raison d'être of the societies responsible. Each would perceive itself and its monumentally bound allies as having "true" warranting capacity to intervene beneficially in the well-being and balance of the cosmos, while constituting the others as producing material warrants that were false and dangerous, indeed polluting to the cosmos, thereby generating and, to various degrees, sustaining standing opposition.

Implications and Conclusion

The warranting model has important methodological and epistemological implications. When monumental constructions are seen as warranting devices, we are justified in interpreting them as evidence of tendencies toward monopolistic claims over collective labor and against the labor output of the deviant "other." Style variations map out disputing jurisdictional claims among and even within territories over what forms of material features will constitute collective interventions in the world as being fully felicitous ceremonial activity of the intended types. Not only does variation in monumental construction, then, realize and manifest regional alliances and hostilities, but in monopolizing local collective labor it tends to spawn local factionalism. Factional conflict is largely concerned with determining what rules of style will prevail, and these are action rules. When these rules underwrite large-scale construction, then they mediate competition over what particular forms communal features must take in order to be material warrants, and such negotiation reaches out to potential allies and enemies, both close to hand and distant.

However, I want to stress that despite the competitive strains implicated in monumental construction, at the same time this competition over the rules leaves largely unscathed the world beliefs that the factions share, that enemies share, and that distant partners share. In sum, therefore, local and regional variation in the material patterning of earthworks would largely map the dynamics of this competition while reproducing a largely unchanging set of world beliefs. The latter, such as the sacred-earth principle, must remain largely unchanged for they are the source of rationality for the whole process. In short, the warranting model theoretically grounds a dual postulate. First, the world beliefs of the prehistoric Eastern Woodlands had wide regional and deep temporal continuity as social knowledge. Second, as a result of competing local factions and regional alliances and hostilities, the styles of material form used in realizing the warranting rules of action would have been quite variable and regionally "patchy." In this way we can account for quite radical material cultural variation without being committed to the further claim that such variation entailed deep cultural structural transformation. Indeed, all this suggests that deep cultural structural continuity is the largely unnoted condition that underwrites and makes possible this observable variation termed style.

The evidence recently marshaled by Lepper actually supports my earlier interpretation of Newark as the Rosetta stone of Hopewell earthwork culture. When treated in terms of the warranting model, this interpretation can be used to enter into the social and cultural universe of the Central Ohio Valley, thereby transforming the temporal and spatial variation among the earthworks and their related assemblage into empirical evidence for grounding interpretive models of its sociopolitical history. Detailed field excavations at enclosure sites will provide critical tests of my interpretations, and I am confident that such studies will not only confirm the general validity of these interpretations but, like Lepper's recently introduced data, reveal additional complexities that governed the construction of enclosures.

Notes

1. This is a brief summary of a full-scale interpretation of the Hopewell earthworks that I published elsewhere (Byers 1987, 1992), focusing on those elements that are relevant to this discussion.

2. There are several other differences that I cannot go into in this chapter. A more complete analysis of the two types will be found in Byers (1987).

3. Excavations of other earthworks have established that embankments were usually built up through a series of additions (Essenpreis and Moseley 1984; Lepper 1993; Riordan 1986, 1995). An excavation of this (protected) feature would probably reveal a series of cumulative additions.

4. Also, I will point out that the sacred-earth principle can be used to account for the "uniqueness" of the Hopewell site itself (fig. 8.9). This manifests a C-R motif. I have characterized the large C-form embankment as the infix element of the Paint Creek type since, as at Seip and Liberty Works, it contains the major Hopewell mounds, most of which have strong mortuary associations (e.g., Mounds 23 and 25). The (C) element is inside the C-form, and the Paint Creek Square element is attached to the latter.

Chapter 9

Defensive or Sacred?

An Early Late Woodland Enclosure in Northeast Ohio

Stephanie J. Belovich

Large prehistoric villages, earthen fortifications, and a topography featuring steep slopes and high plateaus have come to characterize the northern Ohio Whittlesey Tradition. Colonel Charles Whittlesey, for whom the tradition was named, recorded a number of sites with these characteristics in the nineteenth century. The plateaus on which these sites are found overlook major river valleys and their tributary streams. Topographic setting and the presence of earthen walls and ditches suggested a defensive function to Whittlesey (e.g., 1871) and subsequent writers. Limited excavations at some of these sites indicated a Late Prehistoric (A.D. 950–A.D. 1560) temporal placement. Most archaeologists therefore assumed that all such sites, and especially those initially recorded by Whittlesey, were fortified villages once occupied by maize agriculturalists. Data from the Greenwood Village site challenge this assumption and suggest that not all hilltop enclosures are defensive, nor can they be uncritically assigned to the Late Prehistoric Whittlesey Tradition.

Defining the Whittlesey Tradition

As Ohio's surveyor general, sometime prior to 1850 Colonel Charles Whittlesey had begun to collect information on earthworks, caches, and mounds located in Ohio. He continued this practice throughout the 1850s and 1860s, publishing some of his information in 1850 and 1867. In 1871 Whittlesey published a summary of earthwork data pertaining to northeast Ohio in a work entitled *Ancient Earth Forts of the Cuyahoga Valley, Ohio*, in which he recorded the existence of eleven "ancient earth works" (fig. 9.1). Numbers 1 through 9 were located along both banks of the Cuyahoga River in Cuyahoga and Summit counties. Numbers 10 and 11 were located in Medina County. Work No. 10 was situated between two small unnamed streams near the city of Granger, Ohio, while No. 11 was located along the west bank of the east branch of the Rocky River within the city of Weymouth, Ohio.

All of these works except Nos. 8 and 10 are situated atop steeply sided and relatively isolated plateaus, and all consist of one or more ditches and embankments. Access to all but three of the works (Nos. 8, 9, and 10) is by way of narrow hogbacks, across which at least one of the earthen embank-

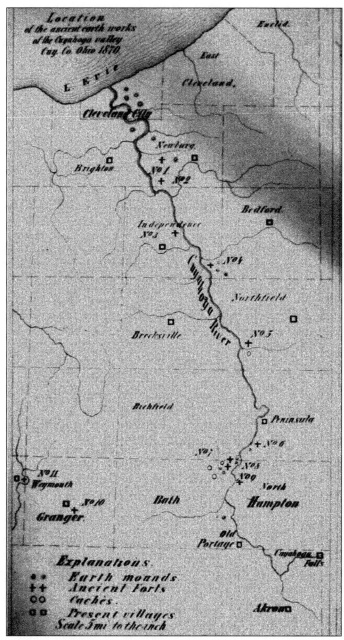

Fig. 9.1. Whittlesey's 1871 map showing the locations of the forts and other earthworks he recorded in the Cuyahoga River Valley.

ments stretch. Eight works (Nos. 1, 2, 3, 5, 6, 7, 8, and 10) had "gateways" or "openings" still visible at the time of Whittlesey's visit. Three of them (Nos. 4, 5, and 11) had mounds within or near the areas enclosed by the earthworks. Whittlesey called nine of these ancient works "forts" and two (8 and 10) "earthworks." Neither earthwork No. 8 nor 10 is located atop a steeply sided plateau. Both are constructed on flat, lower ground; in fact No. 10 is near a swamp. Whittlesey (1871:2) concluded that the open and easily accessible location of both "precludes the idea of a design for a fort."

The elevated topographic locations of the other earthworks, as well as the presence and orientation of the ditch and embankment lines, suggested to Whittlesey (1871:5) "a military purpose." He referred to these enclosures as "forts" and described each with reference to potential defensibility. Whittlesey's opinions were first published in 1850 and later republished (1867 and 1871), gaining authority with each reissue. Other early writers offered the same interpretations for similar sites throughout Ohio (Atwater 1820; Moorehead 1890, 1895). The identification of earthen hilltop enclosures as defensive works gained wide regional acceptance by the mid-nineteenth century. Whittlesey's conclusions thus were accepted by scholars without additional excavation or challenge.

Limited efforts to relocate Whittlesey's "forts" were made during this century. These attempts, as well as more frequent excavations that took place at sites not recorded by Whittlesey, served to strengthen Whittlesey's initial assessment. For example, Greenman (1937) relocated and partially excavated Whittlesey Fort No. 3, the Tuttle Hill site (33Cu7-1) (fig. 9.2). This site, located in Independence, Ohio, is situated on a bluff overlooking the west bank of the Cuyahoga River (Whittlesey 1871:11) and consists of a pair of earthen walls with outer ditches enclosing an area of about four acres. Another earthen wall (*sans* ditch) is situated perpendicular to this pair of earthen walls, but along the east bluff edge of the site. A gateway once existed between these lines. Finally, a horseshoe-shaped "outwork" is reported along the east bluff edge just outside the enclosure (Whittlesey 1871:plate III). At the time of Greenman's excavations, these earthworks were no longer visible.

Within weeks of the Tuttle Hill excavations, Greenman conducted excavations at the nearby South Park (33Cu8) site, located about one mile south of Tuttle Hill. Though not one of Whittlesey's "forts," the South Park site is located atop a promontory connected to the surrounding highland by a narrow neck of land about 20 ft wide (Greenman 1937). Greenman (1937:307) found "no signs of fortifying walls or ditches . . . nor [were they] remembered by residents of the region."

Both sites, Tuttle Hill (Whittlesey Fort No. 3) and South Park, are rich in pit features and cultural materials and also yielded artifacts and other traits that suggest a strong cultural relationship between the sites. Greenman con-

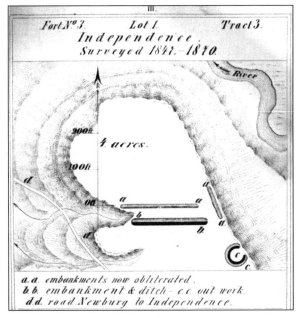

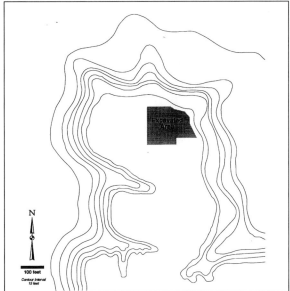

Fig. 9.2. Fort No. 3, the Tuttle Hill site (33Cu7-1): *top*,
Whittlesey's 1871 map; *bottom*, Greenman's
1937 map (adapted from Greenman 1937,
courtesy Ohio Historical Society)

cluded that South Park, even though it had no earthen embankments or ditches, was a Late Prehistoric fortified village similar to Tuttle Hill. Greenman must have assumed (though he never explicitly stated) that the absence of fortifications at South Park was the result of plowing that reduced or eliminated the earthworks, as was the case at Tuttle Hill. Since Tuttle Hill is one of Whittlesey's "forts," Greenman proposed a new cultural focus, named after Whittlesey, to which he assigned these two sites (Greenman 1937:351). The definition for Whittlesey-period sites thus became firmly established to mean Late Prehistoric fortified villages situated atop steeply sided promontories. Greenman drew up an extensive trait list (1937:357–366), based on topography and artifact assemblages. This allowed other researchers to identify additional sites belonging to his "Whittlesey Focus."

Excavations at other Whittlesey Focus sites (Greenman 1935a, 1935b, 1937; Morgan and Ellis 1943; Murphy 1971) produced similar material-culture remains, but did not recover adequate data on subsistence patterns, spatial organization, and site function. As noted by Belovich and Brose (1992:3), "With little evidence these sites were assumed to represent large fortified villages whose inhabitants focused on maize agriculture."

In the late 1960s, David S. Brose recognized that most of what was known about the Whittlesey Focus was based on Greenman's trait lists and untested assumptions derived from them (Brose 1973a and 1992). In an attempt to clarify the geographic and chronological boundaries of the Whittlesey Focus, Brose (1973a, 1992) conducted extensive excavations at the South Park site (33Cu8). These excavations uncovered many large refuse and storage pits, house patterns, and a rich artifact assemblage, and revealed evidence for long-term occupations spanning nearly seven hundred years. Within the midden, three stratigraphically distinct occupations were identified that suggested an increasing reliance on maize-bean-squash agriculture and eventual year-round village occupation.

The earliest occupation at the South Park site dates from A.D. 950 to 1250, the middle occupation from A.D. 1250 to 1450, and the latest occupation from A.D. 1550 to 1650 (Brose 1973a, 1992). The latter component included a single line of very large postmolds that ran across the southern edge of the site. The postmolds were 12–15 in (30–40 cm) in diameter and 40–60 in (100–150 cm) apart. Brose stated that "in the notes of some early collectors there were indications of a ditch and earthen wall which ran across the narrow neck of land to the southeast of the plateau," but his excavations failed to find any evidence for these earthen constructions (Brose 1973a:34). Given the postmolds and the clear similarities in topography and artifact assemblage to the Greenman-defined Whittlesey Focus, Brose (1973a, 1992) concluded that the line of posts represents a stockade or palisade and that the last occupation at South Park (A.D. 1550–A.D. 1560) was a large, year-round fortified agricultural village. Information on domestic structures, site patterning, ditch and earthen fortifications, ceramic and lithic assemblage, and seasonal scheduling led Brose to concur with the previous interpretations of Whittlesey period sites.

Brose (1976a, b; Brose et al. 1981) continued his research on the Whittlesey Tradition in the area of the Cuyahoga River Valley, conducting two important surveys between 1970 and 1981. A significant result of both surveys is that they located a number of sites that were not hilltop, fortified agricultural villages, but could be assigned to the Whittlesey Tradition based upon their ceramic and lithic assemblages. These surveys and the previous excavations led Brose (1992) to develop a new settlement model for the Whittlesey Tradition in northeast Ohio.

The investigations reported below help refine that model by demonstrating the fallacy of the long-held hypothesis that all hilltop enclosures were defensive, and that all of them can be assigned to the Whittlesey Tradition. This reinterpretation is based largely on data collected during excavations conducted at Whittlesey Fort No. 5, the Greenwood Village site (33Su92). Although the site initially was assigned to the Whittlesey Tradition because it was one of Whittlesey's "forts," detailed investigations at the Greenwood Village site proved that the original interpretation was in error.

History of Research at Greenwood Village, 1847–1982

The Greenwood Village site was recorded by Charles Whittlesey (1850:2) in 1847 and mentioned in his *Descriptions of Ancient Works in Ohio* (Whittlesey 1850) as "Work in Northfield, Summit County." Whittlesey described the site's geographic setting and called the work a "fortification." He mentioned the presence of three wells, two mounds, and five ditch/embankment lines:

> The engineers who selected the site of this fortification, understood very well the art of turning natural advantages to good account. . . . On all sides, the gulleys are from eighty to one hundred and ten feet deep. . . . The earth is as steep as it will stand; and, in fact, is subject to slides. . . . Before the ground was cultivated, the ditches are said by Milton Arthur, Esq., the owner of the land, to have been so deep that a man standing in them could not look over the wall.
>
> . . . In the gully on the north the water is permanent at all seasons, running over green shales and sandstones. . . . But the ancient inhabitants appear to have dug wells within the fort, at the points indicated by large black dots, which the old settlers say were stoned up, like our wells.. . . At the north end of the ditch of the *inner* wall, at the neck, there was a narrow space left as a passage into the work, but none in the outer wall. . . .

It is not very evident why a few rods of ground were cut off by lines at the south-west angle, nor why part of the ditch was made on the inside on the north and west.

It is very remarkable that, while all the works in northern Ohio are of a military character, there are no evidences of attacks by a foe, or of the destruction or overthrow of any of them. (Whittlesey 1850:17–18)

This description refers to an accompanying map that evidently was drawn by Whittlesey (fig. 9.3). Though generally accurate, it lacks specific details. For example, the narrow "hog back" is actually oriented east by northeast and not due east as shown. The long axis of the plateau is oriented northwest, and the Cuyahoga River and canal lie more to the west of the site than the map suggests. These inaccuracies reappear in all of Whittlesey's later maps. Inaccuracies notwithstanding, the 1850 map is the most accurate of all the maps Whittlesey published of the site.

In *Early History of Cleveland, Ohio*, Whittlesey (1867) describes the site in much the same fashion as before, with some new information, a little more detail, and minor rewording of his description and speculations. In this publication he refers to Greenwood Village as "Ancient Fort, Summit County." The relevant portions of the text read as follows:

A road leading west from the center to the river, passes along a very narrow ridge, or "hogs back," between two gullies, only wide enough for a highway. Before reaching the river bluffs, this neck of land expands right and left, where there is a level space of about two acres, elevated near two hundred feet above the canal and river. Where this area begins to widen out on the land side, there are two lines of banks, with exterior ditches, which are forty feet apart, and extend across the neck, without entrances or gateways. From the top of the breast work to the bottom of the ditch, is now from four to five feet.

. . . It is remarkable that there is, within this area, another set of lines on the side towards the river, reducing the fortified area to about one-half the space, whose edges are at the bluffs. Two projecting points are cut off by these lines, and left outside the works. In this way, much of the natural strength of the position is lost. . . . There are also two low mounds, *m, m,* on the east side. Where the bluff is not as steep as it is elsewhere, there is a parapet thrown up at the crest. A part of the earth on the north and west side, was taken from the inside, which indicates a state of siege, or at least some pressing haste when this part of the line was finished. Perhaps their enemies had gained a foothold in the level space outside the lines.

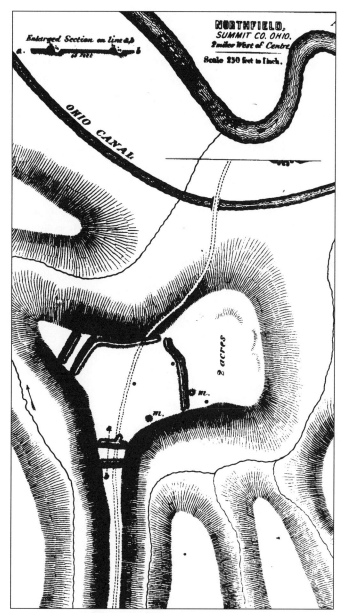

Fig. 9.3. Whittlesey's 1850 map of Fort No. 5, the Greenwood
Village site (33Su92) (reproduced from Belovich and
Brose 1992, courtesy of The Cleveland Museum of
Natural History)

... On the west side of the river is another ancient fortification, opposite this, and it is stated there is in the township of Independence, on the bluffs, north of Tinker's Creek, near its mouth, another work of the same character. There are no doubt others which are known to the inhabitants not yet surveyed or described. (Whittlesey 1867:36–39)

Four years later Whittlesey (1871) compiled all of his collected information on earthworks and aboriginal occupations in the Cuyahoga River Valley in *Ancient Earth Forts of the Cuyahoga Valley, Ohio*, and assigned formal names to the many earthworks he recorded. Because all of these sites included some type of earthwork (ditches, enclosures, embankments, or mounds), Whittlesey called them "forts" and numbered them in order. Greenwood Village is identified as "Fort No. 5."

The fort "on the bluffs, north of Tinker's Creek, near its mouth," briefly mentioned in the last paragraph of the 1867 publication, is not mentioned in the 1871 summary. I believe this cryptic notation refers to Fort No. 4, which is actually located on the south side of Tinker's Creek. Raymond Baby and students from Case Western Reserve University relocated Fort No. 4 in 1946 and renamed it the Russell site (33Cu10). Their map places the site on the floodplain south of Tinker's Creek instead of on the bluff as Whittlesey stated. In 1971 field crews directed by Brose collected Adena-like materials from the area indicated by Whittlesey's 1871 map (but not his 1867 description) as the location of Fort No. 4. At that time, the site was named the Soldat Mound and Village site (33Cu20). After limited field reconnaissance of this area in 1995, I concluded that the Soldat Mound and Village site probably was Whittlesey Fort No. 4. In 1995 the National Park Service permitted a local university to conduct excavations at the site. A report on this work has recently been completed, but as yet it is not available from the Park Service (Finney 1997). Field testing of the area identified by Baby in 1946 as the location of Fort No. 4 also needs to be done before it can be determined which location actually is Fort No. 4.

Sometime after the survey of 1847, and after the 1850 and 1867 publications, Whittlesey became aware of the existence of "caches" on an adjacent ridgetop to the south of Greenwood Village (Fort No. 5). He combines a description of these caches with a new description and map of the Greenwood Village site (fig. 9.4) in his 1871 publication (Whittlesey 1871:12–13):

> When this fort was surveyed in 1847, the ancient pits across the ravine on the east were not known. Mr. L. Austin, of this city, first apprised me of their existence and went with me to the spot. I cannot say that there is any connection or relation between them and the fort. There are similar pits but more regular and circular in and around the space A, which were regarded by the early settlers as wells, because most of them contained water.

. . . With the assistance of Messrs. A. B. and Lorin Bliss, of Northfield, I made trenches through some of those. . . . No relics, ashes or charcoal was discovered in them, such as are invariably found in the ancient pit dwellings of England. My present conviction is that they are caches, and the work of the red men.

Referring back to Fort No. 5, he states:

Along the sharp ridge or "hogs back," *ee*, there is barely room for a single team to pass. On this side there was no gateway or entrance, but at the west end of the inner parapet, there was a very narrow passage around it. The main entrance was evidently from the river side, near where the present road ascends the hill. Inside the lines the ground was much richer than without them. The mounds are small, and have not been explored. Pieces of flint, pottery and wrought stone implements, are numerous in the space A. They are of the Indian type. The caches at B C, are on a level with the fort, and the ravine between them is sixty and seventy feet deep. As their strongest apprehensions of attack were from the country side, it is not probable that the fortress would have its magazines so far away, more than fifty rods distant, in an exposed position, beyond a very difficult gulf. As the present red race have made similar pits for storing their corn, and wild rice, it is reasonable to attribute all works of that kind to them. But in no instance, have the northern tribes been known to have occupied earth forts at, the period when they were first known to the whites, and rarely if ever since. We must therefore regard the forts, as the work of a different and older race.

The map accompanying the 1871 text was extensively modified (fig. 9.4) from that of 1850. The western extension to the innermost embankment crossing the narrow hogback entrance to the site disappeared completely. Whittlesey also changed the orientation of the Ohio Erie Canal and the Cuyahoga River to flow east, and the north arrow now pointed east. The shape of the plateau was changed, as were the spatial relationships between the embankments. Finally, the arrangement of the mounds was changed and their number increased from two to three. As Belovich and Brose noted (1992:6), "These revisions seem so extensive that it is clear that Whittlesey not only never revisited the site, but he even failed to revisit his own notes apparently drawing the later maps from memory, if he drew them at all."

In 1970 Brose conducted a systematic, environmentally stratified, archaeological survey of northeast Ohio (Brose 1973a, 1976a, and 1976b). One of the sampling quadrants tested encompassed four plateaus along the western bluffs of the Cuyahoga River on properties then owned by the Greenwood Village Development Company. Limited field testing produced cultural material characteristic of the Whittlesey Tradition (Belovich and Brose 1983; Belovich 1985a; Belovich and Brose 1992). Artifacts and site-patterning data suggested that the Greenwood Village site was a complex of three or four ridges containing a small fortified agricultural village, with small hunting or gathering camps located on the adjacent ridges (Brose 1973a, 1976a, and 1976b). Brose (1973a, 1992) thought the Greenwood Village complex represented a fall-through-spring occupation between A.D. 1300 and A.D. 1400—relatively late in the Whittlesey period.[1]

In 1979 Brose and Belovich surveyed the 32,000-acre Cuyahoga Valley National Recreation Area (CVNRA) for the National Park Service (Brose et al. 1981). A goal was to identify and relocate Whittlesey "forts" and earthworks within the CVNRA boundaries. The literature review and examination of historical maps showed that five of Whittlesey's nine forts (Nos. 4, 5, 6, 7, and 9) and one earthwork (No. 8) lay within park boundaries, and that the plateau Brose labeled Greenwood Village "West" in 1971 very likely was Whittlesey Fort No. 5. Field testing of this plateau proved disappointing. Only three of the ten shovel tests yielded artifacts, none of which were diagnostic. Dense vegetation prevented observation of any earthworks. Of the five "forts" initially identified within park boundaries, only Nos. 5 and 7 and earthwork No. 8 could be located. (See Belovich 1985a for more detail.)

In 1982 Brose and I obtained permission from the National Park Service to test Whittlesey Fort No. 5 with the expectation that testing one of these "forts" could further understanding of the defensive nature of these sites.

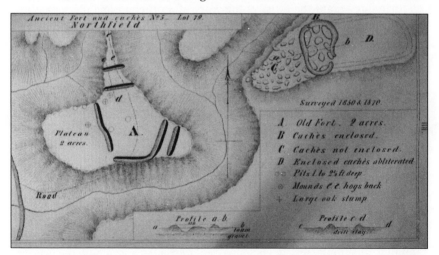

Fig. 9.4. Whittlesey's 1871 map of Fort No. 5, the Greenwood Village site (33Su92).

Naming and numbering problems were sorted out (see Belovich 1985a), and the official designation for the site, first discovered by Whittlesey in 1847, became 33Su92, the Greenwood Village site.

The Greenwood Village Site

Based on its location on an isolated plateau and the presence of extensive earthworks and ditches, the Greenwood Village site, like so many other Whittlesey sites, was assumed to be a Late Prehistoric fortified agricultural village. To test this assumption, four areas of the site were investigated (fig. 9.3): the eastern narrow entrance to the site; the area inside the lines where "the ground was much richer" (Whittlesey 1871:13); the inner ditch/embankment line, which reduced "the fortified area to about one-half" (Whittlesey 1867:38); and the areas outside the lines, where Whittlesey noted the ground was not as "rich" (Belovich 1985a; Belovich and Brose 1992).

Excavations and Features

The excavations in 1983 and 1984 revealed that one of only two clearly identifiable ditch/embankment lines was the innermost one along the southern point of the plateau. All others appeared to have deteriorated (Belovich 1985a). While no mounds were observed, undulations across the eastern narrow hogback possibly represented the exterior ditch/embankment line recorded by Whittlesey. Portions of the "highway" reported by Whittlesey as passing through the site from east to west, and down the western slope to the Ohio Erie Canal, were clearly visible (Belovich 1985a:33). Subsequent literature and map searches established that this narrow path was a roadway in 1838 (Brose et al. 1981); today it is a nature trail, constructed and maintained by the National Park Service.

The twenty-four test units at the Greenwood Village site encompassed approximately 77 m² (fig. 9.5) and revealed sixteen features (Belovich 1985a; Belovich and Brose 1992). Limited excavation outside the earthwork yielded little cultural material and no features, confirming Whittlesey's (1871:13) observation that "Inside the lines the ground was much richer than without them."

Most of the features within the enclosure were hearths that were shallow, basin shaped, and rock filled. Similar features were recorded at the Bugai site (Halsey 1976) and the early Late Woodland Lichliter site near Dayton, Ohio (Allman 1957). Very few postmolds, no house patterns, and no midden or habitation debris indicative of long-term village occupation were found (Belovich 1985a and 1985b; Belovich and Brose 1992). Three features require further elaboration. Features 6 and 10 were located within the enclosure, while Feature 3 was part of the eastern ditch and embankment line.

Feature 6, a cluster of over 200 pottery sherds, contained the fragments of a nearly complete, Fairport Harbor Cordmarked, *var.* Willoughby vessel (fig. 9.6) (Brose 1992). This vessel may have broken while sitting in a shallow pit or depression on the ground surface (Belovich 1985a; Belovich and Brose 1992).

Feature 10 lay no more than a meter east of Feature 6 and was about 2 m in diameter and nearly a meter deep. The six layers identified within this bowl-shaped firepit were composed of dark brown silts mixed with charcoal. The sides and base were lined with a thin layer of burned, red-orange, silty glacial gravels. Only four pieces of lithic debitage were recovered from this great firepit, but pottery was plentiful. Most sherds were cordmarked and grit tempered, although two were fabric marked and five had decorated rims. Feature 10 also yielded burned soils, dense charcoal deposits, nearly 300 kg (657 lb) of fire-cracked rock, and samples suitable for radiocarbon and thermoluminescence dating. No botanical remains were recovered, and the bone fragments were exceedingly small (Belovich 1985a).

Feature 3 was a prepared rock pavement encountered at one of the undulations crossing the eastern narrow hogback entrance to the site. Work in this area revealed the undulation to be the innermost of two lines of ditches and

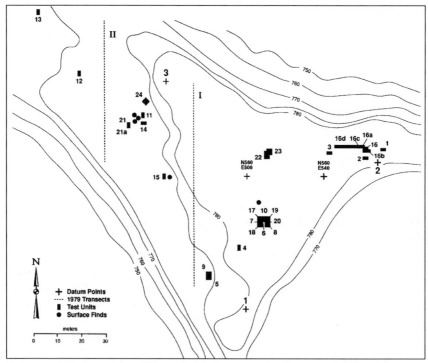

Fig. 9.5. 1983–1984 map of the excavated areas at the Greenwood Village site (33Su92) (adapted from Belovich 1985a).

embankments that Whittlesey recorded (fig. 9.3). The aboriginal ditch lay to the east and adjacent to the embankment. Feature 3 is 20–25 cm thick along its entire length and consists of cobbles and tabular, sedimentary sandstones and shales, none larger than 30 x 17 cm. The stone probably was gathered from the streambeds at the base of the plateau (Whittlesey 1850). The cobbles usually lay on their flat sides overlying a silty-sand, glacial till matrix 15–30 cm in thickness (see Belovich 1985a:fig. 11 and plate 5). Similar stones lay along the eastern slope of the embankment, some at increasing depths within the ditch. I believe they were used as facing to retard erosion along the eastern, outer slope of the embankment. The glacial till, silty-sand glacial till matrix, and the prepared rock pavement together formed a very stable foundation for the embankment. Feature 3 was less than 2.5 m wide, corresponding to the width of the base of the embankment. No evidence of a palisade was observed (Belovich 1985a; Belovich and Brose 1992).

Test units showed that the prepared rock pavement continued for an additional 9.1 m (nearly 30 ft) to the west and the construction remained the same (Belovich 1985a:figs. 12 and 13 and plate 6). Whittlesey's 1850 map indicates a western extension to the embankment, but this extension is obscured or not illustrated on his later maps (Whittlesey 1867, 1871). In 1850 Whittlesey (1850:18) stated that "At the north end of the ditch of the *inner* wall, at the neck, there was a narrow space left as a passage into the work, but none in the outer wall," but later he noted that "there are two lines of banks with exterior ditches . . . [that] extend across the neck, without entrances or gateways" (Whittlesey 1867:38). In 1871 Whittlesey (1871:13) stated that "On this side there was no gateway or entrance, but at the west end of the inner parapet, there was a very narrow passage around it." He further notes that "The main entrance was evidently from the river side, near where the present road ascends the hill" (Whittlesey 1871:13). Examination of Whittlesey's text and maps suggests that there were two gateways or entrances into the site. The first was a very narrow space providing passage "around" the northern end of the inner embankment. The second was the "main entrance," which was an opening located on the river side of the enclosure where two ditch/embankment lines converged.

Whittlesey's memory lapses notwithstanding, the western extension of the prepared rock pavement seems to be an additional passage into the enclosure. This extension formed a pedestrian walkway or ramp leading into the main habitation area on the plateau, and the rock found within the ditch represents facing for controlling erosion. Figure 9.7 shows a reconstruction of Feature 3 (Belovich 1985a, 1985b; Belovich and Brose 1992).

The few postmolds identified at the site contained no cultural material, but all were located within the enclosure near or adjacent to features assignable to

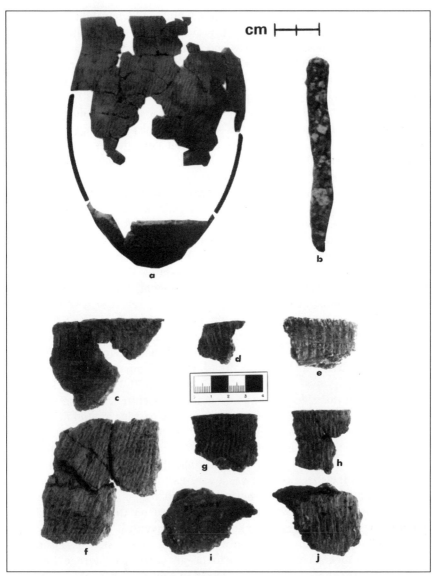

Fig. 9.6. Grit-tempered ceramics from the Greenwood Village site (33Su92): *a*, reconstructed Fairport Harbor Cordmarked *var. Willoughby* pottery vessel from Feature 6; *b*, cross section of vessel rim showing large grit-tempering; *c–e*, cordmarked sherds with two to four horizontal incisions; *f*, fabric-marked body sherd; *g–h*, cordmarked rim sherds; *i–j*, horizontal cordmarked interior and vertical marked exterior body sherd (*a* and *b* adapted from Belovich and Brose 1992, Fig. 7).

the primary occupation at the site. The posts may have supported windbreaks, spits, or drying racks for the firepits with which they are associated.

Artifacts

The Greenwood Village lithic assemblage contains artifact types that occur across Ohio, Indiana, Illinois, Michigan, Kentucky, West Virginia, and western Pennsylvania and New York, in contexts dating from Middle Woodland to Late Woodland times (Schatz 1957; Allman 1957, 1961; Converse 1963, 1984; Prufer 1965, 1967, 1981; Reidhead and Limp 1974; Halsey 1976; Oplinger 1981; Ormerod 1983; Belovich 1985a; Justice 1987; Shott 1990). Of particular interest are the projectile points and shale discs and knives (Allman 1957, 1961; Halsey 1976; Oehler 1950; Belovich 1985a; Justice 1987).

The 89 chipped-stone artifacts include 6 cores, 22 bifacial tools or fragments, 9 scrapers, 2 drills, 1 perforator, and 24 projectile points or fragments. Most projectile points fall into two typological categories: "fishspears" and a Chesser Notched/Anthony Side Notched/Lowe Flared Base projectile point cluster (fig. 9.8) (Belovich 1985a; Justice 1987). The "fishspears" are small, crudely flaked points with diamond or humpbacked cross sections (Prufer 1967; Converse 1963 and 1984). Several points resemble Chesser Notched (Prufer 1967; Justice 1987), Lowe Flared Base (Reidhead and Limp 1974; Justice 1987), and Anthony Side Notched (A. Lee 1986); these types are very similar and are characterized by shallow side notches, weak shoulders, and square or narrowly rounded tangs (Belovich 1985a). While the dating of "fishspears" is problematic (Prufer 1967; Converse 1963, 1984; Belovich 1985a; Justice 1987), the Chesser Notched/Anthony Side Notched/Lowe Flared Base projectile point cluster dates to between A.D. 300 and A.D. 700 (e.g., Belovich 1985a; Converse 1963, 1984; Justice 1987; Prufer 1967). The 25 slate and groundstone tools include knives, hoes, discs, celts, picks, abraders, hammerstones, cupstones, and grinding stones (Belovich 1985a:plates 11–15) (fig. 9.9).

Of the 714 pottery sherds, over 97 percent are grit-tempered; a few limestone-tempered sherds are present. The predominant surface treatment is cordmarking (n = 410), with a medium-to-coarse cordage that is usually vertically oriented (see fig. 9.6). The surface treatment of the remaining sherds was either fabric marking (2 percent) or indeterminate (41 percent) (Belovich 1985a).

Vessels are simple subconoidal forms, with weak shoulders, straight necks, and flat to slightly rounded lips. Decoration is rare, but when present consists of two to four thin, weak, discontinuous incisions that cross-cut the cordmarking at the neck (see fig. 9.6 c–e) (Belovich 1985a). The vessel recovered from Feature 6 (fig. 9.6a) cannot be completely reconstructed but is 26 cm in diameter and held an estimated 7077.7 cc.

A thermoluminescence assay on similar sherds from the Stanford Knoll site (33Su99) yielded a date of A.D. 620, while a radiocarbon determination placed virtually indistinguishable ceramics as early as A.D. 235 (A. Lee 1986).

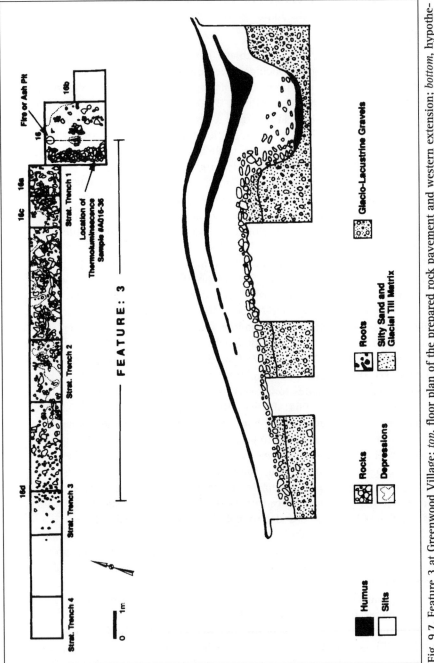

Fig. 9.7. Feature 3 at Greenwood Village: *top*, floor plan of the prepared rock pavement and western extension; *bottom*, hypothesized reconstruction of innermost ditch and embankment line (adapted from Belovich and Brose 1992, Figs. 9 and 10).

This non-earthwork site is located on a terrace of the Cuyahoga River about four miles south of Greenwood Village. Similar ceramics are also found at the Columbia Road Village site (33Su87), situated on a high plateau along the west bank of the Cuyahoga River (Belovich and Brose 1982). Earthen constructions are not known at this site, but two radiocarbon assays place the site between A.D. 780 and A.D. 1000.

The Greenwood Village ceramics are also similar to several types found at Late Woodland sites throughout Ohio, Michigan, Indiana, western Pennsylvania, New York, and Kentucky (see Belovich 1985a and Belovich and Brose 1992), and variously called Fairport Harbor Cordmarked (Belovich and Brose 1983; Brose 1985), Cuyahoga Cordmarked (Brose and Scarry 1976), Newtown Cordmarked (Oehler 1950; McMichael 1984), Peters Cordmarked (Prufer 1967), Mixter Cordmarked (Shane 1967), Wayne Cordmarked (Fitting 1964), Watson and Mahoning Cordmarked (Mayer-Oakes 1955), or Jack's Reef Corded (Ritchie 1965). Greenwood Village ceramics are most closely related to several types found within northeastern Ohio, specifically Fairport Harbor Cordmarked, *var. Willoughby* (Brose 1985, 1992), and Cuyahoga Cordmarked (Brose and Scarry 1976; Brose 1985). Fairport Harbor Cordmarked dates as early as A.D. 900 (Brose 1985), while Cuyahoga Cordmarked is an earlier type perhaps dating as early as A.D. 600 (Brose and Scarry 1976:185). Some sherds from Greenwood Village are similar to ceramics recovered from the earliest levels at the South Park site, where they date between A.D. 950 and A.D. 1250 (Brose 1973a, 1985, 1992).

Based on the ceramics, the major period of occupation at the Greenwood Village site probably occurred between A.D. 235 and A.D. 1000, which is much earlier than the A.D. 1100 to A.D. 1550 timespan for Whittlesey sites (Brose 1992, 1976a; Whittlesey 1850, 1867, 1871; Greenman 1935a, 1935b, 1937; Morgan and Ellis 1943).

Chronology

There are two sets of radiometric assays for the Greenwood Village site (Belovich 1985a). Five samples were collected from layers within Feature 10 and one from near Feature 10. Three thermoluminescence dates obtained by Alpha Analytic on ceramic sherds suggest an occupation date between A.D. 540 and A.D. 1010; the associated standard deviations range from 170 to 210 years. One of the three radiocarbon determinations (DIC-3072) clearly is aberrant; at two sigma, the associated calibrated date is A.D. 887(1020)1178. The two Beta Analytic assays are fairly compatible and at two sigma suggest an age between A.D. 426 and 973 (calibrated). The cordmarked, grit-tempered ceramics from Feature 3 (the rock pavement) are identical to those recovered from Feature 10, so the temporal placement of the earthwork is secure.

For northeastern Ohio, the Late Woodland period lasts from approximately

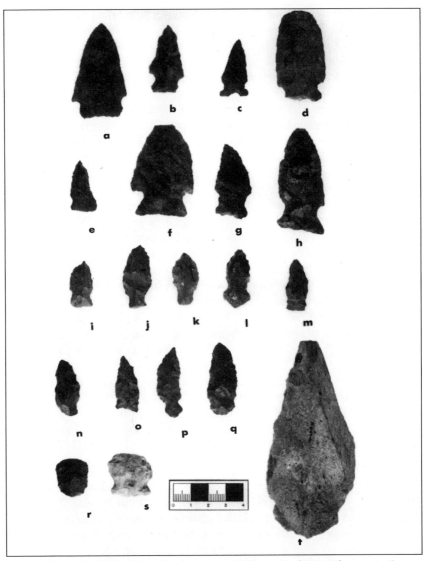

Fig. 9.8. Projectile points from the Greenwood Village site (33Su92): *a–c*, Anthony side-notched projectile points; *d*, side-notched hafter scraper made from an Anthony side-notched projectile point; *e*, reworked projectile point with single, shallow side notch, similar to Lowe flared or Chesser notched types; *f*, corner-notched projectile point similar to Lowe flared type; *g–h*, Chesser notched projectile points; *i–q*, small projectile points with diamond-shaped or humpbacked cross sections, similar to "fishspears"; *r*, thumbnail scraper; *s*, corner-notched, hafted end scraper; *t*, large biface.

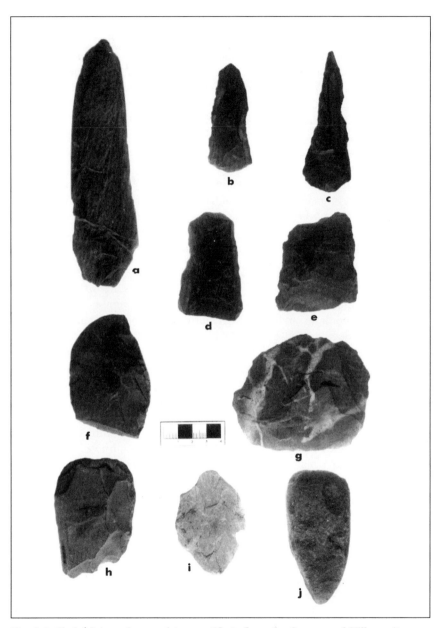

Fig. 9.9. Shale/slate and groundstone artifacts from the Greenwood Village site (33Su92): *a*, lanceolate shale/slate knife; *b–c*, unifacial shale/slate scrapers; *d–e*, triangular shale/slate knives; *f–g*, shale/slate discs; *h*, hoe; *i*, sandstone sinker; *j*, groundstone celt or axe.

A.D. 500 to A.D. 1650. Sites attributed to the period are usually large, fortified agricultural villages. Radiometric dating of these prehistoric villages places them toward the end of the Late Woodland, between A.D. 950 and A.D. 1650. Only within the last few decades have sites attributed to the earlier part of the Late Woodland period (approximately A.D. 500 to A.D. 950) been recognized throughout Ohio, West Virginia, and Kentucky (Brose and Scarry 1976; Belovich and Brose 1983; Belovich 1985a, b; Lee 1986; Dancey 1988; Shott 1990). Although these were once thought to be similar to the later agricultural village sites, clear differences between them in features and artifact assemblages are now recognized.

Based on the dates for Greenwood Village, the Whittlesey Tradition can now be limited to a shorter time span (Brose 1992). The earlier sites are now viewed as early Late Woodland—that is, approximately A.D. 500 to 900 (see Dancey 1988:224). Radiometric dates from Greenwood Village firmly place the site within this early Late Woodland time frame.

Site Function

Functional interpretations of early Late Woodland sites are difficult because these sites contain artifacts and structural elements common to both terminal Middle Woodland and Late Prehistoric sites. The existence of hilltop enclosures is documented for the Middle Woodland period (Riordan 1995; Essenpreis and Moseley 1984), while hilltop, "fortified" agricultural villages have been considered the hallmark for the later Whittlesey Tradition (Greenman 1935b, 1937; Brose 1992). Thus, topographic setting alone is not a useful indicator of possible site function.

In the case of the Greenwood Village site, precious little data suggests a defensive fortification. Indeed, except for its plateau location, all of the evidence from Greenwood Village suggests a nonmilitary purpose. The location on a steeply sided plateau and the presence of extensive earthworks and ditches is what initially led Whittlesey (and others) to make an argument for a fortified village, but a critical review of this evidence serves more to discount the fortification theory than to support it. In fact, even Whittlesey (1850:17) observed weaknesses in its defenses. The entire plateau is not encircled by earthworks. Whittlesey noted that whoever constructed the "fort" "understood very well the art of turning natural advantages to good account," but he also observed that "It is not very evident why a few rods of ground were cut off by lines at the south-west angle, nor why part of the ditch was made on the inside on the north and west" (Whittlesey 1850:17–18). Whittlesey (1867:36–39) suggested that this "indicates a state of siege, or at least some pressing haste when this part of the line was finished. Perhaps their enemies had gained a foothold in the level space outside the lines." But if this was the case, where is the habitation debris that surely would have accompanied a group of individuals living inside the walls of a fort? And where is the evidence for a fight or a siege? The absence of habitation debris was discussed above, but there is absolutely no debris or the slightest evidence for the destruction or razing of the earthworks. Whittlesey (1850:18) also noted that "It is very remarkable that, while all the works in northern Ohio are of a military character, there are no evidences of attacks by a foe, or of the destruction or overthrow of any of them." That observation is telling, but more than a hundred years would pass before alternative explanations for these hilltop enclosures would even begin to be explored.

Another weakness in the fortification interpretation is the fact that Whittlesey (1850 and 1871) notes two passages into the work. One entrance is at the northwest corner of the enclosure (according to Whittlesey's 1850 map), where two ditch/embankment lines converge. The other opening is on the east side of the site, at the northern end of the innermost embankment, where a "narrow passage . . . [went] around it" (Whittlesey 1871:13). In addition to these breaches in the site's "defenses," excavations documented a pedestrian ramp leading into the main enclosure. To construct a ramp from the embankment into the interior of the enclosure appears to be more of a welcoming gesture than a defensive one. Rock pavements and foundations similar to those found at Greenwood Village are also recorded at the Pollock Works and Fort Ancient, both of which are interpreted as serving nonmilitary, nondefensive functions (Riordan 1982, 1995, and this volume; Essenpreis and Moseley 1984:20).

Two additional features of the earthworks at Greenwood Village that support a nondefensive function are the absence of a palisade and, as mentioned above, the presence of an interior ditch along one of the embankments. The interior ditch would not only be of little use to the defenders of the "fort" but the embankment in front of the ditch would actually assist any foe by providing them with the high ground from which to make their assault. This interior ditch also ran along an embankment that cut the plateau approximately in half. "In this way," Whittlesey noted (1867:39), ". . . much of the natural strength of the position is lost." It is difficult to imagine how such a large area could be defended without a sturdy stockade. At Pollock Works, Riordan (1995) observed that the absence of postmolds (indicating palisades) within embankments, and the presence of openings or gateways through the embankments and internal ditches along the length of some of them, negates the notion that these earthworks and the sites they enclose were defensive fortifications.

The scant evidence of domestic use begs questions about how many defenders there were—perhaps not even enough to patrol the perimeter defined by the ditch/embankment lines. Within the enclosure at Greenwood Village there is no evidence for long-term or intensive occupation (Belovich

1985a). Faunal remains are rare; only a few, small, unidentifiable pieces of burned bone were recovered. No botanical remains were recovered. There are no deep storage pits, midden or village debris, or evidence (such as feature overlap) of more than a single occupation. Almost all of the cultural features identified at Greenwood Village are shallow firepits.

In addition to the sparse occupation debris and the absence of a midden zone, there are no house patterns or burials. The Greenwood Village site does not appear to be unique in this regard. Two other sites in northeastern Ohio, Fort Hill (A. Lee and Belovich 1985) and Windsor Fort (A. Lee 1987), also have earthen embankments and ditches, but few artifacts and no evidence for a deep village midden.

Mounds are also reported at the Greenwood Village site, one inside and one outside the enclosure. Construction of embankments, ditches, and mounds would have required considerable time and energy, as would the transport of stone required to construct the foundations, ramps, and facings. While it is usually assumed that these types of construction activities would have required the cooperation and organization of a fairly large group of people, this is not necessarily the case. Shott (1990) discusses ethnographic research (Gorecki 1985) documenting the construction of a ditch measuring 2 m wide, 2 m deep, and 300 m long by only one to six individuals with a limited investment of time and effort. Large corporate groups are not a prerequisite for embankments, ditches, or small mounds.

Shott (1990) also presents a detailed review of some Late Woodland habitation sites in the middle Ohio Valley. Of the twelve Late Woodland sites he discusses, eight are securely early Late Woodland and none were hilltop enclosures. Only four of these open-air settlements had ditches, only three contained associated embankments (two of which were presumed), and none had a palisade. This lack of defensive works does not provide convincing evidence for a social environment in turmoil and human groups in need of defenses.

The artifact assemblage and radiometric dates unequivocally place the Greenwood Village site within the early Late Woodland period. The absence of evidence for domestic activities, including middens (deep or otherwise), storage pits, or postmold patterns suggestive of any type of building, and the absence of any faunal or botanical remains fails to support a village interpretation.

An interpretation more compatible with the data from Greenwood Village and other similar early Late Woodland hilltop enclosures is that the earthworks define important religious or social spaces (Clay 1985; Essenpreis and Moseley 1984; Riordan 1995, and this volume). It may now be possible to identify at least two functionally different early Late Woodland site types: hilltop enclosures and open-air settlements. Hilltop enclosures would function as ceremonial or social gathering spaces. The open-air settlements, located at or near sources of fresh water, would be villages for closely related kin groups. These kin groups would gather at the hilltop enclosures for their religious or social activities. Greenwood Village provides an example of such an early Late Woodland hilltop enclosure, while sites such as Childers (Shott 1990) and Water Plant (Dancey 1988) are examples of open-air settlements. A ditch or ditch and embankment surrounding an open-air village certainly would not be required but, when present, might be interpreted as a way of establishing a religious or social connection with the hilltop sites.

Traditions of mound and earthwork construction, initiated during the Early Woodland, continued through the Middle and Late Woodland periods, well into the Whittlesey period (Belovich 1986). Classic Hopewell ceremonialism ended by no later than A.D. 500. Although the "interaction sphere" and participation in trade networks for exotic materials and artifacts waned, the Woodland societies still existed. Kin groups occupying nearby villages continued to establish special areas like Greenwood Village upon which to construct earthworks, build mounds, and perform rituals. Ceremonies and social gatherings may have been maintained in a much modified form. Adapting to changes over time, such as the lack of exotica formerly provided by the Hopewell Interaction Sphere (Brose 1974; Brose et al. 1981), or changes in the significance and meaning that these items once held, may have changed early Late Woodland ceremonialism considerably from that of the preceding Middle Woodland period.

Rituals and ceremonies themselves do not preserve, so we are limited to the tangible material culture that is recoverable through archaeological investigation. We thus are limited in our ability to discover subtle changes in the use of sites that structurally do not appear to change. We cannot know, for example, the specific activities that occurred at each and every enclosure. Were they religious, political, or social in character? While we do not know the specific social activities or religious rituals that took place at sites like Greenwood Village, we can discern that the activities were not related to military activities. Rather, the earthworks were likely to have defined a significant space or symbolically expressed group identity.

Summary

One of the most important tasks in archaeology is to relocate archaeological sites discovered and reported in the distant past. In this way mysteries are solved, old records and files are cleaned up, and new knowledge is obtained. This task was undertaken for the Greenwood Village site. Careful analysis of site structure, features, artifacts, and radiometric dates allowed a test of the assumption that all hilltop enclosures in northeast Ohio represent fortified agricultural villages dating very late in prehistory. Data obtained from the Greenwood Village site clearly are not consistent with a Whittlesey-period placement, nor with the site's classifiction as a fortified agricultural village.

The ceramics and lithics from the Greenwood Village site are inconsistent with a Late Prehistoric age, but rather reflect an occupation dating between A.D. 600 and 800. Surfaces on ceramics are usually cordmarked, and coarse grit-tempering predominates. Vessel forms are simple subconoidal shapes, with weak shoulders, straight necks, and flat to slightly rounded lips. Decoration is rare. In contrast, ceramics common to Whittlesey Tradition sites have considerable decoration and rim treatment with many types and subtypes.

The lithic assemblage from Greenwood Village contains early Late Woodland diagnostics, such as slate discs and knives, and projectile points attributed to the Chesser Notched/Lowe Flared Base/Anthony Side Notched cluster. Small, crudely flaked points with diamond or humpbacked cross sections, generally referred to as "fishspears," are also common. This assemblage contrasts with those of Whittlesey sites, which are usually characterized by small triangular Levanna and Madison points.

Subsurface features at Greenwood Village are characterized by small, shallow hearths that are basin shaped and rock filled. All of the feature types identified at Greenwood Village are common to early Late Woodland sites. In contrast, typical features identified at Whittlesey sites are large, deep storage pits, postmolds indicating house patterns, thick midden deposits, prepared firepits, and cooking hearths. Finally, six radiometric dates corroborate all the other evidence by placing the occupation of the Greenwood Village site at about A.D. 750.

Besides being located on a high plateau with very definite natural boundaries, portions of Greenwood Village are outlined by a series of ditches and embankments. While embankments and ditches seem to bring to mind visions of forts and territories to be defended, the absence of a palisade, the variability of ditch placement, and the presence of gateways and rock-paved entrance ramps clearly indicate that the Greenwood Village earthworks did not function as a fortification. In contrast, embankments and ditch constructions at Whittlesey sites are known (or presumed) to be associated with palisades (Morgan and Ellis 1943; Greenman 1935a, 1935b; Brose 1992). They also lack interior ditches, paved-rock entrance ramps, or openings and gateways through their earthen walls.

The findings at the Greenwood Village site have implications for interpretations of other presumed Whittlesey hilltop enclosures. Additional research at sites similar to Greenwood Village is necessary before we can obtain a clear picture of the early Late Woodland period and its role in the transition from Middle Woodland horticulture to Whittlesey Tradition agriculture. Other Whittlesey "forts" must be relocated and tested before definitive statements can be made regarding their specific cultural placement. A good place to start might be an investigation of Fort Nos. 4 and 7, and earth-work No. 8, as well as "the west side of the river" where Whittlesey (1867) recorded "another ancient fortification." At the very least, it should be antic-ipated that such investigations will provide further evidence that not all hill-top enclosures are defensive forts and that all should not be uncritically assigned to the Late Prehistoric Whittlesey Tradition.

Notes

Most of the events discussed here took place in the early to mid-1980s, when Dr. David S. Brose was department head and Mr. Alfred M. Lee and I were associate curators of archaeology at The Cleveland Museum of Natural History. This project was no different from any other in that its successful completion was due to the contributions of many organizations and individuals.

Thanks go first to the National Park Service's Midwest Archaeological Center for granting permission to conduct excavations at the site. I also wish to thank Jan Dial-Jones of the Center for loaning field forms and artifacts for me to review.

Catherine Hovey, my highly skilled and good-humored field supervisor, deserves special mention. Her contributions were innumerable. The efforts of Sean Coughlin, David McNickle, Dennis Griffin, Laura Pompignano, Judy Placko, Andrew Kovalcik, Daniel Krumlauf, and Mark Ohlberg were of particular importance during the research. Several illustrations were modified and reproduced courtesy of The Cleveland Museum of Natural History and The Ohio Historical Society, while much-appreciated photographic assistance came from RPM and Harald of Photoguy Products, Inc.

I wish to thank Randall Boedy for his observations and helpful discussions, Jeff Richner for useful information, and the reviewers for their suggestions and comments. Their input improved the manuscript. Without the support of David Brose, this research could not have been accomplished. Finally, I wish to extend my gratitude to Robert Mainfort and Lynne Sullivan. Their encouragement, prompt response to queries, and patience have made preparation of this chapter a pleasant experience.

1. Confusion surrounds the location of the 1971 excavations of the Greenwood Village site that led Brose to these conclusions. The 1971 materials were quite extensive and must have come from a site with not only much better preservation than was present at Greenwood Village, but with much more cultural debris and extensive midden deposits as well. The 1971 survey investigated four adjacent plateaus, which were labeled Greenwood Village "North," "South," "East," and "West" (Belovich and Brose 1983). Greenwood Village West is the Greenwood Village discussed in this chapter and is considered to be Whittlesey Fort No. 5. The Whittlesey materials recovered in 1971 are not associated with the construction of the earthworks and ditches at the enclosure, nor do they represent any significant occupation within it. The Whittlesey-period materials recovered in 1971 probably came from Greenwood Village North, South, or even East (Belovich 1985a:184–185; Brose 1992).

Chapter 10

The Socioeconomic Role of Late Woodland Enclosures in Northern Lower Michigan

Claire McHale Milner and John M. O'Shea

Earthwork enclosures throughout the world are typically interpreted as defensive fortifications or ceremonial structures. The former function is proposed when earthen walls are surrounded by deep ditches and topped by wooden palisades to deter attackers. The latter function may be expressed by the enclosure's special form, construction techniques, or location (Belovich and Brose 1992; Belovich, this volume). In both cases, it is argued that the considerable effort to build them demonstrates their significance to survival, either as a means to withstand attack or to propitiate sacred beings through ritual.

The same has been said for the hundreds of enclosures within Michigan (Fitting 1975; Hinsdale 1925, 1931; Quimby 1965). Speculation about the function of earthwork enclosures in the Great Lakes region began in the nineteenth century (Leach 1885; Thomas 1894). Early in the twentieth century, Hinsdale (1925, 1931) reported that over one hundred enclosures existed in Michigan. Some of these enigmatic structures were the focus of one of the first archaeological dissertations at the University of Michigan (Greenman 1927a).

Despite such long-standing interest in Michigan earthworks, surprisingly little is known about their age, contents, and role in the lives of the people who constructed them. With few exceptions (Krakker 1983), earthworks are seldom placed in broader social contexts. They are often treated as unique finds rather than as part of settlement systems. Despite their dramatic appeal, few Michigan earthworks have been extensively tested by professional archaeologists. Even their existence often cannot be confirmed due to a high rate of destruction and initial misidentification.

In this chapter we investigate the role of the northernmost Michigan enclosures constructed during the Late Woodland period (fig. 10.1). This cluster of earthworks includes three on the Missaukee County preserve, four along the Rifle River and the Walters-Linsenman Earthwork in Ogemaw County, and the Mikado Earthwork in Alcona County.[1] Reanalysis of the Mikado Earthwork in the light of new data from nearby habitation sites suggests that these enclosures were neither fortified villages nor exclusively ceremonial structures. Instead, they were places for trade between social groups that had access to different resources.

We then address the changing role of Michigan earthworks throughout their existence. These earthworks are distributed across diverse environments and social landscapes. They are found in lowland coastal settings as well as the high plains interior, and from the southern Carolinian to the northern Canadian biomes (fig. 10.2). When earthworks were constructed, cultural systems also varied widely, from nomadic foragers to settled agriculturalists. This variability, however, does not preclude a common thread linking many enclosures involving their role in demarcating the social landscape.

Previous Interpretations

Despite variation in age, location, and cultural context, most researchers have assumed that all Michigan enclosures were fortifications. Krakker (1983:376) argues that the presence of earthworks in southeastern Michigan indicates an increase in raiding among populations, particularly after A.D. 1350, due to population growth and agricultural intensification. He carefully restricts this

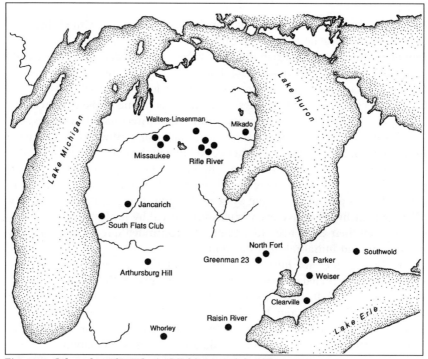

Fig. 10.1. Selected earthworks in Michigan and Ontario.

interpretation to the southeastern Michigan examples, pointing out that the average size difference between southern and northern earthworks implies regional differences in earthwork function or population size (Krakker 1983:441). There is no consideration of alternative interpretations, perhaps because so little is known about the southeastern Michigan earthworks.

In a similar vein, Cleland (1966:33) argues that the earthworks in northern Lower Michigan were fortifications. He asserts that they were inhabited by agriculturalists who moved into the climatically less favorable north during warmer conditions prior to A.D. 1300. Built to fend off attacks from local hunter-gatherers who were defending scarce resources, these outposts were abandoned by the invaders with the onset of cooler, moister conditions and declining agricultural yields after the fifteenth century. Cleland based this model on early historic reports of intertribal conflict along the Carolinian-Canadian ecozone border farther west (Hickerson 1962).

The excavator of the Mikado Earthwork (Carruthers 1969:288–290) dismisses competition between southern agriculturalists and northern hunters over scarce resources but agrees that the northern earthworks were defensive. Protective earthworks were built as agriculturalists expanded into new terri-

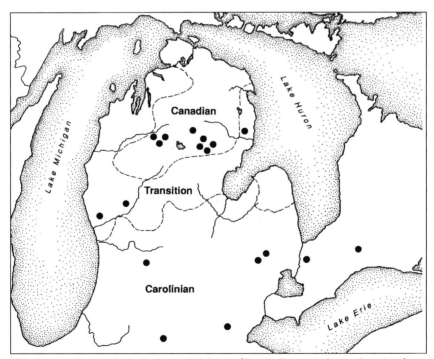

Fig. 10.2. Biotic provinces in Lower Michigan (dots indicate enclosure locations).

tories, a process that inevitably followed increased reliance on agriculture throughout the Great Lakes. To account for the diversity of ceramic styles at Mikado, Carruthers argues that the northern enclosures were used by agricultural groups drawing people that practiced different ceramic traditions from the north and south.

The exception to the prevailing defense model for earthworks throughout Michigan is the interpretation of the eleventh-century Whorley Earthwork in Branch County. Low debris density, numerous and wide gaps, an enigmatic post arrangement, a large empty space, and the absence of an exterior moat led Speth (1966) to argue that Whorley was built for ceremonies that required periodic cleaning of a central plaza. In addition, a 270-foot gap in the earthwork along a creek makes the earthwork accessible by canoe. Interestingly, Whorley, like Mikado, is one of the few earthworks that has been tested by professional archaeologists.

Because South Flats Club Earthwork in Muskegon County did not have a palisade, Quimby (1965) suggested that it may have been a ceremonial structure. He argued that such a conclusion would only be warranted if the earthwork proved to be Middle rather than Late Woodland in age. In other words, he assumed that ceremonial activity involving earthen construction was restricted to Hopewell and that earthworks built by Late Woodland peoples were defensive.

Recent work in Ohio, the heartland of Hopewell activity, counters this chronological presumption. Some Ohio earthworks dating from A.D. 800 to A.D. 1200 contain structural features built with Middle Woodland–like construction techniques. They also lack palisades and evidence for long-term occupation and have numerous gates and single-use fire pits. Belovich and Brose (1992) argue that these earthworks represent a continuation of Middle Woodland earthwork construction for ceremonial purposes and are not fortified villages. Obviously, proof of age and formal similarities are insufficient to establish earthwork function.

Antiquity of the Earthworks

Most of the defense models are grounded in the assumption that all of the Michigan earthworks are a Late Woodland phenomenon. Radiocarbon dates and ceramics have shown that many Michigan earthworks were constructed from about A.D. 900 to A.D. 1500 (table 10.1). Recently, however, Scott Beld (1993, 1994) conducted excavations at the Arthursburg Hill Earthwork in Ionia County, Michigan, which yielded Early Woodland ceramics, thus extending enclosure construction back about a millennium.

The precise age and cultural affiliation of most Michigan earthworks are uncertain. Only those earthworks with either radiocarbon dates or ceramic data are listed in table 10.1. Of the 17 vessels that have been recovered from three Rifle River earthworks, some fit late Younge-phase types, which suggests a thirteenth-century age and cultural ties to southeastern Michigan. Obviously, the Rifle River assemblages are too small to date accurately within the Late Woodland period. In contrast, the larger Mikado assemblage contains some similar types, but has a wider diversity of materials and a fifteenth-century radiocarbon date, suggesting that it is later than the Rifle River enclosures. Rifle River III, however, yielded scalloped-lip vessels that may be roughly contemporaneous with the Mikado assemblage. Despite scarce data, it appears that some, if not all, of the northern earthworks date to the Late Woodland period and may be contemporaneous with the securely dated Mikado earthwork.

The Northern Lower Michigan Case Study

Despite alternative proposals and shaky chronological control, it has been assumed that the only northerly earthwork in Michigan to be extensively tested was a fortification. Mikado Earthwork lies within a heavily dissected morainic landscape sixteen miles west of Lake Huron along a tributary of the Pine River in northeastern Lower Michigan. The site was investigated by Greenman (1927a) in 1926, followed by amateur tests in 1957 (Moll, Moll, and Cornelius 1958). Carruthers (1969) worked at Mikado as part of the Edge Area study by the University of Michigan Museum of Anthropology in 1966 (Fitting 1966).

Perched on a steep bluff above a creek and a mixed conifer swamp, the earthwork is roughly circular and encompasses about 84,000 square feet. The exterior ditch is cut by eight intermittent gaps or entrances, although some gaps may be recent in origin. Postmolds on top of the wall indicate that a palisade had been placed on top of the earthwork. Approximately 1900 square feet of excavations exposed three hearths, each associated with a cluster of pits, postmolds, and debris.

In the 1960s little was known about the late prehistory of northern Lower Michigan, making it difficult to assess the site's cultural and historical significance. As a result, Mikado's ceramic assemblage was linked primarily to the Wolf phase of the well-known southeastern Michigan Younge Tradition, although ties with Ontario, northwest Ohio, New York, and Wisconsin were recognized (Carruthers 1969).

Another twenty years lapsed before a reassessment of Mikado was possible. In the 1980s, the University of Michigan excavated several contemporaneous sites within 30 miles of Mikado Earthwork (O'Shea and Milner n.d.). A fifteenth-century radiocarbon date and stylistic parallels with the habitation-site ceramics confirm that Mikado was occupied during the late Juntunen

Table 10.1. Ages of selected Michigan and Ontario earthworks

Site	County	Date	Temporal phases/ceramic types	References
Mikado	Alcona	A.D. 1450±100 (M-777)	Late Juntunen/Wolf phases	Carruthers 1969; Milner and O'Shea 1990
Rifle River I	Ogemaw		Younge phase/Riviere ware	Dustin 1932; Hinsdale 1931
Rifle River II	Ogemaw		Younge phase/Macomb Linear	Dustin 1932
Rifle River III	Ogemaw		Peninsular Woodland	Dustin 1932; Brose 1978
Rifle River IV	Ogemaw			Dustin 1932
Boven/Missaukee III	Missaukee	A.D. 1470±100 (M-100)	Peninsular Woodland	Greenman 1927b; Gibson and Herrick 1957; Hinsdale 1924; Moll, Moll, and Cornelius 1958; Brose 1978
Missaukee I	Missaukee	A.D. 1200[a]		Same as above
Missaukee II	Missaukee	A.D. 1200[a]		Same as above
Walters-Linsenman	Ogemaw	A.D. 1350±75 (M-779)		Cornelius and Moll 1961; Brose 1978
Whorley	Branch	A.D. 1080±100 (M-1758)		Speth 1966
South Flats Club	Muskegon	A.D. 960	early Late Woodland?	Quimby 1965
Arthursburg Hill	Ionia		Early Woodland?	Beld 1993, 1994
Jancarich	Newaygo		early Late Woodland?	Prahl 1966
North Fort	Macomb	A.D. 1350±70 (Beta-4074)	Wolf phase	Greenman 1927a; Krakker 1983
Southwold	Ontario		Late Ontario Iroquois	G. Wright 1966
Parker	Ontario		Wolf phase	T. Lee 1958
Weiser	Ontario		Wolf phase	Kroon 1972

a. A 1200±75 (M-790) radiocarbon date was recovered from a mound near the Missaukee earthworks (Fitting 1975:177). The relationship of this mound to the Missaukee earthworks is unknown, but a Late Woodland age for their construction is possible, given that one of the earthworks is within 600 feet of the mound (UMMA site files).

phase that extends from A.D. 1400 into the early seventeenth century (Milner and O'Shea 1990). The Mikado Earthwork lies along the southern margin of the Juntunen ceramic tradition, which stretches from northern Lower Michigan into the Lakes Superior and Huron basins.

Although comparisons are limited by differing scales of investigations and perhaps seasonality of occupations, the late-Juntunen-phase habitation sites provide the means to evaluate the special-purpose nature of Mikado (fig. 10.3). These sites include two single-component sites (Gordon-McVeigh and Hampsher) and three multicomponent sites (Scott, Robb, and Gaging Station) with late Juntunen components. A special-purpose site, Black River Cache, furnishes additional evidence for the organization of Late Prehistoric populations in northern Lower Michigan.

Internal Evidence from Mikado

Aspects of Mikado's earthwork cast doubt on a fortification interpretation. The exterior ditch is cut by eight gaps that vary in width from 12 to 40 feet and occur at irregular intervals, varying from 55 to 170 feet. There is also a lengthy opening of 155 feet without wall or ditch. Numerous large breaches

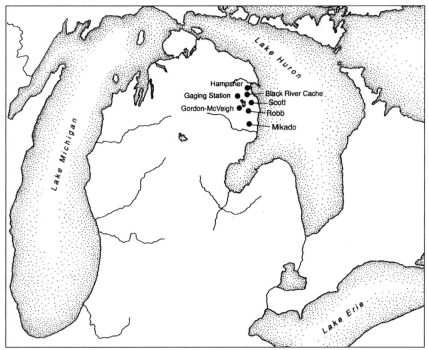

Fig. 10.3. Locations of late-Juntunen-phase sites in northeastern Lower Michigan.

would not have provided much protection, although the longest unfortified gap occurs at a steep gully and wooden palisades crossed at least some of the openings. Unfortunately, the original number and size of entrances is uncertain due to erosion.

If Mikado was a fortified village established in hostile territory, an intensive occupation by a large group of people might be expected. The perimeter is over 1000 feet long and would require many warriors to defend the community. Excavations, however, yielded few artifacts and features considering that the earthwork encloses 84,000 square feet. A total of 34 features and approximately 1300 artifacts were recovered.

The lack of storage pits, houses, middens, and extensive feature superpositioning points to a short-term, low-density, special-purpose occupation rather than a long-term fortified village. Three hearths were associated with clusters of pits, usually containing little debris. Although there are postmolds, no house pattern was discernible. The only superpositioning among features occurred in Areas B and D, where several pits were covered with debris from nearby hearths (Carruthers 1969:244, 250).

Carruthers (1969:227) suggests that some of the pit features were not related to domestic activities; rather, they were borrow or stump-removal pits dug during construction of the embankment and excavation of the outlying ditch. In fact, he argues that most of the occupation occurred during earthwork construction, with little or no evidence of subsequent occupation. Finally, although the area around the earthwork was not tested, refuse was not visible in a nearby gully, a natural place for depositing waste.

In contrast, structures at three of the nearby habitation sites are indicated by posts, contents, and soil texture. At the Scott and Gaging Station sites, there are several large, irregularly shaped living floors consisting of compacted layers of trampled artifacts, burned bones, and ash. Posts and hearths occur in the vicinity of these enigmatic features. Evidence for a structure is clearest at the Gordon-McVeigh site. A large post and an adjacent hearth were found at the base of a thick midden. Although the entire perimeter of the structure was not uncovered, some smaller posts were found along one edge (O'Shea and Milner n.d.). From the nature of these features, it is obvious that nearby contemporaneous sites were more intensively occupied than the Mikado Earthwork.

Carruthers (1969:265) claims that the density of ceramic vessels at Mikado was low relative to densities at other Late Woodland sites but does not provide comparative data. Our research demonstrates that the densities of features, vessels, and lithics at Mikado fall below densities at the habitation sites in northern Lower Michigan (table 10.2). Admittedly, Scott, Robb, and Gaging Station data are suspect because these sites were occupied over a longer span of time, extending back into the Middle Woodland at the Gaging

Table 10.2. Occupation density at northeastern Lower Michigan sites

Site	Excavated (m²)	Features/m²	Features	Vessels/m²	Vessels	Lithics/m²	Lithics
Mikado (all)[a]	177	0.2	34	0.2	33	1.5	264
Mikado (inside)[a]	115	0.3	34	0.3	33	2.3	264
Scott	67	0.4	24	0.4	29	37.8	2532
Hampsher[b]	23.5	0.3	8	1.5	35	10.2	239
Gaging Station	33	0.5	15	0.8	27	103.3	3409
Gordon-McVeigh	11	0.5	5	2.8	31	15.5	170
Robb	23	0.3	7	--	--	225.2	5180

a. The calculations for Mikado (all) include materials from the earthwork itself. Since habitation debris would not be present on the earthwork, densities for features, vessels, and lithics were also calculated using only excavation units placed inside the earthwork (Mikado [inside]).
b. Only vessels from the Hampsher site found by the University of Michigan are included. The area figure pertains to the University of Michigan's excavations.

Station and Robb sites. Interestingly, however, the densities at Mikado are significantly lower than those from the single-component, late-Juntunen-phase site, Gordon-McVeigh. These results run counter to the expectation, given the constricted spatial nature of earthworks, that densities of debris and features should be higher at Mikado than at open-air sites.

Based on minor feature superpositioning and the diversity of ceramic styles, Carruthers raises the possibility that Mikado was occupied more than once. Most vessel types at Mikado, however, are found in association with each other at the single-component sites. The diversity that Carruthers claims, in fact, is less marked in light of a regional appraisal of late-Juntunen-phase assemblages (Milner 1992, 1994). Homogeneity in paste, color, temper, and construction method further supports a single-component occupation. A concentration of pottery and clay lumps in and around a large hearth in Area B may indicate pottery manufacture at the site (Carruthers 1969:235–238). If people lived at Mikado more than once, reoccupations must have occurred over relatively short periods of time.

Although these data do not support occupation by a large group of people or of long duration, the occupants went to considerable effort to build a large enclosure. Several other lines of evidence, however, call the fortified-village interpretation into question. First, large areas within the earthwork contained few artifacts and no features. These areas were either intentionally swept clean, or not used, or activities occurred there that did not generate domestic refuse (Carruthers 1969:262).

Second, the ceramic assemblage from Mikado Earthwork differs in terms of vessel function from the nearby habitation sites in unexpected ways. Sixty percent of vessels are encrusted with food residues, a direct marker of cooking. This percentage is higher at Mikado than at other Juntunen-phase habitation sites with the exception of the Hampsher site (table 10.3). There are no breaks in the distribution of rim diameters that suggest functionally distinct vessel sizes. However, although rim diameter range and mean are consistent with other Juntunen-phase assemblages, there are several vessels with rim diameters less than 10 cm at Mikado that do not occur on other sites. These differences may indicate that vessels were being used more frequently at Mikado for cooking and serving food rather than for storage or other domestic chores.

Alternatively, the occupation at Mikado may have been short lived, which would account for the limited range of activities using pots. This latter interpretation would then apply to the site most similar to Mikado in terms of vessel function. The Hampsher site would not have been occupied year-round. Because of its location on an exposed ridge on Thunder Bay, off Lake Huron, people would have abandoned the site during the cold, windy

winters. It also has shallow deposits and no evidence of substantial structures, and was probably occupied seasonally.

Lithic data also distinguish Mikado from the habitation sites. Not only
is there a comparatively small lithic assemblage, but there are fewer tools or
cores at Mikado than at the habitation sites (table 10.4). Only 2 percent of
the Mikado lithic assemblage consists of tools or cores, whereas these artifact classes constitute 6 to 10 percent of the habitation sites' assemblages.
These data point to a brief stay at Mikado resulting in only light maintenance activities, rather than a long-term occupation that generated many
tools.

In addition, the Mikado lithic assemblage is distinguished from the other
assemblages by the frequencies of different raw-material types (table 10.5).
The Mikado assemblage is dominated by Bayport chert, which outcrops in
the Saginaw Bay region to the south. In contrast, local cherts, including a
lower-quality chert called Northern Gray and cherts extracted from high-

Table 10.3. Comparison of ceramic assemblages
in northeastern Lower Michigan

| | Rim Diameter (cm) | | | Cooking residue | |
Site	Range	Mean	N	%	N
Mikado	5–27	18.9	15	62	30
Hampsher	9–29	18.3	22	67	39
Scott	12–31	18.6	14	31	29
Gaging Station	12–30	18.9	10	22	27
Gordon-McVeigh	10–27	16.1	10	19	21

Table 10.4. Comparison of lithic assemblages
in northeastern Lower Michigan

Site	% debitage	% cores/tools
Mikado	98	2
Hampsher	90	10
Scott	94	6
Gaging Station	90	10
Gordon-McVeigh	90	10
Robb	94	6

quality nodules found in the glacial till, are proportionately more significant at the nearby habitation sites. With the exception of the rare Norwood chert, Bayport chert is a higher-quality raw material than the locally available materials. The inhabitants at Mikado transported high-quality raw materials from the south or acquired them through exchange rather than scrounged for them in the local till during a prolonged stay at the site.

Because Mikado is closer to Bayport chert sources than the other sites, it is not surprising that Bayport chert is well represented in the Mikado assemblage. Based on the distribution of lithic types at sites throughout eastern Michigan, the decline in the proportion of Bayport chert is not gradual but falls dramatically from nearly 100 percent at sites near the northernmost outcrop of Bayport near Oscoda, Michigan, to 20–40 percent at sites to the north around Hubbard Lake and Thunder Bay. Only the proportion of Bayport at Mikado Earthwork falls in between these amounts, suggesting that raw materials were being moved from both north and south to the site.

Subsistence remains further hint at a unique site function. Mikado yielded over 400 fragments of the corn plant, the largest sample of corn ever found in a northern Michigan site. The recovery of stem and husk fragments indicates that corn was produced locally rather than transported from far away, and the small cob size points to marginal growing conditions (Ford 1974). While the Mikado corn may not have been grown at the site, considering the site's poor soils and its location away from Lake Huron's ameliorating effect, it certainly was produced in this region.

External Relationships

The complex web of ties between Mikado and a number of populations, as suggested by ceramic attributes, is also inconsistent with expectations for fortifications. If the enclosure was built by local populations for protection, the

Table 10.5. Raw material percentages in northeastern Lower Michigan sites

	Percentages of raw material types				
Sites	Bayport	Northern Gray	Norwood	High quality glacial	Other
Mikado	77	4	0	2	22
Hampsher	22	10	1	44	23
Scott	40	33	1	12	14
Gaging Station	20	49	2	13	16
Gordon-McVeigh	28	22	2	25	23
Robb	31	66	2	0	1

ceramic assemblages of Mikado and the nearby habitation sites should have been very similar. If Mikado was occupied by an intrusive population, the material culture should be distinctive from that manufactured at nearby settlements and comparable to the southeastern Younge Tradition. In both cases, a boundary between populations should be marked in media such as ceramics, particularly if hostile conditions were pervasive enough to require the construction of defenses.

A comparison of the ceramic assemblages of Mikado and surrounding sites does not fit either defense scenario. The Mikado ceramic assemblage shares numerous stylistic traits with nearby late-Juntunen-phase sites' assemblages. The proportions of numerous attributes of Mikado pottery are most closely matched by those at Hampsher (see table 10.4). The remarkable similarity in the complex design layouts on vessels from the Mikado and Hampsher sites may indicate direct contact (fig. 10.4).

The Mikado ceramic assemblage, however, is distinguished from most other late-Juntunen-phase assemblage materials not by unique characteristics but by contrastive frequencies of certain attributes. Mikado has lower frequencies of interior and neck decoration, and generally higher frequencies

Table 10.6. Attribute percentages of Late Juntunen Phase ceramic assemblages

Site	Interior decoration %	N	Neck decoration %	N	Brushed-on exterior %	N	Parallel lip %	N	Peaked cast. %	N	Cord motif %	N
Mikado	22.2	27	23.1	13	26.7	30	52.2	23	21.1	19	64.3	28
Hampsher	44.4	36	55.6	27	0	38	18.5	27	5.3	19	52.6	38
Scott	52.4	21	83.3	18	0	24	5.9	17	27.3	11	10.7	28
Gaging Station	60.0	20	71.4	14	0	27	17.4	23	0	15	29.6	27
Gordon-McVeigh	41.2	17	66.7	9	5.3	19	16.7	12	0	5	33.3	21

Table 10.7. Juntunen Phase vessel attributes

Site	Mean rim (cm) Height	N	Thickness	N	Smooth surface %	N
Mikado	2.44	18	83.7	17	96.7	30
Hampsher	2.06	24	84.9	25	97.4	38
Scott	2.35	12	75.9	17	70.8	24
Gaging Station	2.22	11	92.7	11	85.2	27
Gordon-McVeigh	2.11	9	79.3	12	94.7	19

of brushed-on exterior surfaces, parallel lip decoration, peaked castellations, and cord-impressed motifs than any other assemblage (table 10.6). Some of these characteristics are found in southeastern Michigan assemblages, although the cord-impressed motifs that dominate the Mikado assemblage occur only in minor amounts in that area (Krakker 1983:156). Furthermore, Mikado lacks Parker Festooned vessels, the ubiquitous horizon marker of southeastern Michigan Wolf phase sites. Interestingly, most of the traits shared with the Younge Tradition are precisely the attributes that distinguish the late Juntunen (A.D. 1400–A.D. 1620) from the early Juntunen (A.D. 1200–A.D. 1400) subphases, particularly in northeastern Lower Michigan (Milner and O'Shea 1990).

Stylistic attributes of the Mikado assemblage indicate ties to other populations. Certain motifs replicate Late Ontario Iroquois motifs, although they are executed with different decorative techniques. For instance, the short collars decorated with parallel vertical or oblique lines made with cord are found on otherwise late Juntunen vessels and are similar to the collar size and motifs on Huron or Lawson Incised vessels. One Mikado vessel is decorated with a fillet, an element that does not appear on other Juntunen-phase vessels. The chevron motif, ware, and form of this vessel, however, are typical of the Juntunen phase. Fillets occur from the fourteenth into the seventeenth centuries in a number of ceramic traditions, including the Younge Tradition of Ohio, Michigan, and Ontario, and the Whittlesey Focus of Ohio and Pennsylvania (Bettarel and Smith 1973; Krakker 1983; C. Murphy and Ferris 1990).

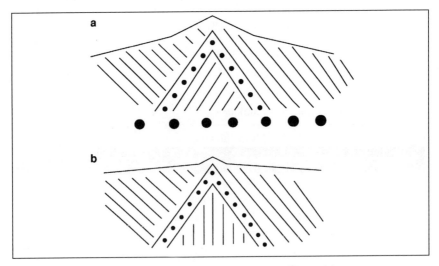

Fig. 10.4. Pottery designs from the Hampsher (a) and Mikado (b) sites.

The uniqueness of the Mikado assemblage is not due as much to unusual traits as to the mixing of Juntunen and non-Juntunen characteristics on single vessels. The vessels with traits obviously derived from other traditions were constructed with sandy clays found in local moraine deposits and fired under the same conditions as the rest of the assemblage, suggesting local production of most if not all vessels. Furthermore, the distinctive characteristics are added to vessels with shapes, sizes, and surface treatments consistent with late Juntunen assemblages (table 10.7).

The observed stylistic similarities and differences signify varying levels of interaction within and outside northern Lower Michigan, particularly with southern agricultural groups. The remarkable matches between Hampsher and Mikado vessels indicate close contact, but there are sufficient stylistic differences between the Mikado assemblage and the other habitation sites to cast doubt that Mikado was occupied by these populations alone. Interaction with southeastern Michigan was so significant that the shared attributes define the late Juntunen phase for northeastern Lower Michigan. The Mikado assemblage, however, lacks many Wolf phase characteristics that would support the idea that Mikado was inhabited by Younge Tradition invaders. There is also evidence for more distant contact to the south and east. Finally, despite the stylistic diversity drawn from other traditions, the Mikado pottery was locally made.

This melding of stylistic markers drawn from different traditions obviously requires a different explanation than has been proposed by the two defense scenarios. People from different areas may have been placing their unique stylistic markers on pottery while participating in joint activities at the Mikado Earthwork, perhaps including pottery manufacture. A cursory look at other Michigan earthworks may shed light on the possible nature of these activities.

Evidence from Other Late Prehistoric Earthworks

The other northern earthworks share characteristics with Mikado that are not consistent with fortifications (table 10.8). They have at least four wide breaches through their embankments, although it is often difficult to determine their original number and size because of the impact of lumbering and erosion. The Rifle River IV enclosure has a 206-foot gap adjacent to a swamp, making it accessible to the outside. Habitation debris is scarce in and around most of the earthworks relative to their large size. If Mikado were the only earthwork to have little debris, it could be considered an isolated case of construction followed by rapid abandonment. In most cases, however, few lithics, ceramics, or fire-cracked rock were recovered. Although few of the earthworks have been tested and it is difficult to observe objects on their

Table 10.8. Dimensions of northeastern Michigan enclosures[a]

Site	Dimensions (ft)	Area (ft²)	Circum. (ft)	Height (ft)	Gap #	Gap Size (ft)	Stockade
Mikado	360 x 350	97,818	1108	6	8	12–155	yes
Rifle River I	208 x 186	30,465	609	5–7	3–6	12	no
Rifle River II	314 x 280	69,244	930	5–7	4–6	15	no
Rifle River III	190 x 139	21,242	541	7	4–6	––	no
Rifle River IV	202 x 145	23,630	408	5–6	2–3	206	no
Boven/Missaukee III	165 x 160	20,728	500	5/6–8	––	––	unknown
Missaukee I	195 x 177	27,158	558	5	2	––	unknown
Missaukee II	151 x 182	21,762	529	5	2	––	unknown
Walters-Linsenman	226 x 200	35,614	688	4–5	4	––	yes

a. Earthwork areas were computed by using the average of the two dimensions. Applied consistently, this method should produce comparable figures of relative area, even if individual estimates are somewhat inaccurate. There are divergent reports on the size of some earthworks. One report claims that Rifle River IV was 216 x 212 feet in size. Carruthers claims Mikado is approximately 84,000 square feet, whereas Fitting claims 96,000. We recalculated the size to make the Mikado estimate consistent with the other earthwork estimates.

overgrown surfaces, it is telling that little debris is found at many earthworks.

Their inaccessible locations (inland amidst dissected topography) seems to support a defensive interpretation. But they are not consistently placed on high ground, as shown by two low-lying earthworks in Missaukee County (Hinsdale 1925:73). The enclosures were not built in areas rich in resources and conducive to food production, nor were they always close to water. Because they were not good places for carrying out daily subsistence activities, inhabitants were vulnerable to attack while collecting distant resources. If fearful enough of attack to build earthworks, people would have stayed nearby for safety; yet there are no known habitation sites near the earthworks.

Also suggestive are the approximately 75 cache pits lying within 600 feet of the Missaukee I Earthwork (Hinsdale 1925:83). If these pits are storage facilities for the inhabitants, it is unclear why they would be located outside of the earthwork's protective perimeter. No cache sites have been found near other enclosures, although this may be due to a lack of recognition of these sites and the low density of archaeological surveys in the area. Furthermore, the identification of archaeological sites has been hampered by the density of secondary forest growth and minimal development in northern Lower Michigan; as a result, the discovery of archaeological sites is an infrequent event (Lovis and O'Shea 1993). Recently, the University of Michigan (O'Shea and Milner n.d.) and the U.S. Forest Service, among others, have located many more cache sites than were known previously in northeastern lower Michigan. Excavations at one such site, Black River Cache, yielded pits found in discrete clusters. Fragments from two late-Juntunen-phase vessels that share many traits with Mikado vessels were also recovered.

Finally, there is evidence to suggest that the northern earthworks fulfilled a different role than earthworks farther south in Michigan. Krakker (1983:441) pointed out that the northern earthworks are on average smaller than the southern earthworks. Based on rough estimates of their area, the mean size of northern enclosures is 38,629 square feet[2] and the mean area of the southern earthworks is 77,877 square feet (tables 10.8 and 10.9). Only two northern earthworks exceed 40,000 square feet, whereas only two southern earthworks are smaller in area. The smaller size of the northern examples does not diminish the effort needed to build the earthworks, and their size is still disproportionate relative to their meager contents. It does suggest, however, that the two sets of earthworks may have been used for different purposes.

One northern earthwork appears to be quite different. According to Cornelius and Moll (1961), there were at least nineteen central-post subrectangular structures with associated storage pits within the Walters-Linsenman enclosure. This earthwork yielded a date of A.D. 1350, placing it within the temporal distribution of the northern earthworks. Its size also falls within the range for the northern sites. Despite these formal and temporal similarities, Walters-Linsenman may have been a fortified village, if the brief description is accurate. In addition to the evidence for intensive site use, this site's cultural affiliation may also differ from neighboring earthworks. Brose (1978:576) claims that the material culture points to ties with western Lower Michigan populations. This divergent case only serves to make the characteristics of the other northern earthworks more distinctive.

An Alternative Explanation for the Northern Lower Michigan Earthworks

Based on their structure, size, and location relative to topography and resources, and the types and densities of features and artifacts, these earthworks (with the exception, perhaps, of Walters-Linsenman) did not function primarily as fortifications, nor were they inhabited by a large group of people for a long time. There is also little evidence to support the argued ceremonial function. Although Mikado may have had an open plaza and may have been a short-term special-purpose camp, there are no other indications of specialized ceremonial activities. There are no distinctive ceremonial vessels, features, or other paraphernalia, although there are possible differences in vessel function between Mikado and the habitation assemblages.

Table 10.9. Size of selected Michigan and Ontario earthworks

Site	Dimensions (ft)	Area (ft^2)
North Fort[a]	--	52,272
Greenman 23[a]	--	143,748
Whorley	135 x 270 (1/2 circle)	45,300
Raisin River[a]	--	10,890
Greenman 24[a]	--	43,000
South Flats Club	90 x 90	6,359
Parker	330 x 174	49,850
Weiser[a]	--	217,800
Clearville	340 x 192	55,543
Southwold	390 x 330	101,736

a. For five of these earthworks only area, not dimensions, were reported.

A more parsimonious explanation can be found when the distributions of the northern earthworks across the physical and social landscapes are considered. These earthworks are located along two ecological boundaries. First, they were built at the headwaters of primary stream systems along the border between the high plains of central Michigan and the climatically ameliorated coastal lowlands. Second, they lie near the transition between the southern Carolinian and northern Canadian biotic provinces (see fig. 10.2).

The earthworks also are placed with respect to social territorial boundaries. They appear near the boundary between the Juntunen and Younge ceramic traditions. Although ceramic style cannot be simplistically equated with all cultural behavior, such a distinct break obviously marks a dramatic shift in interaction intensity. Furthermore, O'Shea (1988) has projected, based on estimated population densities and reconstructed subsistence systems, that Mikado falls on the border between two local settlement systems.

The distribution of earthworks, stylistic patterning of ceramics, possible association with cache pits, and the large quantity of corn suggest a third interpretation. The northern enclosures may have served as rendezvous points for the conduct of trade along the boundaries of the Juntunen territory. From this perspective, the mix of stylistic attributes is an expression of social identification between the Juntunen populations and the farming communities to the south as well as more distant populations. The cache pits were used to store food, probably including corn, and other goods extracted from diverse ecological settings to be exchanged between visiting partners. Such encounters were most likely brief and would have left few features or artifacts. Based on ethnographic descriptions of intertribal trade, such events occurred at the juncture of territories to facilitate access by outsiders (Jackson 1991).

The establishment of trading posts during the thirteenth through the fifteenth centuries may have been a response to increased frequency and severity of food shortages. The onset of cooler conditions associated with the Little Ice Age could have triggered such shortages in the northern Lower Peninsula of Michigan as early as the thirteenth century, considering that agriculture in that region under "normal" conditions was a risky undertaking. Northern populations offset increased subsistence risk by establishing safe places for the regular exchange of food and other goods.

Interestingly, the construction of Mikado and the stylistic shift marking interaction to the south occurs at the same time as a possible fifteenth-century increase in the local population of northeastern Lower Michigan (Milner and O'Shea 1990). Perhaps this settlement shift is related to an increasing emphasis on interaction with southern farming communities.

The Changing Role of Michigan Earthworks

Without better data, we cannot detail the changing role of earthworks in Michigan over time. There are clues, however, that formally similar enclosures built during the Early and Middle Woodland periods also were involved in the social demarcation of the landscape and the integration of regional populations, but within very different cultural contexts.

The recent discovery of an Early Woodland enclosure extends earthwork construction back in time. Mound construction is frequent during the Middle Woodland period, but there are no known Middle Woodland enclosures in Michigan. However, although lacking a built-up earthen base, the circular palisade at the Schultz site in the Saginaw Bay region may be a Middle Woodland formal equivalent to the later enclosures (Fitting 1972). Schultz is considered to be a site where mobile foragers seasonally aggregated. It is located at the center of a rich environment where a large group of people could live for an extended period of time and from where foragers dispersed to small winter camps.

The central placement of these aggregation sites relative to resources and territories differs from the location of the northern Late Woodland enclosures along social and environmental boundaries. These latter marginal locations were chosen because they were neutral locations, a kind of no-man's land, that were visited in comparative safety by people exchanging goods and building social alliances. We would therefore argue that the specific function of some earthworks changed during the Woodland period from that of a seasonal focus for Early and Middle Woodland dispersed foragers to that of a neutral trade rendezvous locality placed at boundaries between major Late Woodland social divisions.

We are not proposing that Michigan earthworks never served defensive or ceremonial roles. Krakker (1983) makes a strong argument for increasing competition that led to the Late Prehistoric construction of fortifications in southeastern Michigan. Ritual probably played an important role in integrating regional populations during the early phases of enclosure construction and in permitting successful interchange among different populations later. Ethnographic examples of the embedding of economic exchange in social and ceremonial activities abound. Trade took place at special sites along with feasting, dancing, and matchmaking. All of these activities promoted social solidarity among participating peoples by providing a shared symbolic milieu in which to operate, physically marked by the earthworks themselves (Jackson 1991). Ritual, however, was not the only motivation for earthwork construction.

The interpretation of the northern Late Woodland earthworks as trading posts is consistent with a variety of data, including the location of the earthworks relative to social and ecological boundaries, a shift in settlement distribution, and comparisons of lithic and ceramic data from habitation and earthwork sites. Constructed at a time when northern populations may have faced food shortages brought on by the Little Ice Age, the earthworks may have provided a safe haven for the exchange of critical resources between socially distant populations.

Notes

1. There is confusion over the original number of earthworks in these counties. Two site numbers have been given to earthworks in Alcona County, but O'Shea and Milner (n.d.) have demonstrated that they refer to only one enclosure. More than five earthworks in Missaukee County and nine earthworks in Ogemaw County have been reported. Only those earthworks for which there are consistent reports of location, size, and contents will be used for this study.

2. The mean size of the northern enclosures decreases further if the small enclosure (20NE115) near the Jancarich site is included (Prahl 1966). With an approximate area of 1256 square feet, this possible Late Woodland enclosure is the smallest such structure in Michigan. Considering its small size relative to other known enclosures, further exploration is needed to confirm its existence.

Chapter 11

Fortified Village or Mortuary Site?

Exploring the Use of the Ripley Site

Sarah W. Neusius, Lynne P. Sullivan, Phillip D. Neusius, and Claire McHale Milner

Archaeologists report many Late Prehistoric earthwork sites in the lower Great Lakes region. These sites, which stretch from northern Ohio through northwestern Pennsylvania, into western and central New York, and to the St. Lawrence River Valley (Belovich and Brose 1992; Cheney 1859; Edson 1875, 1894; Labar 1968; Larkin 1880; Parker 1907, 1922; Ritchie 1928; I. Smith and Herbstritt 1976; Squier 1851; Sullivan et al. 1995; Thomas 1894; Whittlesey 1871), contain embankments forming enclosures or walls across natural promontories. Most of the earthworks themselves and many of the sites were obliterated during the nineteenth and early twentieth centuries, but the interpretation of this group of sites remains an important task in understanding the cultural history of the region.

Located at the edge of Lake Erie in Chautauqua County, New York (see fig. 1.1), the Ripley site has been the focus of our research in southwestern New York State since 1987 (Sullivan et al. 1995; Sullivan 1996). The site originally contained a small oval or C-shaped enclosure, truncated by the Lake Erie shoreline (fig. 11.1); this earthwork was plowed down during the nineteenth century. The Ripley site has figured prominently in regional archaeology since 1907, when Arthur Parker published a report of his 1906 excavations (Parker 1907).

Parker interpreted the site as a single-component, protohistoric Erie Indian village and cemetery. All subsequent discussions of Erie archaeology refer to the Ripley site as a significant Erie village (e.g., White 1978; Widmer and Webster 1981). MacNeish (1952) even used the site as the type site for Erie pottery.

Our reanalysis of existing collections, coupled with excavations over 1988, 1990, and 1992, leads us to question Parker's interpretation of the site with respect to ethnic affiliation, occupational history, and function. In this chapter we focus on the occupational history and use of the site. Understanding these aspects of the Ripley site has significant implications for reconstructions of regional cultural dynamics. Comparative data from other enclosure sites in the region are essential for evaluating our interpretations, but these data are not readily available.

Models of Enclosure Site Use

The excellent ethnographic and ethnohistorical data for Northern Iroquoian cultures provide the basis for many models used in archaeological interpretation in New York State (Champlain 1907; L. Morgan 1851; Sagard-Theodat 1939; Tooker 1994). A consistent feature of these sources is the description of the palisaded villages in which Northern Iroquoians lived (e.g., Fenton 1978). Tuck (1978:326) projects this description backward to at least A.D. 1300. He envisions a basic pattern of stockaded villages in defensible locations, but with periodic settlement relocations, as is typical of shifting cultivators.

Fortified villages also shape archaeological understanding of Late Pre-historic earthwork sites in the lower Great Lakes region. The prevailing view is

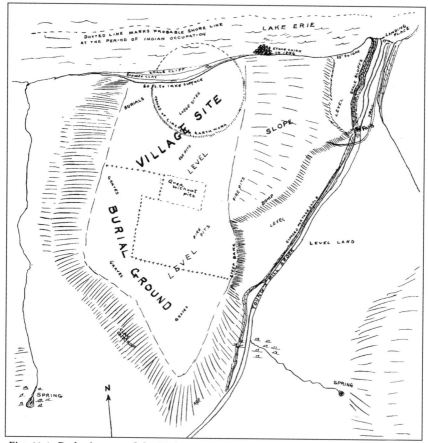

Fig. 11.1. Parker's map of the Ripley site; note location of earth ring (reproduced courtesy of the New York State Museum).

that the earthen enclosures represent defensive features associated with palisades. The defensive function of the earthworks has become an integral part of a model that posits population growth, dependence on horticulture, a greater degree of sedentism, and increased competition for land as aspects of cultural dynamics during late prehistory. When interpreted as features associated with the defense of settlements, the earthworks imply intergroup conflict not unlike that which occurred after European contact (Brose 1976a, 1978; Johnson et al. 1979; Stothers and Graves 1983; White 1961, 1963; Widmer and Webster 1981).

This widely accepted model disregards the fact that only some of the excavated embankments provide clear evidence for the presence of palisades (Jones and Jones 1980; Parker 1922; White 1958). Also noteworthy are arguments that much of the intergroup conflict among Northern Iroquoians was a postcontact phenomenon stimulated by the fur trade and that population pressure in the region was never severe (e.g., Ramsden 1977:291–293; Trigger 1981:34).

An alternative interpretation of these northern earthworks is more consistent with models based on midwestern and southeastern sites, where mounds and other earthworks are often known as ceremonial features sometimes associated with mortuary activities. One of the earliest investigators of the earthworks of the lower Great Lakes, Thesus Apoleon Cheney (1859), proposed that at least some of the earthworks were ceremonial in nature and not necessarily associated with habitation sites. In the middle of this century, Guthe (1958) had a similar perspective, noting that the lack of evidence for palisades and the shallow refuse deposits in some of the enclosures were not consistent with interpretation of the sites as fortified villages. The shallow deposits indicated to Guthe that the length of occupation of these sites was disproportionate to the time invested in constructing the embankments.

A ceremonial interpretation of the enclosures, particularly one associated with mortuary ritual, is consistent with general understanding of tribal societies such as those historically known to have inhabited the Great Lakes region. In this model, the earthworks serve as markers of special disposal areas for the dead. The argument can be made that both defensive structures and special disposal areas for the dead might be linked to pressures brought about by a sedentary lifestyle and increased dependence on plant cultivation. Chapman (1981) associates maintenance of formal disposal areas for the dead with the development of more complex kinship structures and corporate groups, including territorially based descent groups, as a result of the need to control critical resources. Markers, such as earthworks, may serve as symbols of group identity, and mortuary ritual serves as a mechanism for social integration.

Among Northern Iroquoians, the Huron Feast of the Dead, which involved periodic placement of the dead in formal ossuaries covered with mounds, functioned in this way (Heidenreich 1978:374–375). Moreover, ossuary sites are reported in the lower Great Lakes region, where they are sometimes associated with enclosures (e.g., Schock 1974:94; Squier 1851). It is therefore not unreasonable to expect that the cultural traditions of other tribal groups in this region may have involved formal cemeteries with earthen markers.

Thus, despite a consistent tendency by regional researchers to interpret all enclosure sites as fortified villages, there are at least two viable models for interpreting these sites of the lower Great Lakes. The enclosure sites would seem to have equal potential to be either fortified villages or specialized mortuary sites. As indicated by the other chapters in this volume, the question of defensive versus ceremonial functions for enclosures is not unique to this region. Nevertheless, a central problem remains how to identify and distinguish differential site uses.

The Ripley Site Case

The Ripley site has a long and complex history of professional and amateur investigation (Sullivan 1996), but the most important previous work at the site was that of Parker (1907). Parker's work is significant not only because he was a pioneer in Iroquoian archaeology (Brose 1973b:92; Sullivan 1992) but because, as noted earlier, he established what has become the accepted interpretation of the Ripley site, namely, that this site was a single-component protohistoric Erie Indian village and cemetery dating to the late sixteenth or early seventeenth century. Based on his 1906 excavations, he identified a village area in association with the enclosure itself and a cemetery area to the south and west of the village. Parker's excavations concentrated on the location of pits, especially graves, and the collection of a large sample of materials for the New York State Museum.

The original goal of our research at the Ripley site was to compare an Erie village with better-known Iroquois sites in New York, such as the Seneca villages to the east. We initially accepted Parker's interpretations as basic assumptions, but as the research progressed, it became clear that the data were incongruent with these assumptions. Our reanalysis has led us to posit two possible functions for the site, each of which is consistent with one of the two models for earthwork site use already outlined. Was the site a single-component, fortified village with an associated cemetery, as has long been assumed, or was it a multiple-component, special-purpose mortuary site?

This dichotomy is somewhat artificial because the site could have been used as a village at one point and as a mortuary site at another, and as Gibson (this volume) points out, separating the sacred from the secular is not necessarily possible. The dichotomy is, however, heuristically useful for our study of site use. We designed the various analyses of the Ripley site materials to test for presumed archaeological correlates of these site uses, and discrepancies from our expectations have become clear. The correlates we propose for each use are listed in table 11.1. (See Sullivan 1996 for a more complete discussion.) Each correlate relates to our assumption that both a full range of domestic and ceremonial activities should have occurred at a village site with a cemetery, while a more restricted range of activities would have taken place at a special-purpose site. This assumption leads to more specific expectations about the kinds of material remains that should be recovered, about the diversity of these remains, and about the spatial distribution of both features and artifacts at the Ripley site. Our findings support a new interpretation for the site's occupational history and use.

Evidence Concerning the Occupational History of the Ripley Site

Parker envisioned a single-component village along the lines of historically known Iroquoian villages. Village-removal sequences constructed by "upstreaming" from historic villages into prehistoric times have been carefully developed for other Northern Iroquoians such as the Seneca (Wray and Schoff 1953; Tuck 1978), but a sequence that includes the Ripley site has never been generated. The village-removal models posit relocation approximately every ten years (Saunders 1987; Sempowski et al. 1988), but a broad perspective on agricultural village longevity may suggest longer site use (Warrick 1988). Nevertheless, a village duration of more than 50 years would be incompatible with archaeological and ethnohistoric estimates for this region.

At present, the ceramic sequence in western New York does not provide very precise indicators of chronology and occupational history. Both the geographic and the temporal range of the three main ceramic types found at the site (Ripley Plain, Niagara Collared, and Lawson Incised) is wide. All of these types might date from the thirteenth through the sixteenth centuries. One possible chronological indicator is the very small number of shell-tempered sherds. Schock (1974) argued that these ceramics represent the very end of the prehistoric sequence (termed by him the "Chautauqua phase") in southwestern New York. The fact that shell-tempered wares make up less than 5 percent of the ceramics from the Ripley site might argue for an earlier prehistoric occupation.

In his study of ceramics in three collections from the Ripley site, Engelbrecht (1996) found remarkable similarity between the ceramics from Ripley and those from the Newton-Hopper site, using the Brainerd-Robinson coefficient and eleven morphological and design attributes. Newton-Hopper is a Late Prehistoric habitation site in the Niagara Frontier near Buffalo.

Table 11.1. Proposed archaeological correlates for Northern Iroquoian village and mortuary sites

Village site	Mortuary site
1. Single component	1. Single or multiple component
2. Domestic, manufacturing, ritual, and other activities present	2. Primarily ritual activities present
3. Some spatial segregation of activities	3. Little or no spatial segregation of activities
4. Longhouses present	4. Structure size and shape variable
5. Rebuilding and superpositioning minimal	5. If multicomponent, rebuilding and minimal superpositioning likely
6. Large proportions of ceramic sherds with cooking residues	6. Small proportion of ceramic sherds with cooking residues
7. Many different functional types of ceramic vessels	7. Restricted set of functional types of ceramic vessels
8. Variable ceramic vessel sizes	8. Narrow size range for vessels, possibly smaller vessels more common than large
9. All stages of lithic-reduction sequence	9. Partial range of toolmaking sequence
10. High diversity of tool types	10. Restricted set of tool types
11. Both high- and low-input tools common	11. Predominance of high-input tools
12. Faunal assemblage dominated by selectively hunted animals	12. Relatively little evidence for selective hunting of key animals
13. Evidence for garden hunting	13. Little evidence for garden hunting
14. Evidence that fishing was important	14. Little evidence that fishing was important
15. High diversity in procurement strategies	15. Little diversity in procurement strategies
16. Diversity of feature types	16. More restricted set of feature types
17. Large storage pits common	17. Few large storage pits
18. Cooking hearths common	18. Cooking hearths uncommon

Engelbrecht's finding is important because it indicates possible cultural affiliation with protohistoric Niagara Frontier groups. Since there are approximately sixty miles between the Ripley and the Niagara Frontier sites, village removal is a poor explanation for these similarities. Most postulated village removals are of only a few miles (Tuck 1978:326). The possibility that mortuary activities might be carried out at such a distance also seems remote.

In considering the ceramic evidence for chronology and occupational history at the Ripley site, two general concerns emerge. First, Ripley is considered the type site for Erie ceramics (MacNeish 1952). If there is reason to question both the dating and the nature of human usage of the Ripley site, as we argue in this chapter, Ripley is not an appropriate type site for this pottery. What are the implications for archaeological understanding of regional ceramic sequences? Second, there is an apparent lack of diversity in regional ceramic assemblages and in the Ripley site assemblage itself. This homogeneity might be taken as an indication of a single component at the Ripley site, except that the ceramic types in question do not have very restricted spatial and temporal signatures or functional significance. Because this phenomenon seems to be regional, we wonder if pottery might not have been a medium used to signal group identity or specialized activities to the degree found elsewhere. A regional reassessment of ceramic typology certainly is needed, and at this time ceramics will not be particularly useful indicators of the Ripley site's occupational history.

Other chronological indicators provide evidence that the Ripley site is not a single- but a multiple-component site. Parker and others recovered European trade items, associated with a small number of graves. This trade material was the basis for Parker's interpretation of the site as protohistoric, with a date no later than A.D. 1610. Recent reexamination of copper and brass trade items (Fitzgerald 1991; Fitzgerald and Ramsden 1988) suggests a date range of A.D. 1550–1580. Bradley and Childs (1991) also place the site in the sixteenth century based on a report, in the site files at the State University of New York (SUNY) at Buffalo, of a copper spiral from the site. Sixteenth-century use of the site, at least for the burial of a few individuals, is clear, but the assumption that this was the only period of occupation for the Ripley site appears to be incorrect based on the results of radiometric dating.

We obtained dates for twelve radiocarbon assays from the Ripley site (table 11.2). We consider the contexts of all but one of these samples (Beta 82410) to be undisturbed and high in integrity. Reconsideration of Feature 92-623B suggests that this feature is a disturbance or a remnant of a feature that was disturbed, perhaps by the earliest excavators of the site. Further analysis of the radiometric information and possibly the dating of additional

Table 11.2. Radiocarbon dates from the Ripley site

Sample	Provenience	Feature type	Radiocarbon date	Calibrated date range
1. Beta 82409	Feature 92-234	Pit, small to medium, shallow	280 ± 60 B.P.	A.D. 1470–1680[a] A.D. 1745–1805 A.D. 1935–1950
2. Beta 82408	Feature 92-440	Postmold	340 ± 60 B.P.	A.D. 1440–1665
3. Beta 82414	Feature 92-678	Fire pit	370 ± 60 B.P.	A.D. 1430–1655
4. Beta 82413	Feature 92-503	Subadult burial[b]	380 ± 50 B.P.	A.D. 1435–1650
5. Beta 82407	Feature 92-83	Fire pit	390 ± 60 B.P.	A.D. 1425–1650
6. Beta 82406	Feature 92-29, Level 2	Pit, large, Indeterminate	410 ± 70 B.P.	A.D. 1410–1650
7. Beta 82410	Feature 92-623B	Pit, large amorphous[c]	420 ± 60 B.P.	A.D. 1415–1640
8. Beta 82415	Feature 92-469	Pit, small to medium, shallow	480 ± 60 B.P.	A.D. 1395–1505[d] A.D. 1595–1620
9. Beta 82412	Feature 92-541	Fire pit	480 ± 50 B.P.	A.D. 1400–1485
10. Beta 82411	Feature 92-257B	Postmold	570 ± 70 B.P.	A.D. 1290–1450
11. Beta 29941	Feature 88-51	Postmold[e]	620 ± 110 B.P.	A.D. 1220–1470
12. Beta 29940	Feature 88-21	Postmold	710 ± 110 B.P.	A.D. 1055–1090 A.D. 1150–1430

a. The two sigma range includes three date intervals on the Pretoria calibration curve.
b. This sample actually came from a small fire pit that appears to be a grave fire directly over this infant's skeleton and to have been part of the burial activities.
c. One possible interpretation for this feature is that it is a remnant of a trench and feature excavation by Parker or another early excavator.
d. The two sigma range includes two date intervals on the Pretoria calibration curve.
e. The sample consisted of an actual piece of charred post weighing 35 gm.

radiocarbon samples needs to be done, but our present assessment is that there are at least two components at the Ripley site.

The most recent of these components is indicated by the first five samples (Beta 82409, Beta 82408, Beta 82414, Beta 82413, and Beta 82407) listed in table 11.2. The assays suggest occupation of the site between the mid-fifteenth and the mid-seventeenth centuries. The intercepts for most predate A.D. 1550, thus predating the late-sixteenth-century occupation suggested by the trade materials. The two sigma-calibrated date ranges all include the late sixteenth century. In the case of one assay (Beta 82409), fluctuations in the curve result in three widely spaced date ranges. Given the material remains from the Ripley site, an interpretation of this date as representative of a sixteenth-century occupation is most plausible. Pair-wise tests of contemporaneity of the conventional radiocarbon dates, as described in Thomas (1986:249–251), Shott (1992), and R. E. Taylor (1987:124–125), indicate the differences between all pairs within this group of dates are statistically insignificant at the .05 level with infinite degrees of freedom (table 11.3). We thus interpret this group of dates as consistent with the previously recognized protohistoric occupation of the Ripley site.

Three of the dated samples are not consistent with a late sixteenth-century occupation. Two of these dates, Beta 29941 and Beta 29940, are reported elsewhere (Sullivan et al. 1995), but the third (Beta 82411) was not obtained until 1995. All three dated samples were carbonized wood from postmolds within several meters of each other, and possibly from the same structure. These dates indicate use of the Ripley site between the mid-eleventh century and the end of the fifteenth century, but the ceramics suggest the site was not occupied prior to the thirteenth century. Pair-wise tests for contemporaneity (table 11.3) indicate that these dates are not statistically different. There is overlap between the two sigma ranges for these three dates and those for the five dates discussed above, but the pair-wise tests for all possible pairs between the two groups indicate statistically significant differences ($t > 1.96$). The conclusion that is most congruent with the radiocarbon dates is that there is a second, earlier component at the Ripley site, dating to the fourteenth or first half of the fifteenth century.

The other four samples did not produce dates that can easily be associated with one or the other of these two periods of use. Beta 82410 probably should be ignored due to the nature of its context, as discussed above. The other three (Beta 82406, Beta 82415, and Beta 82412) remain ambiguous in terms of the proposed components. All of these samples have two sigma date ranges between the very end of the fourteenth century and the middle of the seventeenth century, with intercepts during the fifteenth century. Pair-wise tests indicate possible contemporaneity with other sample dates in both the early and late groups. One possible interpretation is that the Ripley site was

Table 11.3. T-values for pair-wise tests of contemporaneity between radiocarbon sample dates from the Ripley site

Sample dates[a]	1.	2.	3.	4.	5.	6.	7.	8.	9.	10.	11.	12.
1.	—											
2.	.71	—										
3.	1.06	.35	—									
4.	1.28	.51	.13	—								
5.	1.29	.59	.44	.13	—							
6.	1.41	.76	.44	.35	.22	—						
7.	1.65	.94	.59	.51	.35	.11	—					
8.	2.35	1.65	1.30	1.28	1.06	.76	.71	—				
9.	2.55	1.80	1.41	1.41	1.115	.81	.77	0	—			
10.	3.15	2.50	2.20	2.44	1.96	1.62	1.63	.98	1.05	—		
11.	2.72	2.24	2.07	1.98	2.56	1.62	1.60	1.12	1.16	.38	—	
12.	3.44	2.96	2.72	2.72	2.56	2.31	2.32	1.84	1.90	1.08	.58	—

Note: For x=.05, t=1.96; for x=.10, t=1.65.
a. Sample date numbers correspond to those given in table 11.2.

used for a long span of time without a significant hiatus. This interpretation seems less probable than two periods of site use, particularly if the site was a village occupied by shifting agriculturalists.

The radiometric data need more thorough analysis and consideration in terms of the contexts of the samples within the site. Possible old wood effects with respect to the earlier group of dates do not, however, appear to be a consideration. The small size of the postmolds in question suggests that the poles were made from saplings. Since the local climate was not arid, long-term storage of or reuse of saplings seems unrealistic. Moreover, old wood effects are unlikely explanations for the magnitude of difference in the dates.

The radiocarbon data are not the only indicators that the Ripley site may be multicomponent. For example, the size of the burial population (>235 individuals), combined with a normal mortality profile, suggests that the Ripley site was a large village (Wilkinson 1996). Yet, the relatively small site area of about two hectares suggests a small village. Parker even envisioned a village contained within the earthen enclosure, an area of about only one-half acre. So many individuals could not have died within the short, ten-year span assumed for Northern Iroquoian villages unless the village was much larger than suggested by the site size, or unless mortality was more catastrophic than is indicated by the health status, age, and sex ratios represented in the skeletal population.

The archaeological data also provide considerable evidence for superpositioning of structures at the site. In the approximately 500-square-meter area exposed in 1992, we defined 650 postmolds. Structure patterns are not obvious, but the density of postmolds at the northern end of the knoll presents a bewildering array of possibilities that may best be explained in terms of multiple components (fig. 11.2).

These interpretations are complicated by the site's history of pot-hunter disturbances and multiple excavations (Sullivan 1996). For example, one of the earlier dates (Beta 82411) comes from a sample excavated from a postmold that was not recognized at the base of the plow zone. It was found during reexcavation of a pot-hunter's disturbance of a large burial pit. The pot-hunter's disturbance obscured the top of this postmold but did not affect the base of this post, which extended more than 35 cm below the plow zone. Whether the burial pit originally cut into the top of the postmold or was immediately adjacent to it was no longer apparent. The burial itself is not dated, but a reasonable inference is that this postmold represents a separate, earlier use of the site than does the burial. That this postmold, and several others in the immediate vicinity, were somehow associated with burial activities seems an unlikely argument.

In summary, the long-held assumption that the Ripley site represents a single component village occupied during the Protohistoric period must be

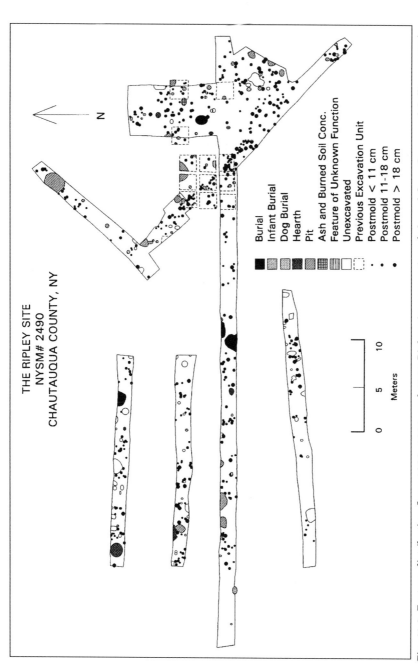

THE RIPLEY SITE
NYSM# 2490
CHAUTAUQUA COUNTY, NY

N

Burial
Infant Burial
Dog Burial
Hearth
Pit
Ash and Burned Soil Conc.
Feature of Unknown Function
Unexcavated
Previous Excavation Unit
Postmold < 11 cm
Postmold 11-18 cm
Postmold > 18 cm

0   5   10
Meters

Fig. 11.2. Feature distribution from 1988, 1990, and 1992 Ripley site excavations (adapted from Green and Sullivan 1997).

questioned on a number of grounds. We argue that, at the very least, there are two components at the Ripley site, one of which represents protohistoric activities, including a number of human burials, and the other of which represents Late Prehistoric usage of the site of an unknown nature.

Evidence Concerning the Use of the Ripley Site

As listed in table 11.1, we propose a number of archaeological correlates for residential, as opposed to mortuary, use of a site. To facilitate a review of the pertinent data, we group these into four general sets of activities: food preparation, food storage, resource procurement, and manufacturing. We also investigate some aspects of the site plan. Comparisons of these activity sets with respect to particular subsets of the Ripley site data produce interesting, if somewhat ambiguous, results. One obvious possibility is that the multicomponent nature of the Ripley site has complicated the evidence for site use. Given the current probability of at least partial superpositioning of components, the nature of each component at the Ripley site may never be completely clear. Nevertheless, we are engaged in detailed spatial analyses that we hope will allow us to be more conclusive. Another result is that our explorations concerning site use have found some intriguing evidence for deviation from our expectations concerning Northern Iroquoian village sites.

Food Preparation

One possible distinction between a village and a mortuary site has to do with the nature of food preparation and storage. We expect that food preparation took place mainly as a routine, daily necessity of life at a village. Food also may have been prepared at a mortuary site, but is likely to have been done in the context of ritual feasting. Food storage, on the other hand, is an activity more likely to occur at residential sites where people would need stocks of food to survive the long northern winters. The ceramic assemblage and pit features are two data sets that offer information relevant to these activities.

Given the routine, daily necessity of food preparation, we expected that a large percentage of vessels from a village site would show evidence of this activity. One indicator of vessel use for food preparation is charred food residues adhering to vessel walls. The frequency of food residues in the older ceramic collections from the Ripley site is not reliable because the pottery was scrubbed. In the more recently collected samples, only 12 percent of the intact rims have residues. Assessing whether this percentage is congruent with a year-round residential site is difficult without adequate comparative data, but we surmise that it is low.

Another possible indicator of food preparation activities is the presence of fire pits and hearths. This class of feature is relatively uncommon at the Ripley site; only 30 (6 percent) of the 508 features other than postmolds reported at the site are fire pits or hearths, and these appear to reflect activities other than food preparation. Early investigators describe most of the fire pits as "grave or ceremonial fires" because these features often occur over or immediately adjacent to a burial. We excavated one such feature in 1992.

We also expected more variety in cooking activities at a village site than at a mortuary site and that this diversity would be reflected in the functional types of vessels: the variety would be greater at a village. The mean diameter is 19.6 cm for the 75 vessels from our excavations that could be measured, but the range is from 6 to 36 cm and the distribution is unimodal with relatively long tails around the mean (fig. 11.3). Although lacking provenience, Engelbrecht's (1996) larger vessel samples hint of several distinct size modes including a category that consists of vessels greater than 32 cm in diameter. Engelbrecht (1996) also found that the whole vessels tended to be smaller, ranging from 7 to 19 cm, than those calculated from the rim fragments. Consistent with this finding, the most intact vessel from our excavations is only 8 cm in diameter. The wide size range among the Ripley vessels suggests that vessels were being made to perform a wide variety of tasks. This finding is more consistent with our expectations for a village than for a mortuary site.

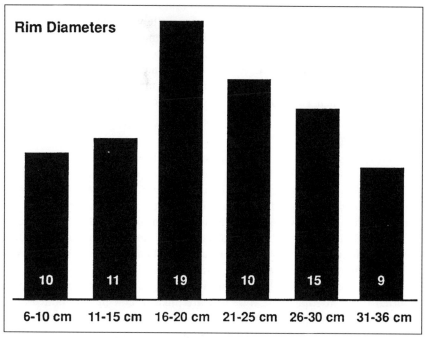

Fig. 11.3. Ceramic vessel diameters at the Ripley site.

There also is no indication of a subset of finer wares that would fit our notion of ceremonial vessels. Ninety-five percent of the assemblage is grit-tempered, and 81 percent of the vessels have smooth surfaces. Sixty-three percent of the vessels, usually classified as Ripley Plain or Niagara Collared, have undecorated exteriors. Another 21 percent are categorized as Lawson Incised, a type decorated with simple oblique or vertical stamps across the collars. The remaining 16 percent consists of a variety of rare types. Although many vessels in the recently excavated samples are too fragmentary to assign to a type, Engelbrecht (1996) observed 25 types in addition to the three well-represented types (Ripley Plain, Niagara Collared, and Lawson Incised) in the older collections. None of this material can easily be understood as better-made ceremonial ware.

The data potentially related to food preparation thus are mixed in terms of our expectations for a village versus a mortuary site, but our expectations may be overly simplistic. The low incidence of carbonized residues on the pottery and the relatively low frequency of fire pits and hearths, plus the fact that these features do not appear to be associated with food preparation, suggests that heating or cooking of food was not a common activity at the site. Yet, while pottery was being used for a wide range of tasks, no special ceremonial wares were used. Functional variation in Northern Iroquoian ceramics is an issue that has received little attention, and when it has, little variation is found. Allen's (1988) study of ceramics from Seneca village assemblages was inconclusive in defining functional categories. It may be that these ceramic assemblages are so undifferentiated that these data are not useful indicators for recognizing specialized activities. Furthermore, burial ceremonies may have been accompanied by feasting, which could result in a similar vessel assemblage as routine domestic consumption.

Food Storage

Food storage is also an activity we presumed to be common at a village site, especially in a climate with a long winter and short growing season. One indicator of food storage is the presence of storage pits. Pits for storage of perishable foods are most effective in minimizing decomposition if their form is characterized by a low surface-to-volume ratio (DeBoer 1988:3). Although the differential use of pits is rarely discussed for Northern Iroquoian groups, the use of subterranean storage is considered by Chapdelaine (1993:185–188) to be an expected activity at village sites.

The purposes for which the majority of the 221 nonburial pit features reported from the Ripley site were dug are unclear. Few pits contained artifacts, nor did they appear to have been used for refuse disposal; other than some organic staining, the fill generally was very clean. The lack of in situ contents relating to primary uses of these features leaves form and size as the only vehicle for assessing pit functions.

Using a sample of 110 well-documented pits representing all excavations at the Ripley site, Green and Sullivan (1997) employed cluster and discriminate analysis to create a typology of pits based on form and size (fig. 11.4). Seventy-four percent of the pits were small to medium-sized (18 to 183 cm) in diameter and shallow (3 to 82 cm) in depth. The uses of these pits is problematic; Stewart (1975) suggests that pits in this size range likely were used for caching a variety of objects. Twelve percent of the pits were very large (198 to 472 cm) in diameter, and shallow (26 to 79 cm) relative to their breadth. We speculate that these are borrow pits and evidence of soil-recovery activities associated with construction and maintenance of the earth ring. Fourteen percent of the pits were large (86 to 315 cm) and deep (76 to 137 cm). Of these larger pits, only nine (8 percent of the sample) conform to the idealized shape for perishable food storage. Storage of perishable food thus does not appear to have been the major reason for digging pits at the Ripley site. In contrast, the number of reported graves (n = 218) at the site nearly equals the number of all other types of pit features.

As noted above, Chapdelaine considers pit features to be an integral part of Northern Iroquoian habitation sites. The evidence for food storage, as indicated by pit features of the optimal form, is scarce at the Ripley site. The use of the vast majority of pits at the site is unknown. Most of these features fall into a size range that Stewart (1975) suggests were small caches. Even if her interpretation is correct, there is no evidence of what was being cached or for what purpose.

In an effort to better understand the pit features at the Ripley site, the Ripley data were compared with those from four other Northern Iroquoian sites, including three village sites, the Boland, Farrell Farm, and Snell sites, and one multicomponent seasonal encampment, the Faucett site (fig. 11.5). The goal here was to determine if the pits at Ripley could be considered typical of those found at Northern Iroquoian villages. The results of this comparison were surprising enough to lead Green and Sullivan (1997) to reconsider their initial assumptions about the character of pit assemblages at special-purpose and village sites. First, just as at Ripley, the most common pit at two of the three village sites and at the special-purpose site is small and shallow. Only one of the villages has large numbers of pits that compare favorably with food-storage facilities. This finding suggests that the pit assemblages at villages are not uniform and will not be easy to predict.

An even more surprising result is that the greatest variety of pits among all five sites is at the Ripley site. In this respect, the assemblage of pits at Ripley clearly is different from those at those sites defined as villages, but suggests a broader, rather than a more restricted range of activities. The pit assemblage at the multicomponent, special-purpose Faucett site is more diverse than the assemblages at any of the three villages and is most like the assemblage from Ripley. Whether this diversity can be attributed to the multiple components at Faucett or to its function as a seasonal resource processing station or to some combination of these factors is not clear.

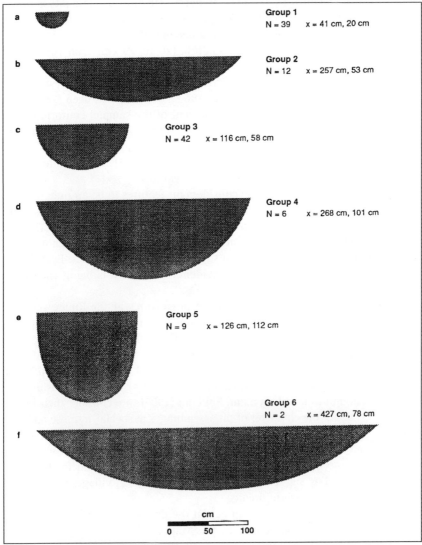

Fig. 11.4. Profiles of pit types at the Ripley site; x=mean diameter, depth (adapted from Green and Sullivan 1997).

We surmise that the diversity of the pits at the Ripley site is a product of the multiple components and divergent uses of the site related to these components. Nonetheless, the lack of refuse disposal in the pit features is incongruent with long-term residential use of the site, and the scarcity of large storage pits does not compare well with common perceptions of Northern Iroquoian village sites. The analysis of the pit features at the Ripley site not only makes apparent our lack of understanding of these features, but shows that the variety of pits at residential sites, even in the same region and of similar time periods, differs considerably. Of particular interest is the variation in representation of storage pits. Investigation of this diversity may shed light on differences in subsistence and settlement practices and could help evaluate DeBoer's (1988) contention that subterranean storage is associated with semisedentary rather than year-round habitation.

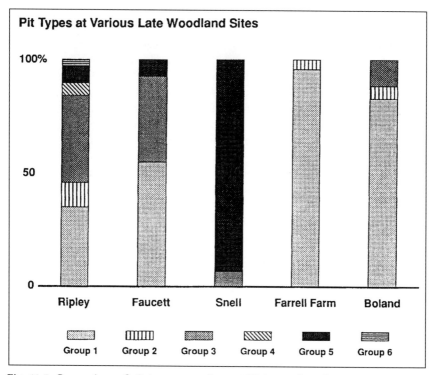

Fig. 11.5. Comparison of pit type proportions at Ripley and northen Iroquoian sites; groups as in fig. 11.4 (adapted from Green and Sullivan 1997).

Resource Procurement

We expected that the assemblage of plant and animal remains at a residential site formerly inhabited by maize agriculturalists should reflect aspects of resource procurement associated with this subsistence base. Gardens would be near the residences, and garden hunting (hunting of animals attracted to garden plots and edges; see Linares 1976; S. Neusius 1990, 1994) would be an important strategy for procuring meat. We also expected that animals indicating selective hunting would be well represented at a village and that incidental collecting of animals would be low. The reverse was proposed for special-purpose mortuary sites. Fishing, especially given the Ripley site's location on Lake Erie, additionally would be important if the site was residential. And finally, we expected the diversity of procurement strategies and range of represented species in the faunal assemblage at a mortuary site to be more restricted than at a village, both because everyday household debris would not be represented and because the species composition might be associated with ritual.

Only limited data on plant use are currently available from the Ripley site because flotation was not employed by the early investigators. Some information is available from food residues on ceramic sherds. A chemical analysis of residues on sherds from nine sites in western New York, conducted by SUNY Buffalo, indicates that the residues from Ripley are anomalous in that they are not compatible with the soils immediately adjacent to the site (Fie et al. 1990). This study suggests that the foodstuffs cooked in these pots, whether cultigens or wild plant foods, did not grow in locations adjacent to the site. Instead, they appear to have grown on the Allegheny Plateau to the south and east. If so, they were transported to the Ripley site for use there. This practice is not consistent with the interpretation that the site is a village occupied by agriculturalists because the lake plain on which the site is located is the best agricultural soil in the region.

The animal procurement strategies suggested by the faunal assemblage also do not conform very well to our expectations for a village site. A comparison of the Ripley faunal assemblage with those from four Andaste villages (S. Neusius 1994) found differences between the Ripley site and these villages with respect to reliance on selective hunting as opposed to incidental collecting of animals.

Figure 11.6 shows that selective hunting is more important in the assemblages from the Andaste villages. In the Ripley assemblage selective hunting strategies, including cervid, bear, beaver, and raccoon hunting, are represented by 30.6 percent of the number of individual species present (NISP) and by 22.9 percent of the minimum number of individuals (MNI). Cervid hunting appears to have been the most important of these strategies, being rep-

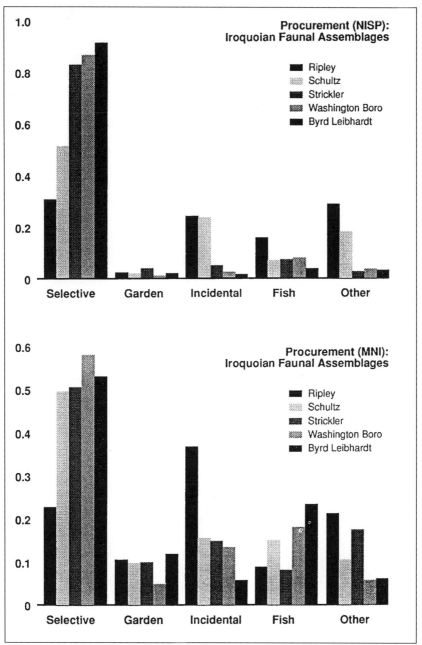

Fig. 11.6. Types of animal procurement strategies at the Ripley site and Andaste villages.

resented by 19.0 percent of the NISP and 8.8 percent of the MNI. Approximately 75 percent of the "other" procurement category, which includes specimens that are not easily assigned to a type of procurement, is from bones assigned only to Artiodactyla. Many of these specimens probably are cervid, although they are too fragmented to identify to family. Adding these specimens to selective procurement would increase the proportional representation of selective hunting to 51.5 percent based on NISP and 28.1 percent based on MNI. These percentages still are not compatible with an interpretation of selective hunting as a predominant strategy.

In contrast, the figures for incidental collecting suggest that this form of procurement was moderately significant at Ripley and less so at the Andaste villages. Incidental collecting is represented by 23.8 percent of the NISP and over 36.8 percent of the MNI at Ripley. Animals included here are foxes, canids, weasels, squirrels, and porcupine. These percentages are not as high at the Andaste villages, although the Schultz site is most like Ripley. The composition of the Ripley assemblage indicates that these types of animals were procured about as often as were those animals assumed to have been selectively hunted. The MNI causes this category to look even more important, but this illusion is because incidental collecting includes small numbers of specimens from a variety of different taxa, all of which are necessarily represented by at least one MNI. The result is that caution is wise in assuming that incidental collecting is the predominant approach to animal procurement at the Ripley site. Nevertheless, these animals likely were incidentally collected, and the Ripley assemblage is atypical with respect to reliance on incidental hunting.

These characteristics of the Ripley faunal assemblage argue against the interpretation of this site as a village according to our expectations. The low proportion of species associated with garden hunting (1.4 percent of the NISP; 3.3 percent of the MNI) and moderately low proportion of fish (15.4 percent of the NISP; 8.8 percent of the MNI) in the Ripley faunal assemblage also do not compare favorably with our initial expectations for a village site. The faunal assemblages from the Andaste villages (see fig. 11.6), however, have representations of fish and garden hunting species similar to those from Ripley.

The lack of difference between the Ripley site and Andaste village faunal assemblages with respect to evidence for garden hunting or for fishing is surprising because garden hunting is a common strategy among agriculturalists (Linares 1976; S. Neusius 1990, 1994). Our expectation was that garden hunting would be evident in assemblages from village sites and not in assemblages from special-purpose mortuary sites (see table 11.1). This strategy is not clearly present at either the Ripley site or at the Andaste villages, and the lack of evidence may mean that garden hunting was not, after all,

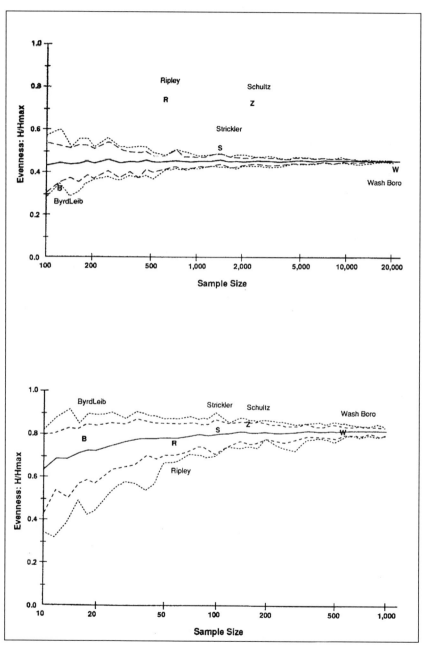

Fig. 11.7. Predicted and actual diversity of animal procurement strategies at the Ripley site and Andaste villages; *upper*, NISP; *lower*, MNI.

an important strategy for Northern Iroquoian agriculturalists. Whether this is the case deserves to be explored more fully as doing so undoubtedly would provide important insights concerning temperate agricultural adaptations (S. Neusius 1996a).

The moderately low exploitation of fish at the Ripley site is also intriguing. As S. Neusius (1996b) has noted, it is counter-intuitive that people living in a sedentary village alongside Lake Erie would not exploit fish. That fish utilization apparently was not very high initially suggested to us that the site was neither residential nor a seasonal fishing camp, but similar levels of fish use in the Andaste village assemblages suggest another explanation should be sought, such as the seasonality of use, the productivity of the fishery, or cultural practices.

In another respect, the Ripley faunal assemblage is similar to those of the Andaste villages. We expected the diversity of the faunal assemblage to be low if the Ripley site was a specialized mortuary site and high if it was a village. S. Neusius (1994) has found the evenness of the Ripley assemblage to be surprisingly high (.613 based on NISP and .635 based on MNI). Moreover, when the four Andaste faunal assemblages are used to build a model for expected faunal diversity following Kintigh (1984, 1989, 1994), the results are surprising (fig. 11.7). The evenness value for the Ripley site assemblage using NISP is well above the 95 percent confidence interval for predicted values with an N equal to the Ripley sample assemblage, but the evenness value using MNI is very close to the predicted value. The same observation can be made for two of the four Andaste faunal assemblages (Schultz and Strickler), suggesting that the aggregate model obscures significant variability in diversity within Andaste village sites. The tentative conclusion is that the diversity of the Ripley site faunal assemblage is not really outside the range of diversity expected at a Northern Iroquoian village. This finding may mean that faunal assemblages from village sites vary so much that high diversity in faunal resource use cannot be considered typical.

Overall, the data related to resource procurement imply that our expectations for faunal assemblages at Northern Iroquoian village sites were too simplistic. Especially intriguing is the finding that the faunal assemblage at the Ripley site is similar to those at the Andaste villages in that neither garden hunting nor fishing appears to be an important procurement strategy. The implication that garden hunting may not be an important strategy for Northern Iroquoian groups is interesting because this strategy is a common practice among agriculturalists worldwide.

On the other hand, a clear pattern of residential use of the Ripley site in terms of resource procurement is not apparent in the data either. Two findings in particular are incongruous with our expectations for a village site. First, the scant evidence for plant use suggests that foodstuffs cooked in pots at the site did not grow in locations adjacent to the site, a circumstance that seems inconsistent with interpretation of the Ripley as a residential site occupied by farmers because the site is located on and adjacent to the best agricultural soil in the region. Second, the data on faunal resource procurement indicate that species consistent with an incidental collecting strategy, rather than selective hunting, are more important in the Ripley assemblages than the compared villages. This latter finding is especially interesting because those species that were incidentally collected are those potentially valued for reasons other than as food sources (i.e., for their pelts and quills), and could be construed as having ritual, ornamental, and/or ceremonial connotations. Yet the diversity of the Ripley site faunal assemblage is not really outside the range of diversity found at the other Northern Iroquoian villages. Once again, the results of our analyses are ambiguous with respect to site use.

Manufacturing

Data on flaked stone tool manufacture provide the most direct insights to manufacturing at the Ripley site. We expected the full range of flint-knapping activities to have been performed at Ripley if the site was a village and that a high diversity of tool types and both expedient and well-crafted tools

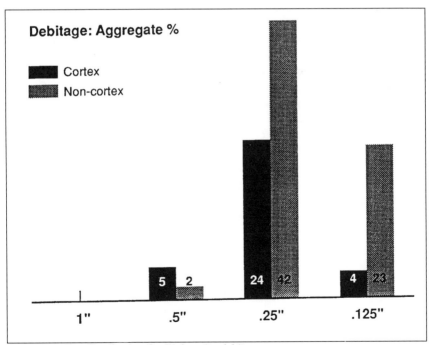

Fig. 11.8. Size distribution for Ripley site debitage.

would be present. In contrast, we expected that if the site was used primarily for mortuary purposes, there would be little evidence for tool manufacture; most of the tools would be well crafted and possibly used as ritual gifts or offerings, and the range of tool types would be limited.

The lithic assemblage at the Ripley site does not represent the full range of flint-knapping activities. Although cores are relatively common, they are notably small in size with a mean weight of only 18 gm. The majority of these cores are bipolar (68 percent), and all appear to represent use of the pebbles and cobbles from the glacial till that is available on or near the site. A common component of this till is Onondaga chert derived from outcrops to the north.

Mass aggregate analysis using nested screen sizes of 1 inch, 0.5 inch, 0.25 inch, and 0.125 inch (Ahler 1989) was performed for the lithic debitage (fig. 11.8). The sample includes 27,108 pieces of debitage that were sorted by presence or absence of cortex for each size grade. Only 32 flakes are greater than one inch in size, with 31 of these largest flakes possessing cortex. Only 1,871 (7 percent) of the flakes are between one inch and one-half inch in size, and 75 percent of these possess cortex. The largest fraction of the debitage is between 0.5 and 0.25 inch in size. Of this 66 percent of the sample (17,963 flakes), 24 percent retains cortex. The remaining 27 percent (7,242 flakes) are less than 0.24 inch in size, with 4 percent retaining cortex.

The small size of the flakes and the relative lack of cortex indicate that the primary flint-knapping activities were the final stages of tool production and resharpening, with some of the debitage coming from small cobble, bipolar reduction. Few or none of the activities on the site relate to flake or initial biface production. The core and debitage analysis indicates that raw material for tool production was not brought to the site. Most of the tools were brought to the site in complete or nearly complete form with only the final stages of production or resharpening represented in the debitage. The local till was used somewhat for expedient types of tools, as indicated by the presence of bipolar cores manufactured from the till cobbles and a modest amount of debitage in the two larger-size grades. These patterns are more congruent with a site used for specific purposes than with a year-round residential base where many types of toolkits would have been prepared for use at a variety of locations.

We also reasoned that a full range of lithic tool types would not be found at a mortuary site. Our original reanalysis of Parker's collection revealed an unusual lack of diversity in tool types (fig. 11.9). Sixty-two percent of the 214 modified tools are projectile points. Only 30 percent of the tools are other types of bifaces; 7 percent are unifaces and 2 percent drills or gravers. There are only 29 flakes, 56 cores, and 70 utilized flakes in his sample. Nearly all of the tools are complete specimens (93 percent), and they reflect a large amount of technological input. We originally proposed that the unusual nature of the assemblage reflects the manufacture and use of these items primarily as mortuary inclusions (P. Neusius 1996).

The analysis of tools from our excavations (conducted in 1988, 1990, and 1992) reveals a distinctly different picture (see fig. 11.9). From this sample of 536 flaked tools, 37 percent are projectile points, 32 percent are other bifacial tools, 25 percent are unifacial tools, and 6 percent are drills or gravers. This distribution represents a more diverse range of activities than seen in Parker's collection. The difference between the two samples may be the result of different contexts being sampled. Parker's emphasis was primarily on burial features, while the more recent excavation sample was drawn predominantly from nonburial features and midden. Another possibility is that the samples originate from different components.

Site Plan

Our initial investigations of spatial patterning at the site do not confirm Parker's view that the cemetery was segregated from the habitation area.

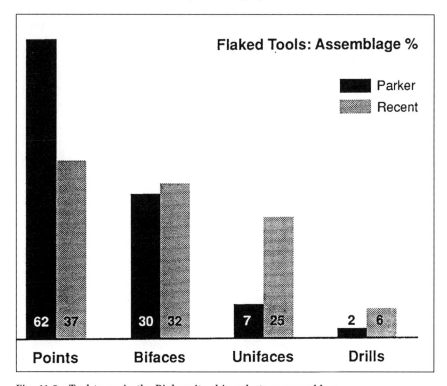

Fig. 11.9. Tool types in the Ripley site chipped-stone assemblage.

Though this kind of segregation is documented at other Northern Iroquoian villages, it is not confirmed by our excavations. Features in the southern third of the site are limited to burial pits, but the postmolds, cache pits, and other features of what Parker assumed was the residential area are interspersed with graves. These include both adults and subadults; the burial practices for these two ages groups vary (Sullivan and Coffin 1996).

Summary of Analyses

A number of lines of evidence lead us to question Parker's interpretation of the Ripley site as a village. There are fewer sherds with cooking residues than we would expect for a residential site, and chemical analyses of these residues have suggested that the foodstuffs in Ripley pots were brought to the site from some distance rather than grown nearby. In addition, the lithic debitage primarily represents the final stages of tool production and resharpening with some bipolar core reduction of glacial pebbles occurring as well. The species representation in the faunal assemblage is high for specimens indicative of incidental collecting and low for specimens indicative of selective hunting strategies. Moreover, comparisons with Andaste village sites suggest that these attributes are, as we expected, atypical for villages. There also are indications that the Ripley feature assemblage is unusual. The most common type of pit found at Ripley, other than a burial pit, is small, shallow, and empty. Hearths (other than possible grave fires) and large pits with the optimal form for food storage are relatively rare. Finally, the spatial segregation of domestic and mortuary activities that we anticipated for a village is not evident.

We initially thought the obvious conclusion from the data is that the site is a special-purpose mortuary site (Sullivan et al. 1995). There are, however, other indicators that do not conform to our expectations for a mortuary site as opposed to a village. Most of these indicators relate to our expectations about the lack of diversity in activities performed at a mortuary site. We thought that, in contrast to a village site, only a limited range of activities would take place at such a special-purpose site. We reasoned that this low diversity would be reflected in the various artifact and feature assemblages. We seldom have found this to be the case at the Ripley site.

In some ways the Ripley material remains are surprisingly diverse. This is true for ceramic vessel size, for the lithics from our excavations as opposed to those in Parker's collection, for faunal assemblage diversity, and for the features when compared with village sites. One conclusion is that there is more variability in Late Prehistoric villages than we realized, especially with respect to diversity. Our ideas about ceremonial ceramic usage, garden hunting, and fishing similarly are not supported by our analyses and require reassessment.

Although we cannot at this point be definitive about the past uses of the Ripley site, we can be unequivocal about the inaccuracy of Arthur Parker's description of the site as a protohistoric, fortified village with a cemetery. A more reasonable interpretation is that the site was used for mortuary purposes during the sixteenth century and, as early as the thirteenth century, as a small, seasonal encampment. In any case, Ripley was never the kind of village envisioned by Parker and accepted in the subsequent references to the site. The site's occupational history and its use are more complex, but nevertheless significant for regional prehistory.

Conclusion

We have discussed the evidence that the Ripley site is not a single-component, fortified village with an associated cemetery dating to the late sixteenth century. This interpretation was Parker's (1907) conclusion at the beginning of this century, and it has been assumed to be basically correct since that time. Our conclusion that Parker was wrong is of obvious significance to understanding the Ripley site itself, but it also has broader importance.

First, if the Ripley site is not a fortified village, then not all enclosure sites in the lower Great Lakes region are fortified villages. Archaeologists cannot assume that the presence of enclosures implies the past existence of a palisade. Enclosures must have served functions other than fortification, such as marking special disposal areas for the dead. Indeed, we believe enclosures served a wide variety of purposes and that these purposes may have changed through time and according to location. Thus, we would not argue that the Ripley site is an appropriate model even for all enclosure sites in the immediate region. Other chapters in this volume further support this position that archaeologists need to be more flexible in modeling enclosure use.

Second, given that enclosure uses vary, the archaeologist's job is to determine the probable occupational history and function of particular enclosures. These investigations should be possible even when the embankments in question are no longer evident, as is the case at the Ripley site. The task is the delineation of archaeological correlates for various site uses. These correlates should establish expectations for artifact assemblages, subsistence data, and the nature of features and spatial patterning.

We hope the analyses at the Ripley site illustrate that this approach is fruitful. In the Ripley case, we have learned both from results that validate our expectations and from results that prove we do not understand adequately the cultural complexity of the phenomena we were modeling. In either case, we recommend studies of site use as an important research goal.

Sarah W. Neusius, Lynne P. Sullivan, Phillip D. Neusius, and Claire McHale Milner

Finally, because the Ripley site is not what archaeologists have long assumed, assumptions about cultural dynamics in the lower Great Lakes must be reexamined. These include assumptions about the nature of known sites and even further consideration of the region's ceramic sequence. What kinds of cultural groups existed in this area during late prehistory and protohistory and how can we recognize them? Was there a need to defend sites with earthen fortifications? When did earth moving have other significance? Could intergroup contacts have been more benign prior to European contact? Obviously, despite a long history of archaeological interest, there is a great deal yet to be learned.

One way to understand more about these topics is to continue discussing the significance, sacred and secular, of enclosure sites, as the contributors to this volume are doing. For while the controversy over a mysterious race of "Moundbuilders" may have been settled long ago (Silverberg 1970), the reanalysis of the Ripley site demonstrates that archaeologists have only just begun to understand the complex cultural phenomena represented by the mounds and earthworks of the eastern United States.

Note

We wish to acknowledge the National Science Foundation for support of this research (Grant SBR9207643), but that agency is not responsible for the content of this article.

References Cited

Ahler, Stanley
1989   Mass Analysis of Flaking Debris: Studying the Forest Rather Than the Tree. In *Alternative Approaches to Lithic Analysis*, ed. D. O. Henry and G. H. Odell, 85–118. Archaeological Papers of the American Anthropological Association, No. 1.

Allen, Kathleen
1988   Ceramic Style and Social Continuity in an Iroquoian Tribe. Ph.D. diss., State University of New York, Buffalo.

Allman, John C.
1957   A New Late Woodland Culture for Ohio:. The Lichliter Village Site Near Dayton. *Ohio Archaeologist* 7(2):59–68.
1961   Late Woodland Stone Discs from Preble County, Ohio. *Ohio Archaeologist* 5(4):128–130.

Applebaum, E.
1996   Holy Stones. *Detroit Jewish News* 109(26):47–51.

Atwater, Caleb
1820   Description of the Antiquities Discovered in the State of Ohio and Other Western States. *Archaeologia Americana* 1:105–267.
1833   *The Writings of Caleb Atwater*. Columbus, Ohio: Scott and Wright.

Autin, Whitney J., Scott F. Burns, Bobby J. Miller, Roger Saucier,
     and John I. Snead
1991   Quaternary Geology of the Lower Mississippi Valley. In *The Geology of North America*. Vol. K-2. Geological Society of America.

Baby, Raymond S.
1954   Archaeological Explorations at Fort Hill. *Museum Echoes* 27(11):86–87.

Baby, Raymond S., and Suzanne Langlois
1979   Seip Mound State Memorial: Nonmortuary Aspects of Hopewell. In *Hopewell Archaeology: The Chillicothe Conference*, ed. D. S. Brose and N. Greber, 16–18. Kent, Ohio: Kent State University Press.

Bacon, Willard S.
1993   Factors in Siting a Middle Woodland Enclosure in Middle Tennessee. *MCJA* 18(2):245–281.

Barrett, John C., Richard Bradley, and Martin Green
1991   *Landscape, Monuments and Society*. Cambridge: Cambridge University Press.

Beers, F. W.
1866   *Atlas of Licking County, Ohio.* New York: Beers, Soule, and Co.
Beld, Scott
1993   Lyons Township Archaeological Survey, S92–313. Archaeological
        Survey Completion Report. Lansing: Bureau of History, Michigan
        Department of State.
1994   Ionia County Archaeology, Phase II, S93–319. Historical
        Preservation Grant. Lansing: Bureau of History, Michigan
        Department of State.
Belovich, Stephanie J.
1985a   The Greenwood Village Site (33Su92): An Early Late Woodland
        Site along the Cuyahoga River. Master's thesis, Kent State
        University, Kent, Ohio.
1985b   Evaluative Testing at the Greenwood Village Site (33Su92): 1984
        Season. Archaeological Research Report 56:1–100. Cleveland:
        Cleveland Museum of Natural History.
1986   The Staas Site (33Cu224): 1985 Excavations. Archaeological
        Research Report 40:1–112. Cleveland: Cleveland Museum of
        Natural History.
Belovich, Stephanie J., and David S. Brose
1982   Survey and Evaluative Testing within the Cuyahoga Valley N.R.A.:
        Sites 33Su87 and 33Su102. Archaeological Research Report
        40:1–86. Cleveland: Cleveland Museum of Natural History.
1983   Evaluative Testing at Greenwood Village Site (33Su92).
        Archaeological Research Report 47:1–141. Cleveland: Cleveland
        Museum of Natural History.
1992   Late Woodland Fortifications in Northern Ohio: The Greenwood
        Village Site. *Kirtlandia* 47:3–23.
Bender, Barbara
1985   Prehistoric Developments in the American Midcontinent and in
        Brittany, Northwest France. In *Prehistoric Hunter-Gathers*, ed. T. D.
        Price and J. A. Brown, 21–57. New York: Academic Press.
Bettarel, R., and H. Smith
1973   *The Moccasin Bluff Site and the Woodland Cultures of
        Southwestern Michigan.* Anthropological Papers 49. Ann Arbor:
        Museum of Anthropology, University of Michigan.
Bhaskar, R.
1979   *The Possibility of Naturalism.* Atlantic Highlands, N.J.: Humanities
        Press.
Black, Glenn A.
1967   *Angel Site.* 2 vols. Indianapolis: Indiana Historical Society.

Blitz, John H.
1993   Locust Beads and Archaic Mounds. *Mississippi Archaeology*
        28(1):20–43.
Bradley, Richard
1991   Monuments and Places. In *Sacred and Profane*, ed. P. Garwood, D.
        Jennings, R. Skeates, and J. Toms, 135–140. Monograph 32.
        Oxford: Oxford University Committee for Archaeology.
Bradley, J. W., and S. T. Childs
1991   Basque Earrings and Panthers' Tails: The Form of the Cross-Cultural
        Contact in Sixteenth-Century Iroquoia. In *Metals in Society: Theory
        Beyond Science and Technology*, ed. R. Ehrenreich, 7–17.
        Philadelphia: MASCA Research Papers in Science and Technology.
Brain, Jeffrey P.
1971   The Lower Mississippi Valley in North American Prehistory.
        Manuscript. On file, Arkansas Archeological Survey, Fayetteville.
Brinton, D. G.
1890   Folk-lore of the Modern Lenape. In *Essays of an Americanist*,
        181–192. Philadelphia: David McKay.
Brose, David S.
1973a   A Preliminary Analysis of Recent Excavations at the South Park
        Site, Cuyahoga County, Ohio. *Pennsylvania Archaeologist*
        43(1):25–42.
1973b   The Northeastern United States. In *The Development of North
        American Archaeology*, ed. J. E. Fitting, 84–115. Garden City, N.Y.:
        Anchor Press/Doubleday.
1974   The Everett Knoll: A Late Hopewellian Site in Northeastern Ohio.
        The Ohio Journal of Science 74(1):36–46.
1976a   An Initial Summary of the Late Prehistoric Period in Northeastern
        Ohio. In *The Late Prehistory of the Lake Erie Drainage Basin: A
        1972 Symposium Revised*, ed. David S. Brose, 25–47. Cleveland:
        Cleveland Museum of Natural History.
1976b   Locational Analysis in the Prehistory of Northeast Ohio. In
        *Cultural Change and Continuity: Essays in Honor of James Bennett
        Griffin*, ed. Charles E. Cleland, 3–18. New York: Academic Press.
1978   Late Prehistory of the Upper Great Lakes Area. In *Handbook of
        North American Indians*, vol. 15, ed. B. G. Trigger, 569–582.
        Washington, D.C.: Smithsonian Institution.
1985   The Woodland Prehistoric Occupation of Summit County, Ohio.
        Kirtlandia 41:35–61.
1992   *The South Park Village Site and the Late Prehistoric Whittlesey
        Tradition of Northeast Ohio*. Monographs in World Archaeology
        20. Madison: Prehistory Press.

Brose, David S., S. Belovich, M. Brooslin, R. Burns, J. Hall, H. Haller,
C. Pierce, and C. Ubbeohde
1981   Prehistoric and Historic Archaeological Investigations of the
Cuyahoga Valley National Recreation Area, Ohio. Archaeological
Research Report 30:1–524. Cleveland: Cleveland Museum of
Natural History.
Brose, David S., and N'omi Greber
1979   *Hopewell Archaeology*. Kent, Ohio: Kent State University Press.
Brose, David S., and John F. Scarry
1976   Boston Ledges: Spatial Analysis of an Early Late Woodland
Rockshelter in Summit County, Ohio. *Midcontinental Journal of
Archaeology* 1(2):179–228.
Brown, James A.
1979   Charnel Houses and Mortuary Crypts: Disposal of the Dead in the
Middle Woodland Period. In *Hopewell Archaeology: The Chillicothe
Conference*, ed. D. S. Brose and N. Greber, 211–219. Kent, Ohio:
Kent State University Press.
1981   The Search for Rank in Prehistoric Burials. In *The Archaeology of
Death*, ed. R. Chapman, I. Kinnes, and K. Randsborg, 25–37.
Cambridge: Cambridge University Press.
Brown, S. P.
1817   *The Western Gazetteer; or Emigrant's Dictionary* . . . Albany, N.Y.:
H. C. Southwick.
Bushnell, David I., Jr.
1909   *The Choctaw of Bayou Lacomb, St. Tammany Parish, Louisiana*.
Bulletin 48. Washington, D.C.: Bureau of American Ethnology.
Byers, A. M.
1987   The Earthwork Enclosures of the Central Ohio Valley: A Temporal
and Structural Analysis of Woodland Society and Culture. Ph.D.
diss., State University of New York, Albany. University Microfilms,
Ann Arbor.
1991   Structure, Meaning, Action and Things: The Duality of Material
Cultural Mediation. *Journal for the Theory of Social Behaviour*
21:1–26.
1992   The Action-Constitutive Theory of Monuments: A Strong
Pragmatist Version. *Journal for the Theory of Social Behaviour*
22:403–446.
Campbell, J. P.
1813   Antiquities of the Western Country. Manuscript. On file, Draper
Collection of Manuscripts, Wisconsin State Historical Society, Madison.
1816a   Of the Aborigines of the Western Country. *The Port Folio*, Fourth
series, 1(6):457–463.

1816b   Of the Aborigines of the Western Country. *The Port Folio*, Fourth series, 2(1):1–8.

Carruthers, Peter
1969   The Mikado Earthwork. Master's thesis, University of Calgary.

Champlain, Samuel de
1907   *Voyages of Samuel de Champlain*, 1604–1618, ed. E. L. Grant. New York: Charles Scribner's Sons.

Chapdelaine, Claude
1993   The Sedentarization of the Prehistoric Iroquoians: A Slow or Rapid Transformation? *Journal of Anthropological Archaeology* 12:173–209.

Chapman, R.
1981   The Emergence of Formal Disposal Areas and the Problem of Megalithic Tombs in Prehistoric Europe. In *The Archaeology of Death*, ed. R. Chapman, I. Kinnes, and K. Randsborg, 71–81. Cambridge: Cambridge University Press.

1995   Ten Years After—Megaliths, Mortuary Practices, and the Territorial Model. In *Regional Approaches to Mortuary Analysis*, ed. L. A. Beck, 29–51. New York: Academic Press.

Charles, Douglas K., and Jane E. Buikstra
1983   Archaic Mortuary Sites in the Central Mississippi Drainage: Distribution, Structure, and Behavioral Implications. In *Archaic Hunters and Gatherers in the American Midwest*, ed. J. L. Phillips and J. A. Brown, 117–145. New York: Academic Press.

Cheney, T. A.
1859   Illustrations of the Ancient Monuments in Western New York. In *Thirteenth Annual Report of the Regents of the University of the State of New York on the Condition of the State Cabinet of Natural History*, 37–72. Albany.

Clay, R. Berle
1985   Peter Village 164 Years Later: 1983 Excavations. In *Woodland Period Research in Kentucky*, edited by D. Pollack et al., 1–41. Frankfort: Kentucky Heritage Council.

1987   Circles and Ovals: Two Types of Adena Space. *Southeastern Archaeology* 6(1):46–56.

1988   Peter Village: An Adena Enclosure. In *Middle Woodland Settlement and Ceremonialism in the Mid-South and Lower Mississippi Valley*, ed. R. C. Mainfort, Jr., 19–30. Archaeological Report 22. Jackson: Mississippi Department of Archives and History.

Cleland, Charles E.
1966   *The Prehistoric Animal Ecology and Ethnozoology of the Upper Great Lakes Region*. Anthropological Papers 29. Ann Arbor: Museum of Anthropology, University of Michigan.

Connaway, John M.
1977   *The Denton Site, a Middle Archaic Occupation in the Northern Yazoo Basin, Mississippi.* Archaeological Report 4. Jackson: Mississippi Department of Archives and History.
1991   "Search . . . ," a Raptorial Review. *Newsletter of the Louisiana Archaeological Society* 18(3):3–4.

Connolly, Robert P.
1996a   Prehistoric Land Modification at the Ft. Ancient Hilltop Enclosure– An Accretive Model of Development. In *A View from the Core: A Conference Synthesizing Ohio Hopewell Archaeology,* ed. P. J. Pacheco, 258–273. Columbus: Ohio Archaeological Council.
1996b   Middle Woodland Period Hilltop Enclosures: The Built Environment, Construction and Function. Ph.D. diss., University of Illinois at Urbana-Champaign. University Microfilms, Ann Arbor.

Connolly, Robert P., and Lauren E. Sieg
1993   Prehistoric Architecture and the Development of Public Space at the Fort Ancient Hilltop Enclosure. Paper presented at the 5th International and Interdisciplinary Forum on Built Form and Culture Research, 2d CSPA Symposium on Architectural Practice, 14–17 September 1993, Cincinnati, Ohio.

Converse, Robert N.
1963   Ohio Flint Types. *Ohio Archaeologist* 13(4):77–121.
1984   Fishspear Points. *Ohio Archaeologist* 34(4):5.
1993   The Troyer Site: A Hopewell Habitation Site, and a Secular View of Ohio Hopewell Villages. *Ohio Archaeologist* 43(3):4–12.

Cornelius, Eldon, and Harold W. Moll
1961   The Walters-Linsenman Earthwork Site. *The Totem Pole* 44(9):1–9.

Cottier, John W., and Michael D. Southard
1977   An Introduction to the Archaeology of Towosaghy State Archaeological Site. In *Investigation and Comparison of Two Fortified Mississippi Tradition Archaeological Sites in Southeastern Missouri: A Preliminary Compilation,* by C. H. Chapman, J. W. Cottier, D. Denman, D. R. Evans, D. E. Harvey, M. D. Reagan, B. L. Rope, M. D. Southard, and G. W. Waselkov, 230–271. *Missouri Archaeologist* 38.

Cox, P. E.
1929   Preliminary Report of Exploration at Old Stone Fort, Manchester, Tennessee. *Journal of the Tennessee Academy of Science* 4(1):1–8.

Dancey, William S.
1988   The Community Plan of an Early Late Woodland Village in the Middle Scioto River Valley. *Midcontinental Journal of Archaeology* 13(2):223–258.

DeBoer, Warren R.
1988   Subterranean Storage and the Organization of Surplus: The View
        from Eastern North America. *Southeastern Archaeology* 7(1):1–20.
DeBoer, Warren R., and John H. Blitz
1991   Ceremonial Centers of the Chachi. *Expedition* 33(1):53–62.
Douglas, M.
1966   *Purity and Danger.* New York: Praeger.
1970   *Natural Symbols.* London: Barrie and Jenkins.
1975   *Implicit Meanings: Essays in Anthropology.* London: Routledge
        and Kegan Paul.
1982   Primitive Rationing. In *In the Active Voice,* ed. M. Douglas, 57–81.
        London: Routledge and Kegan Paul.
Dragoo, D. W., and C. F. Wray
1964   Hopewell Figurine Rediscovered. *American Antiquity* 30:195–199.
Drake, Daniel
1815   *Picture of Cincinnati and the Miami Country.* Cincinnati.
Drewett, Peter
1977   The Excavation of a Neolithic Causewayed Enclosure on Offham
        Hill, East Sussex. *Proceedings of the Prehistoric Society*
        43:201–241.
DuPratz, M. Le Page
[1774] 1975 *The History of Louisiana.* Facsimile ed. Baton Rouge:
        Louisiana State University Press.
Dustin, Fred
1932   *Report on the Indian Earthworks in Ogemaw County, Michigan.*
        Scientific Publications 1. Bloomfield Hills, Mich.: Cranbrook
        Institute of Science.
Earle, T.
1991   Paths and Roads in Evolutionary Perspective. In *Ancient Road
        Networks and Settlement Hierarchies in the New World,* ed. C. D.
        Trombold, 10–27. Cambridge: Cambridge University Press.
Edson, O.
1875   History of Chautauqua Anterior to its Pioneer Settlement. In
        History of Chautauqua County by Andrew Young, 2–63. Buffalo,
        N.Y.: Matthews and Warren.
1894   *History of Chautauqua County.* Boston: W. A. Fergusson.
Engelbrecht, William
1996   Ceramics. In *Reanalyzing the Ripley Site: Earthworks and Late
        Prehistory on the Lake Erie Plain,* ed. L. P. Sullivan, 53–68. New
        York State Museum Bulletin 489. Albany: State Education
        Department.

Essenpreis, P. S.
1985   1985 Archaeological Investigations at the Fort Ancient State
        Memorial: Borrow Area and Gateway 44. Manuscript. On file, Ohio
        Historical Society, Columbus.
1986   An Architectural Examination of Fort Ancient. Paper presented at
        the 51st Annual Meeting of the Society for American Archaeology,
        New Orleans.
1990   Preliminary Report of the 1988 Investigations at the Fort Ancient
        State Memorial: The South Fort Village and Middle Fort.
        Manuscript. On file, Ohio Historical Society, Columbus.
Essenpreis, P. S., and D. J. Duszynski
1989   Possible Astronomical Alignments at the Fort Ancient Monument.
        Paper presented at the Society for American Archaeology.
Essenpreis, P. S., and M. E. Moseley
1984   Fort Ancient: Citadel or Coliseum? *Field Museum of Natural
        History Bulletin* 55(6):5–26.
Evans, Christopher
1988   Acts of Enclosure: A Consideration of Concentrically-Organised
        Causewayed Enclosures. In *The Archaeology of Context in the
        Neolithic and Bronze Age: Recent Trends*, ed. J. C. Barrett and I. A.
        Kinnes, 85–96. Dept. of Archaeology and Prehistory, University of
        Sheffield.
Evans, J. G., A. J. Rouse, and N. M. Sharples
1988   The Landscape Setting of Causewayed Camps: Recent Work on the
        Maiden Castle Enclosure. In *The Archaeology of Context in the
        Neolithic and Bronze Age: Recent Trends*, ed. J. C. Barrett and I. A.
        Kinnes, 73–84. Dept. of Archaeology and Prehistory, University of
        Sheffield.
Faulkner, C. H.
1968   *The Old Stone Fort.* Knoxville: University of Tennessee Press.
Fenton, William N.
1978   Northern Iroquoian Culture Patterns. In *Handbook of North
        American Indians*, vol. 15, ed. B. G. Trigger, 296–321. Washington,
        D.C.: Smithsonian Institution.
Fie, S. M., J. Fountain, E. D. Hunt, E. Zubrow, R. Jacobi, K. Bartalotta,
        J. Brennan, K. Allen, and P. Bush
1990   The Analysis of Encrustations in Iroquois Ceramic Vessels:
        Implications for the Delineation of Food Resource Areas.
        Manuscript. On file, Dept. of Anthropology, State University of
        New York, Buffalo.

Finney, Fred A.
1997   Archaeological Investigations at Selected Sites in the Cuyahoga
        River Valley, Cuyahoga and Summit Counties, Ohio. Institute for
        Minnesota Archaeology Reports of Investigation No. 467.
        Minneapolis. In press.
Fischer, Fred W.
1965   Preliminary Report on 1965 Archaeological Investigations at
        Miami Fort. Mimeographed. University of Cincinnati.
1967   Miami Fort Site: 1966 Preliminary Report. Mimeographed.
        University of Cincinnati.
Fischer, Fred W., and Charles H. McNutt
1962   Test Excavation at Pinson Mounds, 1961. *Tennessee Archaeologist*
        18(1):1–13.
Fisk, H. N.
1940   *Geology of Avoyelles and Rapides Parish.* New Orleans: Department
        of Conservation, Louisiana Geological Survey.
Fitting, James E.
1964   Ceramic Relationships of Four Late Woodland Sites in Northern
        Ohio. *Wisconsin Archaeologist* 45(4):160–175.
1972   *The Schultz Site at Green Point.* Memoirs 4. Ann Arbor: Museum
        of Anthropology, University of Michigan.
1975   *The Archaeology of Michigan.* Bloomfield Hills, Michigan:
        Cranbrook Institute of Science.
Fitting, James E. (editor)
1966   Edge Area Archaeology. *Michigan Archaeologist* 12(4).
Fitzgerald, W. R.
1991   An Analysis of Brass and Copper from the Ripley Site: The 1906
        Sample. Manuscript. On file, New York State Museum, Albany.
Fitzgerald, W. R., and P. G. Ramsden
1988   Copper Based Metal Testing as an Aid to Understanding Early
        European-Amerindian Interaction: Scratching the Surface.
        Canadian Journal of Archaeology 12:1–10.
Folan, W. J.
1991   Sacbes of the Northern Maya. In *Ancient Road Networks and
        Settlement Hierarchies in the New World,* ed. C. D. Thombold,
        222–229. Cambridge: Cambridge University Press.
Ford, James A.
1936   *Analysis of Indian Village Site Collections from Louisiana and
        Mississippi.* Anthropological Study 2. New Orleans: Louisiana
        Geological Survey.

1951   *Greenhouse: A Troyville–Coles Creek Period Site in Avoyelles Parish, Louisiana.* Anthropological Papers 44(2). New York: American Museum of Natural History.

1955   The Puzzle of Poverty Point. *Natural History* 64:466–472.

1969   *A Comparison of Formative Cultures in the Americas, Diffusion of the Psychic Unity of Man.* Smithsonian Contributions to Anthropology 11. Washington, D.C.: Smithsonian Institution.

Ford, James A., and Clarence H. Webb

1956   *Poverty Point, a Late Archaic Site in Louisiana.* Anthropological Papers 45(1). New York: American Museum of Natural History.

Ford, Richard I.

1974   Corn from the Straits of Mackinac. *Michigan Archaeologist* 20(2):97–104.

Fowke, Gerard

1893   The Archaeology of Ohio. In *Geological Survey of Ohio*, Report 7, Pt. 2.

1902   *Archaeological History of Ohio.* Columbus: Ohio State Archaeological and Historical Society.

1927   *Archaeological Work in Louisiana.* Smithsonian Miscellaneous Collections 78(7). Washington, D.C.

1928   Archaeological Investigations II. *Forty-fourth Annual Report of the Smithsonian Institution Bureau of American Ethnology*, 399–540. Washington, D.C.

Freidel, D. A., and J. A. Sabloff

1984   *Cozumel: Late Maya Settlement Patterns.* Orlando: Academic Press.

Funk, Robert E.

1967   Garoga: A Late Prehistoric Iroquois Village in the Mohawk Valley. In *Iroquois Culture, History and Prehistory: Proceedings of the 1965 Conference on Iroquois Research*, ed. Elisabeth Tooker, 81–84. Albany: New York State Museum and Science Center.

Gibson, E. P., and Ruth Herrick

1957   Spot Hunting in Missaukee County, Michigan. *Michigan Archaeologist* 3(4):94–96.

Gibson, Jon L.

1970   The Hopewell Phenomenon in the Lower Mississippi Valley. *Louisiana Studies* (Fall 1970).

1972   Patterns at Poverty Point: Empirical and Social Structures. *Southeastern Archaeological Conference Bulletin* 15:119–125.

1973   Social Systems at Poverty Point: An Analysis of Intersite and Intrasite Variability. Ph.D. diss., Southern Methodist University, Dallas.

1974   Poverty Point, the First North American Chiefdom. *Archaeology* 27:96–105.

1980   Speculations on the Origin and Development of Poverty Point. In *Caddoan and Poverty Point Archaeology: Essays in Honor of Clarence Hungerford Webb*, ed. J. L. Gibson, 319–348. Louisiana Archaeology 6.

1987   Poverty Point Reconsidered. *Mississippi Archaeology* 22(2):14–31.

1990   Religion of the Rings: Poverty Point Iconology and Ceremonialism. Revised version of a paper presented at the 11th annual Mid-South Archaeological Conference, Pinson, Tennessee.

1992   Poverty Point Chronology: The Long and the Short of It. Paper presented at the 34th annual Caddo Conference, Bossier City, Louisiana.

1993   *In Helona's Shadow: Excavations in the Western Rings at Poverty Point, 1991*. Report 11. Lafayette: Center for Archaeological Studies, University of Southwestern Louisiana.

1994   Before Their Time? Early Mounds in the Lower Mississippi Valley. *Southeastern Archaeology* 13:162–181.

1996   The Orvis Scott Site: A Poverty Point Component on Joes Bayou, East Carroll Parish, Louisiana. *Midcontinental Journal of Archaeology* 20(1):1–48.

Gibson, Jon L., and J. Richard Shenkel

1988   Louisiana Earthworks: Middle Woodland and Predecessors. In *Middle Woodland Settlement and Ceremonialism in the Mid-South and Lower Mississippi Valley*, ed. R. C. Mainfort, Jr., 7–18. Archaeological Report 22. Jackson: Mississippi Department of Archives and History.

Giddens, A.

1976   *New Rules of Sociological Method*. London: Hutchinson.

1979   *Central Problems in Social Theory*. London: Macmillan.

1981   *A Contemporary Critique of Historical Materialism*. London: Macmillan.

1984   *The Constitution of Society*. Berkeley: University of California Press.

Gill, Sam D.

1982   *Native American Religions: An Introduction*. Belmont, Calif.: Wadsworth.

Goldstein, Lynne G.

1995   Landscapes and Mortuary Practices: A Case for Regional Perspectives. In *Regional Approaches to Mortuary Analysis*, ed. L. A. Beck, 101–121. New York: Plenum Press.

Goodelier, Maurice
1977   Economy and Religion: An Evolutionary Optical Illusion. In *The Evolution of Social Systems*, ed. J. Friedman and M. Rowlands, 3–11. London: Duckworth.

Gorecki, P. P.
1985   The Conquest of a New "Wet and Dry" Territory: Its Mechanisms and Its Archaeological Consequences. In *Prehistoric Intensive Agriculture in the Tropics*, ed. I. Farrington, 321–345. BAR International Series No. 232.

Greber, N. B.
1976   Within Ohio Hopewell: Analyses of Burial Patterns from Several Classic Sites. Ph.D. diss., Case Western Reserve University. University Microfilms, Ann Arbor.

1979   A Comparative Study of Site Morphology and Burial Patterns at Edwin Harness Mound and Seip Mounds 1 and 2. In *Hopewell Archaeology: The Chillicothe Conference*, ed. D. S. Brose and N. Greber, 27–38. Kent, Ohio: Kent State University Press.

1983   *Recent Excavations at the Edwin Harness Mound, Liberty Works, Ross County, Ohio.* Special Paper 5. Midcontinental Journal of Archaeology. Kent, Ohio: Kent State University Press.

1989   Astronomy and the Patterns of Five Geometric Earthworks in Ross County, Ohio. Abstract in *World Archaeoastronomy: Selected Papers from the Second Oxford International Conference on Archaeoastronomy Held at Mérida, Yucatán, Mexico, 13–16 January 1986*, ed. A. F. Aveni, 495. Cambridge: Cambridge University Press.

1992   The Seip Geometric Enclosure and Environs: An Estimate of Possible Changes in Community Patterns through Time. Paper presented to the 57th Annual Meeting of the Society for American Archaeology, Pittsburgh.

1996   A Commentary on the Contexts and Contents of Large to Small Ohio Hopewell Deposits. In *Hopewell Archaeology: The View from the Core*, ed. P. J. Pacheco, 150–172. Columbus: Ohio Archaeological Council.

1997   Two Geometric Enclosures in Paint Creek Valley: An Estimate of Possible Changes in Community Patterns through Time. In *Ohio Hopewell Community Organization*, ed. W. S. Dancey and P. J. Pacheco, 207–230. Kent, Ohio: Kent State University Press.

Greber, N. B., and K. C. Ruhl
1989   *The Hopewell Site: A Contemporary Analysis Based on the Work of Charles C. Willoughby.* Boulder, Colo.: Westview Press.

Green, William, and Lynne P. Sullivan
1997   Pits and Pitfalls: An Analysis of Pit Features and Site Function at the Ripley Site. *Northeast Anthropology* 53:1–21.
Greenman, Emerson F.
1927a   The Earthwork Enclosures of Michigan. Ph.D. diss., University of Michigan, Ann Arbor.
1927b   Michigan Mounds with Special Reference to Two in Missaukee County. *Papers of the Michigan Academy of Science, Arts and Letters* 7:1–9.
1928   Unpublished field notes on the excavation of Eagle Mound and the Wells Mound Group. Manuscript. On file, Department of Archaeology, Ohio Historical Society, Columbus.
1935a   Excavation of the Reeve Village Site, Lake County, Ohio. *The Ohio State Archaeological and Historical Quarterly* 44(1):2–64.
1935b   Seven Prehistoric Sites in Northern Ohio. *Ohio State Archaeological and Historical Quarterly* 44(2):305–366.
1937   Two Prehistoric Villages near Cleveland, Ohio. *Ohio State Archaeological and Historical Quarterly* 46(4):305–370.
Griffin, James B.
1952   Culture Periods in Eastern United States Archeology. In *Archeology of the Eastern United States*, ed. J. B. Griffin, 352–364. Chicago: University of Chicago Press.
1967   Eastern North American Archaeology: A Summary. *Science* 156(3772):175–91.
Guthe, Alfred K.
1958   *The Late Prehistoric Occupation in Southwestern New York: An Interpretive Analysis.* Research Records 11. Rochester, N.Y.: Rochester Museum of Arts and Science.
Haag, William G.
1961   The Archaic of the Lower Mississippi Valley. *American Antiquity* 26:317–323.
Haas, Mary R.
1956   Natchez and the Muskogean Languages. *Language* 32:61–72.
1958   A New Linguistic Relationship in North America: Algonkian and Gulf Languages. *Southwestern Journal of Anthropology* 14:231–264.
Hale, E. E., Jr.
1980   Archaeological Survey Report, Phase III, LIC-79-12-55. On file, Ohio Historical Society, Department of Archaeology, Columbus.
Hall, R. L.
1989   The Cultural Background of Mississippian Symbolism. In *The Southeastern Ceremonial Complex: Artifacts and Analysis*, ed. P. Galloway, 238–318. Lincoln: University of Nebraska Press.

Hall, Robert L.
1976   Ghosts, Water Barriers, Corn and Sacred Enclosures in the Eastern
        Woodlands. *American Antiquity* 41:360–364.
Halsey, John Robert
1976   The Bussinger Site: A Multicomponent Site in the Saginaw Valley
        of Michigan with a Review of Early Late Woodland Mortuary
        Complexes in the Northeastern Woodlands. Ph.D. diss., University
        of North Carolina, Chapel Hill.
Harkness, B.
1982   Implications for Ohio Hopewell Polity Suggested by Lithic and
        Iconographic Analysis. Ph.D. diss., University Microfilms, Ann
        Arbor, Michigan.
Harrè, Romano
1979   *Social Being: A Theory of Social Psychology.* Oxford: Basil Blackwell.
Harris, T. M.
1805   *Journal of a Tour into the Territory Northwest of the Allegheny
        Mountains: Made in the Spring of the Year 1803.* Boston:
        Manning and Loring.
Harrison, William Henry
1839   A Discourse on the Aborigines of the Ohio Valley. In *Transactions
        of the Historical and Philosophical Society of Ohio* 1(2). Cincinnati.
Haven, S. F.
1870   Report of the Librarian. *Proceedings of the American Antiquarian
        Society,* 39–41, 27 April 1870.
Heidenreich, Conrad E.
1978   Huron. In *Handbook of North American Indians,* vol. 15, ed. B. G.
        Trigger, 368–388. Washington, D.C.: Smithsonian Institution Press.
Hickerson, H.
1962   *The Southwestern Chippewa: An Ethnohistorical Study.* Memoir
        92. American Anthropological Association.
Hinsdale, W. B.
1924   The Missaukee Preserve and Rifle River Forts. *Papers of the
        Michigan Academy of Science, Arts and Letters* 4:1–14.
1925   *Primitive Man in Michigan.* Michigan Handbook Series 1. Ann
        Arbor: University Museum, University of Michigan.
1931   *Archaeological Atlas of Michigan.* Michigan Handbook Series 4.
        Ann Arbor: University Museum, University of Michigan.
Hively, R., and R. Horn
1982   Geometry and Astronomy in Prehistoric Ohio. *Journal for the
        History of Astronomy. Archaeoastronomy Supplement* 13:S1–S20.
1984   Hopewellian Geometry and Astronomy at High Bank.
        Archaeoastronomy 7:S85–S100.

Hodder, Ian
1982   *Symbols in Action*. Cambridge: Cambridge University Press.
1985   Postprocessual Archaeology. In *Advances in Archaeological Method and Theory*, vol. 8, ed. M. B. Schiffer, 1–26. New York: Academic Press.
1989   This Is Not an Article about Material Culture as Text. *Journal of Anthropological Archaeology* 8:250–269.
Hodder, Ian (editor)
1987   *The Archaeology of Contextual Meanings*. Cambridge: Cambridge University Press.
Holmes, W. H.
1892   Notes upon Some Geometric Earthworks, with Contour Maps. *American Anthropologist* 5:363–373.
Hudson, Charles
1976   *The Southeastern Indians*. Knoxville: University of Tennessee Press.
1984   *Elements of Southeastern Indian Religions*. Leiden, Netherlands: E. J. Brill.
1987   The Southeast Woodlands. In *Native American Religions, North America*, ed. Lawrence E. Sullivan, 139–146. New York: Macmillan.
Jackson, H. Edwin
1991   The Trade Fair in Hunter-Gatherer Interaction: The Role of Intersocietal Trade in the Evolution of Poverty Point Culture. In *Between Bands and States*, ed. Susan A. Gregg, 265–286. Occasional Paper 9. Carbondale: Center for Archaeological Investigations, Southern Illinois University.
Johannessen, Sissel
1984   Paleoethnobotany. In *American Bottom Archaeology*, ed. C. J. Bareis and J. W. Porter, 197–214. Urbana: University of Illinois Press.
Johnson, William, James B. Richardson III, and Alan S. Bohnert
1979   Archaeological Site Survey in Northwestern Pennsylvania, Region IV. Report submitted by the Section of Man, Carnegie Museum of Natural History, to the Pennsylvania Historical and Museum Commission.
Jones, Dennis
1991   The Avoyelles Prairie Terrace-Concentrated Archaeology. *Louisiana Archaeological Society Newsletter* 18(1).
Jones, D., and A. Jones
1980   The Defenses at Indian Fort Road, Tompkins County, New York. *Pennsylvania Archaeologist* 50(1–2):61–71.

Jones, Dennis, and Malcolm Shuman
1989   Atlas and Report on Prehistoric Indian Mounds in Louisiana, vol.
       IV, Avoyelles Parish, Pt. 1. Museum of Geoscience, Louisiana State
       University. Report. On file, Louisiana Division of Archaeology,
       Baton Rouge.
Justice, Noel D.
1987   *Stone Age Spear and Arrow Points of the Midcontinental and
       Eastern United States.* Bloomington and Indianapolis: Indiana
       University Press.
Kincaid, C. (editor)
1983   *Chaco Roads Project Phase I, a Reappraisal of Prehistoric Roads in
       the San Juan Basin.* Albuquerque, N.M.: U.S. Department of the
       Interior, Bureau of Land Management.
Kintigh, Keith W.
1984   Measuring Archaeological Diversity by Comparison with Simulated
       Assemblages. *American Antiquity* 49(1):44–54.
1989   Sample Size, Significance and Measures of Diversity. In
       Quantifying Diversity in Archaeology, ed. R. D. Leonard and G. T.
       Jones, 25–36. Cambridge: Cambridge University Press.
1994   *Tools for Quantitative Archaeology: Programs for Quantitative
       Analysis in Archaeology.* Tempe, Ariz.: Keith W. Kintigh.
Knight, James V.
1986   The Institutional Organization of Mississippian Religion. *American
       Antiquity* 51:675–685.
1989   Symbolism of Mississippian Mounds. In *Powhatans' Mantle:
       Indians in the Colonial Southeast,* ed. Peter H. Wood, Gregory
       Waselkov, and M. Thomas Hatley, 279–291. Lincoln: University of
       Nebraska Press.
Kocsis, Alexander
1973   *Old Stone Fort.* Edited by B. A. Bridgewater. Special Publication 1.
       Manchester, Tenn.: Coffee County Historical Society.
Krakker, James J.
1983   Changing Sociocultural Systems during the Late Prehistoric Period in
       Southeast Michigan. Ph.D. diss., University of Michigan, Ann Arbor.
Kroon, Leonard
1972   Notes on Ceramic Technology from the Weiser Site, Kent County,
       Ontario. *Michigan Archaeologist* 18:215–222.
Labar, R. J.
1968   Report on Archaeological Excavations of Indian Forts 36EL1 and
       36EL2, Highland Township, Elk County, Pennsylvania. Manuscript.
       On file, Section of Archaeology, William Penn Museum,
       Pennsylvania Historical and Museum Commission, Harrisburg.

Larkin, F.
1880   *Ancient Man in America*. Washington, D.C.: Miles Davis.
Leach, M. L.
1885   Ancient Forts in Ogemaw County, Michigan. *Annual Report of the Board of Regents of the Smithsonian Institution, 1884*, 849–851. Washington, D.C.
Lee, Alfred M.
1986   *Excavations at the Stanford Knoll Site, Cuyahoga Valley National Recreation Area*. Archaeological Research Report 65:1–100. Cleveland: Cleveland Museum of Natural History.
1987   *Archaeological Reconnaissance in Ashtabula County, Ohio*. Archaeological Research Report 78. Cleveland: Cleveland Museum of Natural History.
Lee, Alfred M., and Stephanie J. Belovich
1985   Field notes and forms from test excavations in 1985 at Fort Hill (33Cu1). On file, Cleveland Museum of Natural History, Cleveland.
Lee, Thomas E.
1958   The Parker Earthwork, Corunna, Ontario. *Pennsylvania Archaeologist* 28(1):3–30.
Lepper, Bradley T.
1989   An Historical Review of Archaeological Research at the Newark Earthworks. *Journal of the Steward Anthropological Society* 18(1–2):118–140.
1991   Early Archaeological Investigations in Licking County, Ohio. *Ohio Archaeologist* 40(4):6–7.
1992a   A "New" Old Map of the Newark Earthworks. *Licking County Historical Society Quarterly* 2(3):4.
1992b   Just How Holy Are the Newark "Holy Stones"? In *Vanishing Heritage: Notes and Queries about the Archaeology and Culture History of Licking County, Ohio*, ed. P. E. Hooge and B. T. Lepper, 58–64. Newark, Ohio: Licking County Archaeology and Landmarks Society.
1993   The Newark Earthworks and the Geometric Enclosures of the Scioto Valley: Connections and Conjectures. Paper presented at the symposium Hopewell Archaeology: A View from the Core, Ohio Archaeological Council, Chillicothe, Ohio, November 1993.
1995   Tracking Ohio's Great Hopewell Road. *Archaeology* 48(6):52–56.
1996   The Newark Earthworks and the Geometric Enclosures of the Scioto Valley. In *A View from the Core: A Synthesis of Ohio Hopewell Archaeology*, ed. P. J. Pacheco, 224–241. Columbus: Ohio Archaeological Council.

Lepper, B. T., and R. Yerkes
1997   Hopewellian Occupations at the Northern Periphery of the Newark
        Earthworks: The Newark Expressway Sites Revisited. In *Ohio
        Hopewell Community Organization*, ed. W. S. Dancey and P. J.
        Pacheco, 175–206. Kent, Ohio: Kent State University Press.
Licking [pseud.]
1834   Ancient Fortifications. *Western Monthly Magazine* 2:446–447.
Linares, Olga F.
1976   "Garden Hunting" in the American Tropics. *Human Ecology* 4(4):331–349.
Lingafelter, R. C.
1899   Description of Ancient Earth Works Idlewilde Park. Manuscript. On
        file, Licking County Historical Society, Newark, Ohio.
Little, G.
1891   Fort Ancient Survey Notes. Manuscript. On file, Ohio Historical
        Society, Columbus.
Lovis, William, and John M. O'Shea
1993   A Reconsideration of Archaeological Research Design in Michigan.
        Michigan Archaeologist 39(3–4):107–126.
MacLean, J. P.
1879   *The Mound Builders.* Cincinnati: Robert Clarke and Co.
1887   Aboriginal History of Butler County. *Ohio Archaeological and
        Historical Quarterly* 1:64–68.
MacNeish, Richard S.
1952   *Iroquois Pottery Types: A Technique for the Study of Iroquois
        Prehistory.* Anthropological Series 31. Bulletin 124. Ottawa:
        National Museum of Canada.
Mainfort, Robert C., Jr.
1986   *Pinson Mounds: A Middle Woodland Ceremonial Center.* Research
        Series 7. Nashville: Tennessee Department of Conservation,
        Division of Archaeology.
1988   Middle Woodland Ceremonialism at Pinson Mounds, Tennessee.
        American Antiquity 53(1):158–173.
1993   Pinson Mounds and the Middle Woodland Period in the Midsouth.
        Keynote address, "A View from the Core: A Conference
        Synthesizing Ohio Hopewell Archaeology," Chillicothe, Ohio.
Mainfort, Robert C., Jr., and Robert L. Thunen
1986   The "Eastern Citadel": A Circular Enclosure at Pinson Mounds.
        Paper presented to the Society for American Archaeology, New
        Orleans, Louisiana.
Mainfort, Robert C., Jr., and Richard Walling
1992   1989 Excavations at Pinson Mounds: Ozier Mound. *Midcontinental
        Journal of Archaeology* 17(1):112–136.

Marshall, J. A.
1986   Survey and Mapping Fort Ancient, Warren County, Ohio. Paper
       presented to the Midwest Archaeological Conference, Columbus,
       Ohio.
1987   An Atlas of American Indian Geometry. *Ohio Archaeologist*
       37(2):36–49.
Mason, O. T.
1882   Stone Image Found in Ohio. *American Naturalist* 16(2):154.
Mayer-Oakes, William J.
1955   Prehistory of the Upper Ohio Valley. *Annals of the Carnegie
       Museum,* vol. 34. Anthropological Series 2.
McMichael, Edward V.
1984   Appendix A: Type Descriptions for Newtown Series Ceramics. In
       *The Pyles Site (15MS28), a Newtown Village in Mason County,
       Kentucky,* ed. J. Railey, 132–135. Occasional Paper 1. Lexington:
       William S. Webb Archaeological Society.
Middleton, J. D.
1887   Ohio Mounds. *Science* 10(232):32.
Miller, Robert A.
1974   *The Geological History of Tennessee.* Bulletin 74. Nashville:
       Tennessee Department of Conservation, Division of Geology.
Mills, W. C.
1908   Field Notes from 1908 Excavations at Fort Ancient. Manuscript.
       On file, Ohio Historical Society, Columbus.
1922   Exploration of the Mound City Group. *Ohio Archaeological and
       Historical Quarterly* 31:423–584.
Milner, Claire McHale
1992   Diversity within Homogeneity: The Role of Ceramic Style in
       Juntunen Phase Social Differentiation and Risk Buffering. Paper
       presented at the Midwest Archaeological Conference, Grand
       Rapids, Michigan.
1994   Regional Identity and Interregional Interaction during the
       Juntunen Phase, A.D.1200–1620. Paper presented at the Annual
       Meeting of the Canadian Archaeological Association, Edmonton,
       Alberta.
Milner, Claire McHale, and John M. O'Shea
1990   Life after the Juntunen Site? Late Prehistoric Occupation of the
       Upper Great Lakes. Paper presented at the Midwest Archaeological
       Conference, Evanston, Illinois.
Moll, Harold W., Norman G. Moll, and Eldon S. Cornelius
1958   Earthwork Enclosures in Ogemaw, Missaukee, and Alcona Counties.
       The Totem Pole 41(3).

Moorehead, Warren King
1887   Notes on Fort Ancient. Manuscript. On file, Ohio Historical Society,
        Columbus.
1890   *Fort Ancient: The Great Prehistoric Earthwork of Warren County,
        Ohio.* Cincinnati: Robert Clarke and Co.
1895   A Description of Fort Ancient. *Ohio Archaeological and Historical
        Society Publications* 4:362–377.
Morgan, Lewis H.
1851   *League of the Ho-de-no-sau-nee or Iroquois.* Rochester, N.Y.: M. H.
        Newman.
Morgan, Richard G.
1939   Field Notes from 1939 Excavations at the Fort Ancient State
        Memorial. Manuscript. On file, Ohio Historical Society, Columbus.
1940   Field Notes from 1940 Excavations at the Fort Ancient State
        Memorial. Manuscript. On file, Ohio Historical Society, Columbus.
1952   Outline of Cultures in the Ohio Region. In *Archeology of Eastern
        United States*, ed. J. B. Griffin, 83–98. Chicago: University of
        Chicago Press.
Morgan, Richard G., and H. Holmes Ellis
1943   The Fairport Harbor Site. *Ohio State Archaeological and Historical
        Quarterly* 52(3):1–62.
Morgan, Richard G., and Edward S. Thomas
1948   *Fort Hill.* Columbus: Ohio State Archaeological and Historical
        Society.
Morse, Dan F.
1986   Preliminary Investigation of the Pinson Mounds Site: 1963 Field
        Season. In *Pinson Mounds: A Middle Woodland Ceremonial Center*,
        by Robert C. Mainfort, Jr., 96–119. Research Series 7. Nashville:
        Tennessee Department of Conservation, Division of Archaeology.
Murphy, Carl, and Neal Ferris
1990   The Late Woodland Basin Tradition of Southwestern Ontario. In
        The Archaeology of Southern Ontario to A.D. 1650, ed. C. J. Ellis
        and N. Ferris, 189–278. Occasional Publications 5. London Chapter,
        Ontario Archaeological Society.
Murphy, James L.
1971   The Fairport Harbor Site (33LA5), Lake County, Ohio. *The
        Pennsylvania Archaeologist* 41(3):26–43.
1986   Dr. John Poage Campbell: Pioneer Archaeologist of the "Western
        States" (abstract). *ESAF Bulletin* 45:28.
1995   Two Older "New" Maps of the Newark Earthworks. *Ohio
        Archaeologist* 45(2):4–7.

Myer, William E.
1922   Recent Archaeological Discoveries in Tennessee. *Art and Archaeology* 14:141–150.

Neusius, Phillip D.
1996   Lithic Assemblage Variability in the Parker Collections. In *Reanalyzing the Ripley Site: Earthworks and Late Prehistory on the Lake Erie Plain*, ed. L. P. Sullivan, 69–77. New York State Museum Bulletin 489. Albany: State Education Department.

Neusius, S.
1990   Hunting Strategies and Horticulturalists: The Anasazi and Iroquoian Cases. Paper presented at the 6th International Congress of Archaeozoologists, Washington, D.C.
1994   What Can Faunal Remains Tell Us about Site Function? The Ripley Site Experience. Paper presented at the conference Ethnobiology: Perspectives and Practice in the Northeastern United States and Eastern Canada, Rochester Museum and Science Center, Rochester, N.Y.
1996a   Game Procurement among Temperate Horticulturalists: The Case for Garden Hunting by the Dolores Anasazi. In *Case Studies in Environmental Archaeology*, ed. E. J. Reitz, L. A. Newsom, and S. J. Scudder, 273–288. New York: Plenum Press.
1996b   Ripley Site Faunal Analysis and the Parker Collections. In *Reanalyzing the Ripley Site: Earthworks and Late Prehistory on the Lake Erie Plain*, ed. L. P. Sullivan, 78–89. New York State Museum Bulletin 489. Albany: State Education Department.

Oehler, Charles
1950   *Turpin Indians.* Cincinnati Museum of Natural History Popular Publication Series 1. (Revised and reprinted for the *Journal of the Cincinnati Museum of Natural History* 23(2), 1973.)

Oplinger, Jon
1981   *Wise Rockshelter: A Multicomponent Site in Jackson County, Ohio.* Kent State Research Papers in Archaeology 2. Kent, Ohio: Kent State University Press.

Ormerod, Dana E.
1983   *White Rocks: A Woodland Rockshelter in Monroe County, Ohio.* Kent State Research Papers in Archaeology 4. Kent, Ohio: Kent State University Press.

O'Shea, John M.
1988   Marginal Agriculture or Agriculture at the Margins: A Consideration of Native American Agriculture in the Upper Great Lakes. Paper presented at the Annual Meeting of the Society for American Archaeology, Phoenix, Arizona.

O'Shea, John M., and Claire McHale Milner

n.d.   The Hubbard Lake Survey: 1983–1987. Technical Report, University of Michigan, Museum of Anthropology, Ann Arbor. In preparation.

Park, S.

1870   American Antiquities. In *Notes of the Early History of Union Township, Licking County, Ohio*, 35–56. Terre Haute, Ind.: O. J. Smith.

Parker, Arthur

1907   *Excavations in an Erie Indian Village and Burial Site at Ripley, Chautauqua Co., New York*. Bulletin 117. Albany: New York State Museum.

1922   *The Archaeological History of New York*. Bulletins 235 and 236. Albany: New York State Museum.

Phillips, Philip

1970   Archaeological Survey in the Lower Yazoo Basin, Mississippi, 1949–1955. Papers of the Peabody Museum of Archaeology and Ethnology vol. 60. Cambridge: Harvard University.

Prahl, Earl J.

1966   The Muskegon River Survey: 1965 and 1966. *Michigan Archaeologist* 12(4):183–209.

Prufer, Olaf H.

1961   The Hopewell Complex of Ohio. Ph.D. diss., Harvard University.

1964a   The Hopewell Complex of Ohio. In *Hopewellian Studies*, ed. R. L. Hall and J. R. Caldwell, 37–83. Scientific Papers 12. Springfield: Illinois State Museum.

1964b   The Hopewell Cult. *Scientific American* 211(6):90–102.

1965   The McGraw Site: A Study in Hopewellian Dynamics. *Scientific Publications of the Cleveland Museum of Natural History* 4(1).

1967   Chesser Cave: A Late Woodland Phase in Southeastern Ohio. In *Studies in Ohio Archaeology*, ed. O. Prufer and D. McKenzie, 1–62. Cleveland: Press of Western Reserve University.

1981   Raven Rocks: A Specialized Late Woodland Rockshelter Occupation in Belmont County, Ohio. *Kent State Research Papers in Archaeology* 1. Kent, Ohio: Kent State University Press.

1997   Fort Hill 1964: New Data and Reflections on Hopewell Hilltop Enclosures in Southern Ohio. In *Ohio Hopewell Community Organization*, ed. W. S. Dancey and P. J. Pacheco, 311–328. Kent, Ohio: Kent State University Press.

Putnam, Frederic Ward

1891   A Singular Ancient Work. American Antiquarian Society *Proceedings*, 1890, n.s. 7(1):136–137.

Quimby, George I.
1965   An Indian Earthwork in Muskegon County, Michigan. *Michigan Archaeologist* 11(3–4):165–169.
Ramsden, Peter G.
1977   *A Refinement of Some Aspects of Huron Ceramic Analysis.* Mercury Series Paper 68. Ottawa: Archaeological Survey of Canada, National Museum of Man.
Rapoport, A.
1990   *The Meaning of the Built Environment: A Nonverbal Communication Approach.* Tucson: University of Arizona Press.
Reidhead, Van A., and William F. Limp
1974   The Haag Site (12D19): A Preliminary Report. *Indiana Archaeological Bulletin* 1(1):4–19.
Renfrew, Colin
1994   The Archaeology of Religion. In *The Ancient Mind: Elements of Cognitive Archaeology*, ed. C. Renfrew and E. B. W. Zubrow, 47–54. Cambridge: Cambridge University Press.
Riordan, Robert V.
1982   *The Pollock Works.* Report on the 1981 Field Season to the Green County Recreation and Park Department, Xenia, Ohio. Wright State University Laboratory of Anthropology.
1984   *The Pollock Works: Report on the 1982–1983 Field Seasons.* Reports in Anthropology 7. Wright State University Laboratory of Anthropology.
1986   The Pollock Works: Chronology and Construction of a Hilltop Enclosure. Paper presented at the 51st annual meeting of the Society for American Archaeology, New Orleans.
1993a   A Timber Stockade at the Pollock Works. Paper presented at the biannual meeting of the Ohio Archaeological Council. Columbus, Ohio.
1993b   A Construction Sequence for the Pollock Works. Manuscript in possession of the author, Wright State University.
1995   A Construction Sequence for a Middle Woodland Hilltop Enclosure. *Midcontinental Journal of Archaeology* 20(1):62–104.
1996   The Enclosed Hilltops of Southern Ohio. In *A View from the Core: A Synthesis of Ohio Hopewell Archaeology*, ed. P. A. Pacheco, 242–256. Columbus: Ohio Archaeological Council.
Ritchie, William A.
1928   An Early Iroquoian Hilltop Fort near Kane, Pennsylvania. Manuscript. On file, Archaeology Section, William Penn Museum, Pennsylvania Historical and Museum Commission, Harrisburg.
1965   *The Archaeology of New York State.* New York: Natural History Press.

Romain, W. F.
1996   Hopewellian Geometry: Forms at the Interface of Time and
        Eternity. In *A View from the Core: A Synthesis of Ohio Hopewell
        Archaeology*, ed. P. J. Pacheco, 194–209. Columbus: Ohio
        Archaeological Council.
Russo, Michael
1994   A Brief Introduction to the Study of Archaic Mounds in the
        Southeast. *Southeastern Archaeology* 13(2):89–93.
Ryan, Thomas M.
1975   Semisubterranean Structures and Their Spatial Distribution at the
        Marksville Site (16AV1). *Southeastern Archaeological Conference
        Bulletin* 18:215–225.
Sagard-Theodat, Gabriel
1939   *Father Gabriel Sagard: The Long Journey to the Country of the
        Iroquois (1632)*, ed. George M. Wrong. Toronto: Champlain
        Society.
Salisbury, James H., and Charles B. Salisbury
1862   Accurate Surveys and Descriptions of the Ancient Earthworks at
        Newark, Ohio. Manuscript. On file, American Antiquarian Society,
        Worcester, Mass.
Saunders, Joe W.
1995   1994–1995 Annual Report for Management Unit 2, Regional
        Archaeological Program, Northeast Louisiana University.
        Manuscript. On file, Louisiana Division of Archaeology, Baton
        Rouge.
Saunders, Joe W., Thurman Allen, and Roger T. Saucier
1994   Four Archaic? Mound Complexes in Northeast Louisiana.
        Southeastern Archaeology 13(2):134–153.
Saunders, L. P.
1987   Occupation, Interval and Mortality Rate: A Methodological
        Approach. *The Bulletin* (Journal of the New York State
        Archaeological Association) 95:18–22.
Schatz, John W.
1957   Late Woodland Projectile Point Types from Central Ohio. *Ohio
        Archaeologist* 7(4):134–135.
Schele, L., and D. Freidel
1990   *A Forest of Kings*. New York: William Morrow.
Schock, J. M.
1974   The Chautauqua Phase and Other Late Woodland Sites in
        Southwestern New York. Ph.D. diss., State University of New York,
        Buffalo.

SCS (Soil Conservation Service)
1970   *General Soil Map: Avoyelles Parish Louisiana.* Alexandria, La.:
        U.S. Department of Agriculture.
Searle, J. R.
1983   *Intentionality.* Cambridge: Cambridge University Press.
Seeman, Mark F.
1992   Woodland Traditions in the Midcontinent: A Comparison of Three
        Regional Sequences. In *Research in Economic Anthropology,*
        Supplement 6, ed. D. R. Croes, R. A. Hawkins, and B. L. Isaac,
        3–46. Greenwich, Conn.: JAI Press.
1995   When Words Are Not Enough: Hopewell Interregionalism and the
        Use of Material Symbols at the GE Mound. In *Native American
        Interactions,* ed. M. S. Nassaney and K. E. Sassaman, 122–143.
        Knoxville: University of Tennessee Press.
Sempowski, M., L. P. Saunders, and G. C. Cervone
1988   The Adams and Culbertson Sites: A Hypothesis for Village
        Formation. *Man in the Northeast* 35:95–108.
Service, Elman R.
1975   *Origins of the State and Civilization.* New York: W. W. Norton.
Setzler, Frank M.
1933a   Pottery of the Hopewell Type from Louisiana. *Proceedings of the
        United States National Museum,* vol. 8, 1–21. Washington, D.C.:
        Smithsonian Institution.
1933b   Hopewell Type Pottery from Louisiana. *Journal of the Washington
        Academy of Sciences* 23(3):149–53.
1934   A Phase of Hopewell Mound Builders in Louisiana. *Explorations
        and Fieldwork of the Smithsonian Institution in 1933,* 38–40.
        Washington, D.C.
Setzler, Frank M., and W. D. Strong
1936   Archaeology and Relief. *American Scholar* 5(1):109–117.
Shane, Orrin C., III
1967   The Mixter Site: A Multicomponent Hunting Station in Erie
        County, Ohio. In *Studies in Ohio Archaeology,* ed. O. Prufer and D.
        McKenzie, 121–186. Cleveland: Press of Western Reserve University.
1974   Report on Excavations at High Banks, Ross County, Ohio. Paper
        presented at the annual meeting of the Ohio Academy of Science,
        Cleveland.
Sherratt, Andrew
1990   The Genesis of Megaliths: Monumentality, Ethnicity and Social
        Complexity in Neolithic North-west Europe. *World Archaeology*
        22(2):147–167.

Sherrod, Clay, and Martha A. Rolingson
1987   *Surveyors of the Ancient Mississippi Valley.* Research Series 28.
        Fayetteville: Arkansas Archeological Survey.
Shetrone, Henry Clyde
1930   *The Mound Builders.* New York: D. Appleton.
Shott, Michael J.
1990   Childers and Woods: Two Late Woodland Sites in the Upper Ohio
        Valley, Mason County, West Virginia. Archaeological Report 200.
        Program for Cultural Resource Assessment, University of Kentucky,
        Lexington.
1992   Radiocarbon Dating as a Probabilistic Technique: The Childers Site
        and Late Woodland Occupation in the Ohio Valley. *American
        Antiquity* 57(2):202–230.
Silverberg, Robert
1968   *Mound Builders of Ancient America.* Greenwich, Conn.: New York
        Graphic Society.
1970   *The Mound Builders.* New York: Ballantine Books.
Skipwith, H.
1881   Avoyelles Parish. In *Louisiana: Products, Resources, and
        Attractions; with a Sketch of the Parishes,* ed. W. H. Harris. New
        Orleans: New Orleans Democrat-Times Print.
Smith, Bruce D.
1992   Hopewellian Farmers of Eastern North America. In *Rivers of
        Change,* by B. D. Smith, 201–248. Washington, D.C.: Smithsonian
        Institution Press.
Smith, Ira F., and James T. Herbstritt
1976   Preliminary Investigations of the Prehistoric Earthworks in Elk
        County, Pennsylvania. Report prepared for the Allegheny National
        Forest, Pennsylvania Historical and Museum Commission,
        Harrisburg.
SMSS (Soil Management Support Services)
1988   *Keys to Soil Taxonomy.* SMSS Technical Monograph 6. U.S.
        Department of Agriculture, Agency for International Development,
        Cornell University.
Smucker, I.
1873   The Mound-builders' Works in Licking County, Ohio. *American
        Historical Record* 2 (23):481–485.
1875   Address of Isaac Smucker on the Mounds and Earth Works of
        Licking County. In *Minutes of the Ohio State Archaeological
        Convention, Held in Mansfield, O., Sept. 1st & 2nd, 1875.*
        Columbus, Ohio: Paul and Thrall.

1881 Mound Builders' Works near Newark, Ohio. *American Antiquarian* 3(4):261–270.

Sofaer, A., M. P. Marshall, and R. M. Sinclair

1989 The Great North Road: A Cosmographic Expression of the Chaco Culture of New Mexico. In *World Archaeoastronomy*, ed. A. F. Aveni, 365–376. Cambridge: Cambridge University Press.

Speck, F. G.

1931 *A Study of the Delaware Indian Big House Ceremony*, vol. 2. Harrisburg: Pennsylvania Historical Commission.

Speth, John D.

1966 The Whorley Earthwork. *Michigan Archaeologist* 2(4):211–227.

Squier, Ephraim G.

1851 *Antiquities of the State of New York*. Buffalo: George Derby.

Squier, E. G., and E. H. Davis

1848 *Ancient Monuments of the Mississippi Valley*. Smithsonian Institution Contributions to Knowledge, vol. 1, Washington, D.C. [1848]

1973 *Ancient Monuments of the Mississippi Valley*. Reprint. New York: AMS Press.

Stewart, Marilyn C.

1975 A Typology of Pits on the Engelbert Site. Ph.D. diss., State University of New York at Binghamton. University Microfilms, Ann Arbor.

Stothers, D. M., and J. R. Graves

1983 Cultural Continuity and Change: The Western Basin, Ontario Iroquois and Sandusky Traditions: A 1982 Perspective. *Archaeology of Eastern North America* 11:109–142.

Stouff, Faye, and W. Bradley Twitty

1971 *Sacred Chitimacha Indian Beliefs*. Pompano Beach, Fla.: Twitty and Twitty.

Struever, S., and G. L. Houart

1972 An Analysis of the Hopewell Interaction Sphere. In *Social Exchange and Interaction*, ed. E. N. Wilmsen, 47–79. Anthropological Papers 46. Ann Arbor: Museum of Anthropology, University of Michigan.

Sullivan, Lynne P.

1992 Arthur C. Parker's Contributions to New York State Archaeology. *Bulletin of the New York State Archaeological Association* 104:1–8.

Sullivan, Lynne P. (editor)

1996 *Reanalyzing the Ripley Site: Earthworks and Late Prehistory on the Lake Erie Plain*. New York State Museum Bulletin 489. Albany: State Education Department.

Sullivan, Lynne P., and Gwenyth Ann D. Coffin
1996   Mortuary Customs and Society. In *Reanalyzing the Ripley Site: Earthworks and Late Prehistory on the Lake Erie Plain*, ed. L. P. Sullivan, 100–120. New York State Museum Bulletin 489. Albany: State Education Department.

Sullivan, Lynne P., Sarah W. Neusius, and Phillip D. Neusius
1995   Earthworks and Mortuary Sites on Lake Erie: Believe It or Not at the Ripley Site. *Midcontinental Journal of Archaeology* 20(2):115–142.

Swanton, John R.
1911   *Indian Tribes of the Lower Mississippi Valley and Adjacent Coast of the Gulf of Mexico*. Bulletin 43. Washington, D.C.: Bureau of American Ethnology.

1928a   *Social Organization and Social Usages of the Indians of the Creek Confederacy*. 44th Annual Report. Washington, D.C.: Bureau of American Ethnology.

1928b   Sun Worship in the Southeast. *American Anthropologist* 30:206–213.

1931   *Source Material for the Social and Ceremonial Life of the Choctaw Indians*. Bulletin 103. Washington, D.C.: Bureau of American Ethnology.

1946   *The Indians of the Southeastern United States*. Bulletin 137. Washinton, D.C.: Bureau of American Ethnology.

Taylor, C. (editor)
1985   Theories of Meaning. In *Human Agency and Language*, 248–292. Cambridge: Cambridge University Press.

Taylor, R. E.
1987   *Radiocarbon Dating: An Archaeological Perspective*. Orlando: Academic Press.

Thomas, Cyrus
1889   *The Circular, Square, and Octagonal Earthworks of Ohio*. Bureau of Ethnology Bulletin 10:7–33. Washington, D.C.: Smithsonian Institution.

1894   Report on the Mound Explorations of the Bureau of Ethnology. *Twelfth Annual Report of the Bureau of Ethnology*, 1890–1891. Washington D.C.: Government Printing Office.

Thomas, David H.
1986   *Refiguring Anthropology: First Principles of Probability and Statistics*. Prospect Heights, Ill.: Waveland Press.

Thunen, Robert L.
1987   Recent Investigations at the Pinson Mounds Enclosure. Paper presented to the Southeastern Archaeological Conference, Charleston, South Carolina.

1988a   Investigations at the Pinson Enclosure. Paper presented to the
        Southeastern Archaeological Conference, New Orleans, Louisiana.
1988b   Geometric Enclosures in the Mid-South: An Architectural Analysis
        of Enclosure Form. In *Middle Woodland Settlement and
        Ceremonialism in the Mid-South and Lower Mississippi Valley*, ed.
        Robert C. Mainfort, Jr., 99–115. Archaeological Report 22. Jackson:
        Mississippi Department of Archives and History.
1990a   Planning Principles and Earthwork Architecture: The Pinson
        Mounds Enclosure. Ph.D. diss., Northwestern University.
1990b   Pinson Mounds: Recent Excavations at Mound 30. Paper presented
        to the Mid-South Archaeological Conference, Pinson, Tennessee.

Tooker, Elisabeth
1994   *Lewis H. Morgan on Iroquois Material Culture.* Tucson: University
        of Arizona Press.

Toth, E. Alan
1974   *Archaeology and Ceramics at the Marksville Site.* Anthropological
        Papers 56. Ann Arbor: Museum of Anthropology, University of
        Michigan.
1988   *Early Marksville Phases in the Lower Mississippi Valley: A Study
        of Culture Contact Dynamics.* Archaeological Report 21. Jackson:
        Mississippi Department of Archives and History.

Trigger, Bruce G.
1981   Prehistoric Social and Political Organization: An Iroquoian Case
        Study. In *Foundations of Northeast Archaeology*, ed. D. R. Snow,
        1–50. New York: Academic Press.
1990   Monumental Architecture: A Thermodynamic Explanation of
        Symbolic Behavior. *World Archaeology* 22(2):119–131.

Tuck, James A.
1978   Northern Iroquoian Prehistory. In *Handbook of North American
        Indians*, vol. 15, ed. B. G. Trigger, 322–333. Washington, D.C.:
        Smithsonian Institution.

Vescelius, G. S.
1957   Mound 2 at Marksville. *American Antiquity* 22(4):16–20.

Walling, Richard, R. C. Mainfort, Jr., and J. A. Atkinson
1991   Radiocarbon Dates for the Bynum, Pharr, and Miller Sites,
        Northwest Mississippi. *Southeastern Archaeology* 10(1): 54–62.

Warrick, G. A.
1988   Estimating Ontario Iroquoian Village Duration. *Man in the
        Northeast* 36:21–60.

Webb, Clarence H.
1944   Stone Vessels from a Northeast Louisiana Site. *American Antiquity*
        9:386–394.

1968   The Extent and Content of Poverty Point Culture. *American Antiquity* 33:297–321.
1970   Intrasite Distribution of Artifacts at the Poverty Point Site, with Special Reference to Women's and Men's Activities. In *The Poverty Point Culture*, ed. Bettye J. Broyles and Clarence H. Webb, 21–34. Bulletin 12. Morgantown, W. Va.: Southeastern Archaeological Conference.
1971   Archaic and Poverty Point Zoomorphic Locust Beads. *American Antiquity* 36:105–114.
1975   The Fox-Man Design. *Newsletter of the Louisiana Archaeological Society* 2(3):6–7.
1982   *The Poverty Point Culture.* Geoscience and Man 17. 2d ed., rev. Baton Rouge: Louisiana State University.

Webb, W. S.
1941   *Mt. Horeb Earthworks, Site 1, and the Drake Mound, Site 11, Fayette County, Kentucky.* Reports in Anthropology and Archaeology 5(2). Lexington: University of Kentucky.

Weiant, W. S., Jr.
1931   Letter to E. Greenman, 2 January 1931. On file, Department of Archaeology, Ohio Historical Society, Columbus.

White, Marian E.
1958   *The Niagara Frontier Iroquois: Archaeology and History.* Miscellaneous Contributions 11. Buffalo: Buffalo Museum of Science.
1961   *Iroquois Culture History in the Niagara Frontier Area of New York State.* Anthropological Papers 16. Ann Arbor: Museum of Anthropology, University of Michigan.
1963   1962 Excavation at the Henry Long Site. *Science on the March: Magazine of the Buffalo Museum of Science* 43(3):51–56.
1978   Erie. In *Handbook of North American Indians*, vol. 15, ed. B. G. Trigger, 412–417. Washington, D.C.: Smithsonian Institution.

Whittlesey, Col. Charles
1838   Works near Newark. Unpublished field notes on file, Western Reserve Historical Society, Cleveland, Ohio, MSS 2872, Container 2, Folder 2, 276–280. San Francisco: W. H. Freeman.
1850   Descriptions of Ancient Works in Ohio. *Smithsonian Contributions to Knowledge*, vol. 2, article 7, 17–18, plate 7, no. A.
1867   *Early History of Cleveland, Ohio.* Cleveland: Fairbanks, Benedict & Co.
1868   Field book, July 1, 1868. Unpublished field notes. On file, Western Reserve Historical Society, Cleveland, Ohio, MSS 2872.

1871   *Ancient Earth Forts of the Cuyahoga Valley, Ohio.* Western Reserve and Northern Ohio Historical Society Tract 5. Cleveland: Fairbanks, Benedict & Co.

Widmer, R. J., and G. S. Webster
1981   Prehistory. In *Cultural Resources in the Southern Lake Erie Basin: A Predictive Study,* ed. S. A. Curtis and J. W. Hatch, chap. 3. Prepared for the U.S. Army Corps of Engineers by Argonne National Laboratory.

Wilkinson, Richard G.
1996   Population Dynamics, Health and Mortality at the Ripley Site. In *Reanalyzing the Ripley Site: Earthworks and Late Prehistory on the Lake Erie Plain,* ed. L. P. Sullivan, 90–98. Bulletin 489. Albany: New York State Museum.

Willey, Gordon R.
1957   Review of *Poverty Point, A Late Archaic Site in Louisiana,* by James A. Ford and Clarence H. Webb. *American Antiquity* 23:198–199.

Willey, Gordon R., and Jeremy A. Sabloff
1974   *A History of American Archaeology.* San Francisco: W. H. Freeman.

Williams, Stephen, and Jeffrey P. Brain
1983   *Excavations at the Lake George Site, Yazoo County, Mississippi, 1958–1960.* Papers of the Peabody Museum of Archaeology and Ethnology 74, Cambridge, Mass.

Willoughby, Charles C., and Earnest A. Hooton
1922   *The Turner Group of Earthworks, Hamilton County, Ohio.* Papers of the Peabody Museum of American Archaeology and Ethnography 8(3), Cambridge, Mass.

Wilson, D.
1862   *Prehistoric Man.* London: Macmillan.

Wilson, J. N.
1865   Copy of letter to O. C. Marsh. Unpublished manuscript. On file, Western Reserve Historical Society, MSS 3359.
1868   Mounds near Newark. In *Isaac Smucker Scrap Book,* 69–71. On file, Granville Public Library, Granville, Ohio.

Wray, Charles F., and Harry L. Schoff
1953   A Preliminary Report on the Seneca Sequence in Western New York, 1550–1687. *Pennsylvania Archaeologist* 23(2):53–63.

Wright, Alfred
1828   Choctaws: Religious Opinions, Traditions, Etc. *Missionary Herald* 24:178–183, 214–216.

Wright, Gary A.
1966   Eastern Edge Survey: 1965 Season. *Michigan Archaeologist*
        12(4):151–168.
1990   On the Interior Attached Ditch Enclosures of the Middle and Upper
        Ohio Valley. *Ethnos* 55(1–2):92–107.
Wymer, Dee Anne, Bradley Lepper, and William Pickard
1992   Recent Excavations at the Great Circle, Newark, Ohio: Hopewell
        Ritual in Context. Paper presented at the 1992 Midwestern
        Archaeological Conference, Grand Rapids, Michigan.
Wyrick, D.
1866   Ancient Works near Newark, Licking County, O. In *Atlas of Licking
        County, Ohio*, ed. F. W. Beers. New York: Beers, Soule.

Contributors

Stephanie J. Belovich was serving as an assistant curator of archaeology at the Cleveland Museum of Natural History when conducting her research reported here. She received her M.A. from Kent State University in 1985 and is an instructor in human anatomy at the Ohio College of Podiatric Medicine and Case Western Reserve University's School of Dentistry.

A. Martin Byers received his Ph.D. in anthropology from the State University of New York at Albany in 1987. He teaches in the Departments of Social Science and Humanities at Vanier College in Montreal.

Robert P. Connolly is station archaeologist at Poverty Point State Commemorative Area and adjunct assistant professor, Department of Geosciences, Northeast Louisiana University. His 1995 doctoral dissertation at the University of Illinois focused on the built environment of Middle Woodland hilltop enclosures and synthesized seven years of research at the Fort Ancient site.

Jon L. Gibson received his Ph.D. in 1972 from Southern Methodist University. He serves as a professor of anthropology and director of the Center for Archaeological Studies at the University of Southwestern Louisiana at Lafayette. His archaeological and ethnographic research focuses on the Lower Mississippi Valley and other parts of the South, primarily on Poverty Point and folk cultures.

Dennis Jones received an M.A. from the Department of Geography and Anthropology at Louisiana State University in 1985. Formerly associated with LSU as a research associate, he now works as a contract archaeologist in Baton Rouge. He has done archaeological work in Costa Rica, Guatemala, Mexico, and the southeastern United States. His research interests include prehistoric lithic material and earthen architecture.

L. Carl Kuttruff received his Ph.D. from Southern Illinois University in 1974. He is a consulting archaeologist and adjunct assistant professor in the School of Human Ecology at Louisiana State University. He has done prehistoric research in the midwestern and southeastern United States and Mexico and historic archaeological research in the southeastern United States, the Philippine Islands, and the Republic of the Marshall Islands.

Bradley T. Lepper is a curator of archaeology for the Ohio Historical Society and, occasionally, a visiting assistant professor in the Department of Sociology and Anthropology at Denison University. He received his Ph.D. from Ohio State University in 1986 and was the Ohio Historical Society's curator for the Newark Earthworks and Flint Ridge State Memorials for six years.

Robert C. Mainfort, Jr., is Sponsored Research program administrator, Arkansas Archeological Survey, and associate professor of anthropology, University of Arkansas. He has conducted prehistoric and historic archaeological research in the Midsouth for over 20 years. He has published numerous monographs and essays on the Middle Woodland period and is coeditor, with David S. Brose and C. Wesley Cowan, of *Societies in Eclipse* (in press, Smithsonian Institution Press).

Claire McHale Milner is the curator of the Matson Museum of Anthropology at Penn State University. She is conducting doctoral research on the late prehistoric period, A.D. 1200–1600, in the Upper Great Lakes. Her research focuses on social and economic variation in small-scale societies and on the use of pottery style to track such variation.

Phillip D. Neusius received his Ph.D. from the University of Missouri in 1985 and is an associate professor and director of Archaeological Services in the Anthropology Department at Indiana University of Pennsylvania. He has done archaeological research in the Midwest, Plains, Southwest, and Northeast, and he is especially interested in prehistoric lithic technology.

Sarah W. Neusius received her Ph.D. from Northwestern University in 1982 and is a professor of anthropology at Indiana University of Pennsylvania. As an archaeologist and zooarchaeologist, she is particularly interested in human subsistence strategies among diverse groups and has studied Archaic hunter-gatherers in the Midwest, Anasazi horticulturalists in the Southwest, and Northern Iroquoian groups in the Northeast.

John M. O'Shea is curator of Great Lakes archaeology and professor of anthropology at the Museum of Anthropology at the University of Michigan. He received his doctorate from Cambridge University and has done research in the Great Plains and Michigan in the United States and in Hungary. His research focuses on the organization of tribal level societies.

Robert V. Riordan is associate professor of anthropology at Wright State University in Dayton, Ohio. He obtained his Ph.D. from Southern Illinois

University at Carbondale and has conducted field research in southwest Ohio at Woodland and Fort Ancient sites since 1977.

Lynne P. Sullivan received her Ph.D. from the University of Wisconsin–Milwaukee and is associate scientist (archaeology) in the Anthropological Survey of the New York State Museum and adjunct associate professor in the Anthropology Department at the University at Albany, SUNY. She has done archaeological research in the southeastern, midwestern, and northeastern United States and is particularly interested in community organization and sociopolitical developments during late prehistory.

Robert L. Thunen is an assistant professor of anthropology at the University of North Florida. His research interests include ritual architecture, earthwork construction, and the prehistory and early contact period of the southeastern United States. He received his Ph.D. from Northwestern University in 1990.

Index

Florida Museum of Natural History
The Ripley P. Bullen Series
Jerald T. Milanich, General Editor

Tacachale: Essays on the Indians of Florida and Southeastern Georgia during the Historic Period, edited by Jerald T. Milanich and Samuel Proctor (1978); first paperback edition, 1994

Aboriginal Subsistence Technology on the Southeastern Coastal Plain during the Late Prehistoric Period, by Lewis H. Larson (1980)

Cemochechobee: Archaeology of a Mississippian Ceremonial Center on the Chattahoochee River, by Frank T. Schnell, Vernon J. Knight, Jr., and Gail S. Schnell (1981)

Fort Center: An Archaeological Site in the Lake Okeechobee Basin, by William H. Sears, with contributions by Elsie O'R. Sears and Karl T. Steinen (1982); first paperback edition, 1994

Perspectives on Gulf Coast Prehistory, edited by Dave D. Davis (1984)

Archaeology of Aboriginal Culture Change in the Interior Southeast: Depopulation during the Early Historic Period, by Marvin T. Smith (1987); first paperback edition, 1992.

Apalachee: The Land between the Rivers, by John H. Hann (1988)

Key Marco's Buried Treasure: Archaeology and Adventure in the Nineteenth Century, by Marion Spjut Gilliland (1989)

First Encounters: Spanish Explorations in the Caribbean and the United States, 1492-1570, edited by Jerald T. Milanich and Susan Milbrath (1989)

Missions to the Calusa, edited and translated by John H. Hann, with an Introduction by William H. Marquardt (1991)

Excavations on the Franciscan Frontier: Archaeology at the Fig Springs Mission, by Brent Richards Weisman (1992)

The People Who Discovered Columbus: The Prehistory of the Bahamas, by William F. Keegan (1992)

Hernando de Soto and the Indians of Florida, by Jerald T. Milanich and Charles Hudson (1993)

Foraging and Farming in the Eastern Woodlands, edited by C. Margaret Scarry (1993)

Puerto Real: The Archaeology of a Sixteenth-Century Spanish Town in Hispaniola, edited by Kathleen Deagan (1995)

A History of the Timucua Indians and Missions, by John H. Hann (1996)

Archaeology of the Mid-Holocene Southeast, edited by Kenneth E. Sassaman and David G. Anderson (1996)

Bioarchaeology of Native American Adaptation in the Spanish Borderlands, edited by Brenda J. Baker and Lisa Kealhofer (1996)

The Indigenous People of the Caribbean, edited by Samuel M. Wilson (1997)

Hernando de Soto among the Apalachee: The Archaeology of the First Winter Encampment, by Charles R. Ewen and John H. Hann (1998)

The Timucuan Chiefdoms of Spanish Florida, by John E. Worth (1998); vol. 1, *Assimilation;* vol. 2, *Resistance and Destination.*

Ancient Earthen Enclosures of the Eastern Woodlands, edited by Robert C. Mainfort, Jr., and Lynne P. Sullivan (1998)